Settlers at the end of empire: Race and the politics of migration in South Africa, Rhodesia and the United Kingdom

Manchester University Press

STUDIES IN IMPERIALISM

General editors: Andrew S. Thompson and Alan Lester
Founding editor: John M. MacKenzie

When the 'Studies in Imperialism' series was founded by Professor John M. MacKenzie more than thirty years ago, emphasis was laid upon the conviction that 'imperialism as a cultural phenomenon had as significant an effect on the dominant as on the subordinate societies'. With well over a hundred titles now published, this remains the prime concern of the series. Cross-disciplinary work has indeed appeared covering the full spectrum of cultural phenomena, as well as examining aspects of gender and sex, frontiers and law, science and the environment, language and literature, migration and patriotic societies, and much else. Moreover, the series has always wished to present comparative work on European and American imperialism, and particularly welcomes the submission of books in these areas. The fascination with imperialism, in all its aspects, shows no sign of abating, and this series will continue to lead the way in encouraging the widest possible range of studies in the field. 'Studies in Imperialism' is fully organic in its development, always seeking to be at the cutting edge, responding to the latest interests of scholars and the needs of this ever-expanding area of scholarship.

To buy or to find out more about the books currently available in this series, please go to: https://manchesteruniversitypress.co.uk/series/studies-in-imperialism/

Settlers at the end of empire

Race and the politics of migration in South Africa, Rhodesia and the United Kingdom

Jean P. Smith

MANCHESTER UNIVERSITY PRESS

Copyright © Jean P. Smith 2022

The right of Jean P. Smith to be identified as the author of this work has been asserted by them in accordance with the Copyright, Designs and Patents Act 1988.

Published by Manchester University Press
Oxford Road, Manchester M13 9PL

www.manchesteruniversitypress.co.uk

British Library Cataloguing-in-Publication Data
A catalogue record for this book is available from the British Library

ISBN 978 1 5261 4548 2 hardback
ISBN 978 1 5261 8230 2 paperback

First published 2022

The publisher has no responsibility for the persistence or accuracy of URLs for any external or third-party internet websites referred to in this book, and does not guarantee that any content on such websites is, or will remain, accurate or appropriate.

Typeset
by Cheshire Typesetting Ltd, Cuddington, Cheshire

Contents

List of figures	*page* vi
List of tables	vii
Acknowledgements	viii
Introduction	1
1 'The height of my ambition is to become a Springbok': Wartime travel to southern Africa, race and the discourse of opportunity	26
2 'We want new settlers of British stock': Planning for post-war migration	51
3 'Immigration on a Selective Basis': The competing imperatives of minority settler colonialism, 1945–53	73
4 From Britons to 'New Rhodesians' and 'New South Africans': The consolidation of racial nationalism in the 1950s	99
5 The demographic defence of the white nation, 1960–75	124
6 'The last bastion of the British Empire': The politics of migration in the final days of Rhodesia and apartheid South Africa, 1970–94	149
7 'I still don't have a country': The southern African settler diaspora after decolonisation	171
Epilogue	192
Select bibliography	195
Index	216

List of figures

0.1	Raymond Jackson, *Evening Standard*, 18 January 1969	page 2
0.2	Graph showing immigration to South Africa, 1939–2000	3
0.3	Graph showing European immigration to Southern Rhodesia/ Rhodesia, 1946–80	4
5.1	Department of Immigration, *Land of Sunshine* (Pretoria: The Government Printer, 1970)	135
5.2	'Playtime in the Garden', Department of Immigration, *Housing Facilities in the Republic of South Africa* (Pretoria: The Government Printer, 1972)	136
5.3	Department of Immigration and Tourism, *Rhodesia: Assisted Passages to the Land of Sunshine: Golden Opportunity* (Salisbury: The Government Printer, 1965)	138
6.1	Anti-Apartheid Movement (London) poster, 1972. Reproduced with permission from the Anti-apartheid Movement Archive	150

List of tables

3.1	British migration to South Africa and Southern Rhodesia, 1946–54	*page* 74
4.1	British migration to South Africa and Southern Rhodesia, 1951–60	102
5.1	White migration to Southern Rhodesia/Rhodesia and South Africa, 1960–79	127
6.1	European immigration to and emigration from Rhodesia, 1970–79	153
6.2	White immigration to and emigration from South Africa, 1970–94	154

Acknowledgements

Without the assistance and support of many people around the world, completing this book would not have been possible. I would especially like to thank those who made the time to talk to me about their time in Africa. These oral histories have enriched my work and proved crucial for my understanding of the period. In particular, I would like to thank Marieke Clarke, who not only spent time discussing her own experience, but also put me in touch with many others. I am extremely grateful to Fred Brownell, who not only took the time to talk to me, but also lodged his papers on immigration at the National Archives of South Africa. They have been a fantastic resource. I would like to thank the staff at the many libraries and archives I have used, both in the United Kingdom and southern Africa. I owe special thanks to the archivists at the National Archives of Zimbabwe and to the staff at the Cory Library at Rhodes University led by Dr Jeff Peires, who could not have been more welcoming and helpful as I went through the Ian Smith Papers. Marian Eksteen scanned material for me from the National Library of South Africa when the Covid-19 pandemic made international travel impossible. I would also like to thank Christabel Gurney and the Anti-Apartheid Movement archive for kind permission to reproduce one of their posters. I would like to thank Emma Brennan and Paul Clarke at Manchester University Press for their assistance and patience. I am grateful for financial support for research from the Institute of Historical Research, the American Historical Association, and the University of California, Santa Barbara, and for publication from the Scouloudi Foundation in association with the Institute of Historical Research. A version of Chapter 1 appeared as '"Transformation to paradise": Wartime travel to southern Africa, race and the discourse of opportunity, 1939–1950', *Twentieth Century British History*, 26:1 (2015), 52–73. A version of Chapter 7 appeared as '"I still don't have a country": The southern African settler diaspora after decolonisation', in *Cultures of Decolonisation: Transnational Productions and Practices, 1945–1970*, eds Ruth Craggs and Claire Wintle, Manchester: Manchester University

Press, 2016. I am grateful to the editors for permission to include the material here.

I owe a tremendous intellectual debt to Erika Rappaport, whose probing questions, insights and support have been invaluable. For their comments and engaged feedback on various versions and aspects of the book, I would also like to thank Stephan Miescher, Paul Spickard, Jack Talbott, Ruth Craggs, Claire Wintle, Will Jackson, Durba Ghosh, Ashley Jackson, Jonathan Fennell, Radhika Natarajan, Anne Spry Rush, Sandra Dawson, Duncan Money, Stuart Ward, Christian Damm Pederson, Sarah Stockwell, Camilla Schofield, Becky Taylor, Anna Maguire and the anonymous reviewers. Justin Bengry has been an excellent sounding board both in Santa Barbara and in London, and he and Bianca Murrillo read drafts and provided insightful commentary on various conference papers which evolved into chapters. I am also grateful for the intellectual communities in London provided by the Institute of Commonwealth Studies and the Institute of Historical Research. Philip Murphy, in particular, has been a source of helpful advice and feedback on my work. Needless, to say, any errors that remain, are my own.

A network of friends and family across the world assisted me as I tackled the practical difficulties of transnational research. Nichole Sater, John Foss, Abby Dowling, Sarah Watkins, Zamira Yusufjonova, Ryan Abman, Joe Figliulo-Rossworm, Janiene Langford and Richard Bussey all put me up on my many return visits to California and they and Megan Barber, Tara Tubb, Andrea Gill and Sean Kheraj provided much needed solidarity and friendship. In London, Graeme Williams and Amanda Talma-Williams provided a place to stay during my first two summers of archival research and much support since. Zoe Williams provided comic relief and gave up her bedroom more than once. Scott Brodie put up with an extra flatmate at times and his discipline as a writer has been inspiring. Friends in the United Kingdom have made my time here a pleasure and have kindly indulged my excited talk about my most recent research discovery. I would like to thank for their support and friendship Vanessa Rockel, Sarah and Chris Bourn, Jesslyn Holman, Chris Ayles, Miikka Leskinen, and though she did not live to see me finish, Anita Bednarek Brodie.

In Cape Town, Ken and Alison Garlick, and Peter and Cheryl Mann provided places to stay and engaged discussions about South African history, while Gareth Mann hosted a much-needed break from research in Kalitzdorp. Returning to Johannesburg, it was comforting to know that Margie and Peter Griffiths always had a bed for me. I also owe thanks to Alan and Dawn Smith and Sharon Christina Smith-Schuler for their hospitality. I am grateful to Sheena and Johnny Pettit, who put me up both in Centurion and Rayton and who travelled to Durban with me for an oral history interview. In Harare, Peggy Rambanapasi opened her home and even lent her car to someone she had never met. Maria Rambanapasi, not only introduced me to her sister, but also proved a crucial source of information about Zimbabwe.

I owe special thanks to my brother David Smith and his wife Lauren Smith who have been a source of steadfast support and practical help over the years. I am especially grateful to Lauren for looking after my son so that I could write. I would also like to thank Ian and Kate Smith for helping to take care of their cousin and for providing me with all the joys of being an aunt. My son, James Talsma-Smith, has provided a very welcome diversion especially as I worked to finish the book through the uncertainties of the Covid-19 pandemic. My parents, Alastair and Anne Smith have supported my education throughout my life and always encouraged my interest in history, taking me to museums and historic sites for as long as I can remember and patiently waiting (along with David Smith) for me to finish reading all the information available. Their enthusiasm and interest in my work has been crucial. My greatest debt and most profound thanks are to Rob Talsma, who has supported me through this project from the beginning. I had just found the sources on evacuee children that eventually evolved into this project when we began our relationship. Thirteen years, one son and many travels later, I am still grateful for his unflagging support.

London, United Kingdom
October 2021

For Rob and my parents

Introduction

A political cartoon in the *Evening Standard* in January 1969 shows two families on a beach carrying suitcases, with a small boat in the distance. One family, clearly intended to represent migrants from South Asia, is arriving, while the other, a white British family, is leaving. The caption reads, 'Agreed then, you have 14 Upper Pinner Road, we take the boat, and the best of British luck to you!'[1] This image depicts a well-known aspect of post-war British history: the increase in the migration of people of colour from the Commonwealth in the decades after the Second World War. Much scholarship and public attention has focused on this demographic shift and its consequences, exploring the increased diversity that these migrations brought to the United Kingdom as well as the discrimination, hostility and violence faced by many migrants.[2] But it also reflects something that is often overlooked in assessments of this era: high rates of migration *from* the United Kingdom in this period.[3]

The cartoon also speaks to the motivations of emigrants from Britain in the second half of the twentieth century. The prosperous appearance of the departing family and their prior residence in Pinner, a wealthy London suburb, highlight that this was not for the most part a migration driven by economic hardship. Most people who left the United Kingdom in this period were motivated not by privation, but by the promise of greater opportunities and an improved lifestyle abroad. This was often connected to concerns about their prospects and those of their children in a rapidly changing and increasingly multicultural United Kingdom, signalled here by the phrase: 'Best of British luck', and its implied scepticism about the arriving family's chances of success in their new home.[4]

Though there are many studies of migration from the United Kingdom in earlier periods, the focus for the post-war period has largely been on migration *to* the United Kingdom, and especially the migration of people of colour.[5] Rates of emigration were, however, significant in the decades after the Second World War and especially in the immediate post-war decades, the majority of British migrants moved to Commonwealth

"Agreed then, you have 14 Upper Pinner Road, we take the boat, and the best of British luck to you!"

Figure 0.1 Raymond Jackson, *Evening Standard*, 18 January 1969.

countries. From 1946 to 2000, more than 8 million Britons left the United Kingdom and more than 5 million of these migrants moved to countries in the empire and former empire. The proportion was close to 90 per cent in the 1950s, it was 74 per cent in the 1960s, 59 per cent in the 1970s, 46 per cent in the 1980s and dropped to 32 per cent in the 1990s as British migrants increasingly moved to European destinations such as France and Spain.[6]

There was also widespread interest in emigration in the decades after the Second World War. From 1948 to 1975, between 22 and 42 per cent of the British public surveyed by Gallup expressed the wish to emigrate, largely indicating the so-called old Commonwealth (the settler colonies of Australia, Canada, New Zealand, South Africa and Rhodesia[7]) and the United States as their most desired destinations.[8] While this is clearly larger than the number of people who actually left the United Kingdom, these polls indicate public awareness of the possibility of emigration as well as its broad appeal.[9] This was likely influenced by the long history of migration from the United Kingdom, personal knowledge of friends and family who had moved abroad as well as recruitment campaigns that emphasised the opportunities and lifestyle available for white British migrants.

Emigration generally, and to Anglophone settler colonial nations (including the United States) in particular, was a means of social mobility for many Britons in the decades after the Second World War. The history of post-war social mobility in the United Kingdom has largely focused on domestic factors including increased access to education, especially higher education, the benefits of the welfare state and the decline of deference.[10] But as Simon Gunn has argued, social mobility was also connected to spatial mobility.[11] Gunn and others have focused largely on the impact of mobility within the United Kingdom, ranging from the slum clearances, new town schemes and other state programmes that rehoused 4 million people to the 'hyper-mobility' of middle-class professionals whose career progression often depended on a series of geographic moves.[12] *Settlers at the end of empire* broadens this focus to highlight the ways in which post-war social mobility was also achieved through migration abroad, migration made more accessible to white Britons by subsidised schemes and other incentives as these settler colonial nations aimed to bolster their white populations, engineering white flight on a global scale.[13]

Though Australia and Canada received the most migrants, Britons also moved to South Africa and Rhodesia in this period. As reflected in Figure 0.2[14] and Figure 0.3[15] there was a surge in migration in the immediate post-war period to both nations. While migration to South Africa was stable through most of the 1950s, rates of migration to Southern Rhodesia, then part of the Central African Federation were more volatile, reflecting

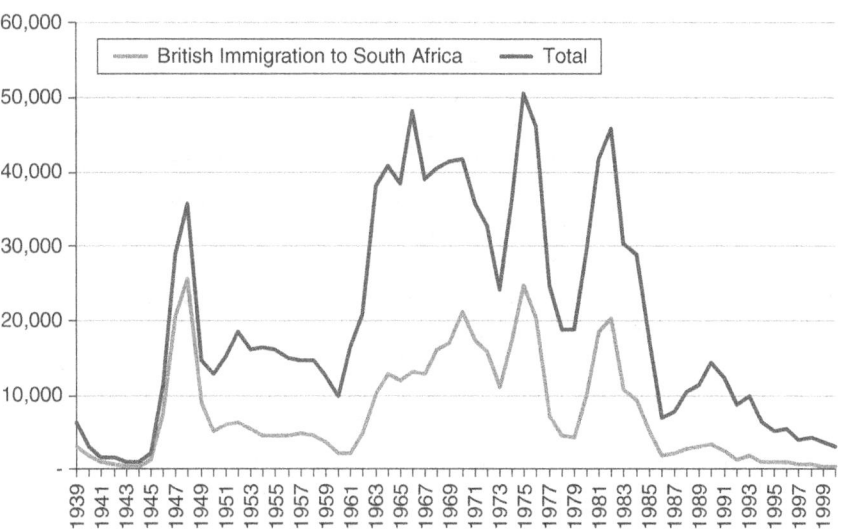

Figure 0.2 Immigration to South Africa, 1939–2000.

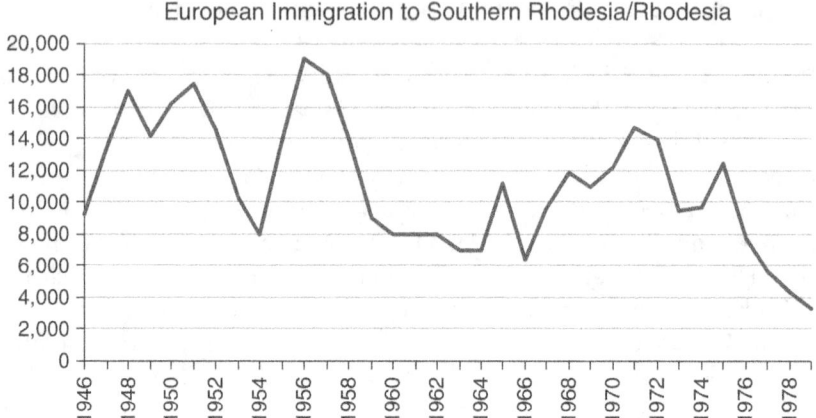

Figure 0.3 European Immigration to Southern Rhodesia/Rhodesia, 1946–80.

economic and political instability. Most significantly, this migration did not end when these countries left the Commonwealth in the 1960s to continue racially based minority rule. To the contrary, British migration to South Africa significantly increased in the 1960s and 1970s, only declining from the early 1980s even as the apartheid regime came under increasing international criticism. Migration also continued to Rhodesia, although at much lower rates, especially by the 1970s due to sanctions and the escalating war between the Rhodesian state and anti-colonial forces. This increase is in part explained by higher rates of emigration from Britain overall at this time, however, another significant factor was the institution in both South Africa and Rhodesia in the 1960s of subsidised migration schemes aimed at increasing their white populations.[16]

The focus of this study is the politics of migration in the United Kingdom, South Africa and Rhodesia across the long era of decolonisation from the Second World War to the collapse of the apartheid regime in 1994. Tracing the evolution of policy and debate surrounding migration alongside the way it was understood and experienced by migrants themselves, *Settlers at the end of empire* applies a transnational lens to the protracted, uneven and complex process of decolonisation. Migration policies, as well as reflecting changing conceptions of the nation and the ideal citizen, at a more practical level are also informed by a government's perceptions of self-interest whether in terms of geopolitics, what might appeal to the electorate or demographic survival. There are many ways in which states can exert influence on migration. Restricting who can enter, reside and work in their territory is only one of the mechanisms available. States can also enact policies of recruitment, offering incentives or publicity to attract specific kinds of migrants and policies of removal, deporting those considered undesirable. Migration policies can also be aimed at existing citizens, whether encouraging them to leave by subsidising migration elsewhere, or encouraging them to stay either by offering incentives or by prohibiting or making emigration difficult by restricting the assets a departing resident could take abroad, for instance.

The employment of these tools of 'demographic governance' in all three states under discussion in the second half of the twentieth century varied depending on the political and economic context and were implemented with varying levels of success.[17] In the United Kingdom in the immediate post-war period, the promotion of emigration to the Commonwealth and the continuation of an open policy towards migration from the Empire and Commonwealth, as formalised by the 1948 British Nationality Act, formed an attempt to strengthen the Commonwealth and thereby Britain's geopolitical position.[18] These policies operated alongside informal attempts to reduce the migration of Commonwealth migrations of colour and the recruitment of white workers, largely from Europe. In the 1940s and 1950s, South Africa and Rhodesia employed restrictive immigration policies, exclusionary not only in terms of race, but also in terms of nationality, class, health and financial standing. Both governments were concerned about the maintenance of the racial hierarchy on which their minority regimes depended and therefore operated selective policies with the aim of attracting 'the right sort' of white migrants who would assimilate well and contribute to the building of these settler colonial societies. Other than a small scale, short-lived programme in Southern Rhodesia in the mid 1950s, neither state offered subsidised fares or other incentives to immigrants in the 1940s and 1950s.[19]

By the 1960s the calculus had changed in all three nations. In the United Kingdom amid racially charged concerns about rising migration from former colonies, the United Kingdom implemented restrictions on migration from the Commonwealth that disproportionally impacted migrants of colour and provided less support to emigration amid concerns about a 'brain drain'. After the Rhodesian Unilateral Declaration of Independence (UDI) in 1965, the British state banned the promotion of migration to Rhodesia and limited the assets that British migrants could take if they moved there. The British government also implemented limited policies of removal, offering voluntary 'repatriation' to migrants from the Commonwealth and deporting Commonwealth migrants convicted of crimes.

The acceleration of decolonisation in other parts of Africa as well as the 1961 South African declaration of republic and the 1965 Rhodesian Unilateral Declaration of Independence made South Africa and Rhodesia increasingly isolated internationally. As a result, rates of white emigration increased while rates of white immigration declined and although they maintained selective immigration policies, both governments began an intensive recruitment of white immigrants offering subsidised passages and other incentives. Both states also implemented measures to discourage white emigration, limiting the assets departing residents could take with them.

These shifts in policy reveal two phases of post-war decolonisation. The first phase, up to the early 1960s, was a period of transition and of experimentation with various ways of resolving the problems of empire after the war. Britain came under pressure, initially from the United States and later from the United Nations and newly independent nations to decolonise. Unwilling to abandon its empire entirely, British policymakers sought a middle ground. They emphasised initiatives in colonial development that had begun in the interwar period and rebranded the Empire as the Commonwealth.[20] One important aspect of this, especially in relation to keeping close ties with the increasingly independent former Dominions, was the British Nationality Act of 1948, and the support provided to British emigration to the Commonwealth. The Federation of Rhodesia and Nyasaland was also an experiment along these lines. In existence from 1953 to 1963, its rhetoric of multi-racialism and 'partnership' was undercut by the continuation of racially based minority rule, including a racially exclusionary selective immigration policy. Though in the implementation of apartheid after 1948 South Africa took a harder line, even there, the attempt to reframe is evident in the policy of 'separate development' and later the elaborate charade of the independent Bantustans.

By the 1960s and 1970s, as the realities of imperial collapse took hold and under increasing pressure to abandon white minority rule, both Rhodesia and South Africa broke formal political ties with the United Kingdom and left the Commonwealth. Their attempts to increase white immigration and reduce white emigration in this period were centred on the demographic defence of independent and increasingly isolated white nations. The migration policies of the United Kingdom in this period included increasing restrictions placed on the immigration of people of colour from the Commonwealth, decreasing support for white British emigration to the Commonwealth and a mechanism for the voluntary removal of people of colour already resident in the United Kingdom. Though less explicit than in South Africa and Rhodesia, the politics of migration in the United Kingdom also aimed towards the demographic defence of an independent post-imperial nation, imagined as white.

There were important differences between these three nations. Though immigrants of colour in the United Kingdom faced bigotry and violence, there was no legal regime of discrimination and dispossession comparable to that of South Africa and Rhodesia. Segregation in Rhodesia also took a less extreme form than in apartheid South Africa. Just as there were opponents of minority rule in both Rhodesia and South Africa, there was also no racist consensus in the United Kingdom and anti-racist movements played an important role in advocating for such protections as the Race Relations Acts of 1965, 1968 and 1976, and in campaigning against apartheid in South Africa and minority rule in Rhodesia.[21]

There were, however, important parallels as well. As Wendy Webster and Bill Schwarz have shown, white communities both in the United Kingdom and in the settler colonies of Africa were portrayed as vulnerable to an onslaught of Black violence whether on an isolated Rhodesian farm or an urban English street.[22] Such rhetoric and imagery obscured the violence committed against people of colour in the United Kingdom and colonised people in Africa, and was used to justify the restriction of immigration to the United Kingdom and the continuation of minority rule in southern Africa. It also contributed to a sense of British decline that led many to emigrate, including to South Africa and Rhodesia.

As this suggests, while the formal political structures of the British Empire were crumbling, imperial ideologies of race persisted. This manifested in different ways and evolved over time in each of the three sites under discussion.[23] As discussed below, there were important differences between Rhodesia and South Africa, with the latter's much longer history of European settlement and large and influential Afrikaner population. In both South Africa and Rhodesia, however, the projects of white nation building had their roots in the nineteenth century, drawing on mythologies of frontier masculinity and imperial conquest. At the same time these projects were forward-looking, both Rhodesia and South Africa were often described and imagined as young nations, who had made remarkably quick progress towards modernity and civilisation due to the industry of their white settler populations.[24] White nationalism in the United Kingdom was also rooted in the past, harking back to an imagined time of racial homogeneity. While each nation drew on and developed its own racial logics in response to local circumstances, there were also convergences, affinities, shared histories and mythologies of whiteness which, while not identical, bore a 'family resemblance'.[25]

Equally, perceptions of race, identity and nation were not homogenous within the United Kingdom, South Africa or Rhodesia. Within the United Kingdom, as elsewhere, people often had multiple and overlapping identities, tied to politics, class, religion, the nations that make up the United Kingdom, or a more local affiliation. Neither were white Rhodesia and white South Africa monolithic cultures, but fractured across lines of ethnicity, national origin, religion, politics, class and, especially in the case of South Africa, language.[26] In all three nations, however, whiteness, whether explicit or implicit, was a crucial component in the conception of the nation that informed the politics and policies of migration. As well as analysing the changing politics of migration in these three nations across the era of decolonisation, *Settlers at the end of empire* shows how imperial migration networks persisted and evolved even as the official political structures of empire collapsed.[27] It highlights the ongoing personal and institutional connections between the settler colonies of southern Africa and the United Kingdom, their major source of white immigrants throughout this period.

A note on sources

Following people's movements or 'life geographies' reveals the limits of the national framework, both conceptually and in terms of the physical location of archives.[28] To understand the entangled histories of the United Kingdom, South Africa and present-day Zimbabwe, this study draws on archives in all of these locations as well as oral history interviews.[29] Despite their limits, state archives are an important source for this project. Reading the colonial archive, as Ann Stoler has argued, 'along the grain' and 'with care', uncovers the fractured and protean workings of the colonial state and the difficulties it faced in sustaining an imperial or, in the cases of South Africa and Rhodesia, a settler colonial order.[30] Memoranda and reports on immigration reveal what Stoler calls 'administrative anxiety', frustration with rates of migration whether too high or too low and concerns about whether immigrants were ideologically and racially suitable to become South Africans, Rhodesians or Britons.[31] These concerns varied over time depending on rates of migration, and the economic and political situation. Rather than determining them, government policy frequently reacted to immigration trends, often unsuccessfully. Yet these reactions, whether detailed plans for immigration schemes that were never implemented, memoranda outlining the elusive ideal immigrant, or concerns about the 'brain drain', provide insight into what constituted 'common sense' and how it changed over time, particularly as the European imperial order was challenged by decolonisation.[32]

Alongside archival sources, I have used oral history to better understand how migrants present their stories and what meaning they attribute to their migration in the larger trajectory of their lives, understanding oral history as a unique means to gain insight into subjectivity.[33] As well as interviewing two post-war migrants to Southern Rhodesia in the United States, I also interviewed those who had returned to the United Kingdom and those who remained in South Africa. I found them in a variety of ways: one was the father of an acquaintance, several contacts came from people who spoke to me after I presented my research at conferences. One interviewee, Marieke Clarke, whom I met at the Britain–Zimbabwe Society meeting in Oxford introduced me to several other people with whom she had remained in touch. I did not conduct any interviews in Zimbabwe in 2011, having received advice against it, as researchers had been mistaken for journalists who were then heavily restricted by the government. In South Africa, I interviewed Fred Brownell, a former immigration official who had written a master's thesis on migration and deposited his papers at the National Archives of South Africa in Pretoria. I found others through happenstance, mentioning my research in a bookstore or through archivists I met. I also interviewed several acquaintances though my own family network. My father, Alastair Smith, moved to Bulawayo in what was then Southern Rhodesia, from Perth, Scotland in 1957 when he was nine years old, and moved to South Africa in 1965 to attend the University of Cape Town, where he met and married my mother, Anne Smith. I was born and raised in Johannesburg until the age of thirteen, when my parents moved to the United States. The trajectory of my family follows the serial migrations of many of my interviewees.

My own subject position and background put me in the position of partial insider and partial outsider to the experience of my interviewees. I am from a different generation and never lived in Rhodesia/Zimbabwe. My time abroad and American-inflected accent mark me as an outsider too. Yet my whiteness and especially my experience of South Africa and Zimbabwe and familiarity with institutions, expressions, language and other aspects of white settler culture allowed me to utilise several areas of connection, which often put interviewees at ease and improved rapport.

My usual method was simply to ask, 'How did your family come to be in Africa?' I found this phrasing to be better than 'Why did your family move to Africa?' which could be read as asking for a justification. Using 'how' rather than 'why' usually elicited a story rather than a reason.[34] In many cases this prompt was enough to lead to more than hour of narrative without further questions. I also asked about national identity, whether interviewees still felt an affinity to Britain and about any ongoing connections or visits back to the United Kingdom. I asked about what impression they had of southern Africa before they moved, and particularly if they had moved in the 1960s or 1970s whether they had a sense of the racial politics beforehand. Another useful question was what surprised them most about their new home. In the case of those who had subsequently left southern Africa I asked about their motivations for leaving. If they had not left, I asked whether they had considered it. I left the decision about whether to use a pseudonym up to the individual interviewee.[35]

Using migrant oral histories, biographies and letters as well as official sources, *Settlers at the end of empire* adds breadth to work that has focused on the political and economic relationships between these nations and the United Kingdom.[36] Such sources demonstrate how migrants present their stories and what meaning they attribute to their migration in the larger trajectory of their lives. Examining sources concerning the decision-making of individual migrants alongside those detailing the implementation of government policy reveals the limited impact of state efforts at social engineering. While the state could exert more control over immigration through exclusion, it was more difficult, even when offering incentives, to recruit either the number or the type of immigrants desired or to dissuade people from leaving. This combination of sources also provides insight into the wide range of forces that shaped this migration, from macro-level economic and political factors, to individual human agency.[37]

Minority settler colonialism and migration

Considering South Africa and Rhodesia together brings into focus their shared characteristics as minority settler colonial regimes. While the settler community in Rhodesia was smaller, more British, and more recent than that of South Africa, in both cases a racially defined settler group formed a demographic minority yet held political and economic power.[38] By the 1940s this power was largely held independently of Britain. Having achieved Dominion status in 1910, South Africa's independence, along with that of the other Dominions was confirmed by the Statute of Westminster in 1931. Though Southern Rhodesia was never a Dominion, its attainment of internal self-government in 1923, its domination of the Central African Federation, and the relative ease with which the Unilateral Declaration of Independence was accomplished in 1965 demonstrate its effective independence. Settler control of these states along with their intention of maintaining such dominance and remaining permanently in southern Africa differentiate these polities from other British colonies with significant British populations such as India. South Africa and Rhodesia were not, as Patrick Wolfe has argued, merely 'colonies that had settlers' but rather a specific variant of settler colonialism, different in their demographic make-up from the other self-governing British settler colonies of Australia, New Zealand and Canada, but similar to them in terms of holding economic and political power independent of the United Kingdom and in the intention of their settler populations to remain permanently.[39]

Their situation as minority settler colonies led both the South African and Rhodesian state to pursue a contingent policy towards the recruitment of British and other white migrants. Though increasing the white population seemed to many the best way to ensure security, this goal had to be balanced with maintaining the racial hierarchy on which these states were constituted and consequently the privileged lifestyle thought to be appropriate for the ruling white minority. This was accomplished to some degree through state policies in both Rhodesia and South Africa that favoured and subsidised the white minority in terms of employment, education, housing, and health care.[40] The concern always remained, however, that this might be unsustainable with the arrival of too many white migrants, especially those judged to be 'undesirable' whether in terms of class, qualifications, political outlook, health or nationality. The recruitment of white migrants was more aggressively pursued by the South African and Rhodesian states under the acute existential threat to these minority regimes in the 1960s and 1970s as they became increasingly isolated internationally, as internal challenges to minority rule accelerated and as white emigration rates soared. Even at this point, however, both states continued to operate selective immigration policies.

By contrast, the British settler colonies that had attained a demographic majority – Australia, Canada and New Zealand – more consistently recruited white and especially British migrants across the post-war period including unskilled workers. Though their immigration programmes fluctuated in scale and form based on economic and political concerns, Canada providing loans, and Australia and New Zealand offering subsidised passages for prospective emigrants, such schemes as well as policies that favoured the admission of British and other European migrants were consistently employed in the decades after the war.[41]

Such policies continued the long-running use of both restriction and recruitment to constitute settler colonial nations in racial terms. Racial restrictions, whether stated outright or implemented through language tests, landing fees or the continuous passage requirement applied to migrants from within the British Empire as well as beyond it.[42] Similarly, restrictions on the health and morality of migrants, including those from the United Kingdom, excluded the admission not only of people of colour but of those who, although classified by these states as white or European, were deemed racially unfit.[43]

By contrast, though immigration restrictions in the United Kingdom were applied to 'aliens' from beyond the empire from 1905 and more consistently from 1914, restrictions were only applied to migrants from the Empire–Commonwealth from 1962 due to concerns about the maintenance of imperial and later Commonwealth unity.[44] That this emphasis on unity might lead to the mass migration to the United Kingdom of colonial subjects was not anticipated by British policymakers, who were often alarmed at this outcome.⁴⁵ Though it ended up facilitating the mass migration of people, including those of colour, from the Empire–Commonwealth, the British Nationality Act of 1948 was not intended to do so. Rather it was an attempt to formalise existing nationality and citizenship arrangements in light of increasing moves by the Dominions to create their own separate citizenship legislation, beginning with Canada in 1946.⁴⁶ But with the increasing arrival of Commonwealth migrants of colour, and a reorientation from the Commonwealth to Europe, the United Kingdom increasingly implemented policies of restriction similar to those that had long been employed by the settler colonies of the British Empire.

Scholarship on British migration

Scholarship on post-war Britain has focused on how non-white migration *from* former colonies dramatically changed the racial and cultural make-up of the United Kingdom. This literature clearly demonstrates the continuing legacy of British imperialism, as manifested in the physical presence of former colonial subjects in the United Kingdom. This shift to a more multicultural Britain, however, was accompanied by an often overlooked exodus of large numbers of Britons to the former empire, including to South Africa and Rhodesia, even as anti-colonial movements intensified and violently contested settler colonial rule in both places. The scholarly focus on immigration to the United Kingdom after 1945 has obscured the ways in which it remained a country of emigration.

Continued migration from the United Kingdom to the settler colonies of the British Empire was, however, another aspect of the British imperial legacy, reflecting in particular the legacy of the racial hierarchies of empire in the relative privilege afforded to white British migrants, who were not only allowed entry to these countries, but often explicitly recruited by them.⁴⁷ As this suggests, after the reality of imperial collapse became clear, the racial hierarchies of empire persisted. *Settlers at the end of empire* highlights connections between the increasing racial conflict in the United Kingdom and migration to places such as South Africa and Rhodesia with explicit racial hierarchies. Scholars have largely treated these as separate phenomena, illustrating Stuart Ward's argument that after 1945 the national framework remains the dominant historical lens.⁴⁸

Though migrants by definition crossed borders, the scholarship on British migration has tended to be framed by the nation state. Recent edited collections have made strides towards a more transnational examination of migration with useful introductory essays. However, with some exceptions, the case studies which make up their individual chapters remain fragmented.⁴⁹ Studies of *emigration* from Britain tend to emphasise the motivations behind migration schemes and the structural factors in Britain that spurred emigration.⁵⁰ Largely in the tradition of social history, these studies have examined how charitable organisations and policymakers attempted to solve social problems through migration, including overpopulation,⁵¹ the perceived surplus of women⁵² and the difficulties of maintaining a middle-class family.⁵³ Scholars have also investigated child migration schemes, finding that although they were intended to give impoverished children a better chance in life while at the same time providing the settler colonies with more British 'stock', many children were taken without family permission and often suffered abuse and terrible conditions.⁵⁴

The literature on *immigration* to the empire has tended to focus on issues of assimilation and the contribution of British migrants to each settler colony, with separate studies of British migration to Canada,⁵⁵ New Zealand,⁵⁶ Australia,⁵⁷ Rhodesia,⁵⁸ and South Africa.⁵⁹ Notable exceptions are Kent Fedorowich's study of the land settlement scheme for veterans of the Great War, Angela McCarthy's study of Irish and Scottish migration to Canada, Australia and New Zealand, Philip Payton's work on Cornish migration, James Belich's work on British migration to what he terms the 'Anglo-World' (the Dominions and the United States), Gary Magee and Andrew Thompson's study of the role of networks and migration in imperial globalisation, and James Hammerton's work drawing on the oral histories of British migrants since the 1960s.⁶⁰

With the exception of Hammerton's and McCarthy's work, this scholarship has, however, largely focused on the nineteenth century and the first half of the twentieth century. In part, this is because of the post-1945 focus on immigration *to* the United Kingdom described above. It also reflects changing perceptions of the meaning of migration as the destination countries increasingly exerted their independence, both within the Commonwealth, or in the cases of South Africa and Rhodesia from the 1960s, outside of it. Stephen Constantine suggests that from around 1940 British migration to the settler colonies 'produced experiences less like overseas settlement and more akin to a diaspora', that rather than moving from Britain to Greater Britain as before, they moved to a different culture.⁶¹ It is clearly true that as Australia, Canada, New Zealand, South Africa and Rhodesia established more independence from Britain and increasingly admitted and even recruited migrants from beyond the United Kingdom, British migration took on a different character than that of the nineteenth century or earlier in the twentieth century. Yet, until late in the twentieth century, well after the Second World War, these countries continued to recruit British migrants, who continued to move in large numbers, making up a significant proportion, and often the majority, of incoming migrants.

Scholarship on British migration to South Africa and Rhodesia has also tended to focus on the nineteenth and early twentieth centuries, while work on the post-war era has been fragmented or largely conducted in the fields of sociology and geography. Studies of Rhodesia do not provide comprehensive coverage of the post-war era. Alois Mlambo's study of migration ends with the establishment of the Central African Federation in 1953 but is mostly focused on the early twentieth century.[62] While including some earlier material the main focus of Josiah Brownell and David Kenrick's work is the post-UDI period.[63] The years of the Federation have largely been ignored by scholars.[64] Examining the period from the Second World War to Zimbabwean independence, *Settlers at the end of empire* shows that much of what Brownell found for the post-UDI period were long-running trends, including the tension between increasing the white population and maintaining its privilege.

The historical literature on British migration to South Africa also fails to provide comprehensive coverage of the post-war era. Edna Bradlow's study ends in 1948.[65] Fred Brownell, who worked in the South African Immigration Department in the 1960s, wrote his master's thesis on South African immigration policy in the post-war era and his work benefits from his first-hand perspective. However, it is primarily a political study, with less attention given to the social and cultural aspects of the migration.[66] The same is true of the work of Sally Peberdy, a political geographer.[67] On the other hand, sociologists have provided a social and cultural analysis of the migration. John Stone's 1973 study and Daniel Conway and Pauline Leonard's 2014 study draw on oral histories and present valuable first-hand accounts of the perspective of migrants.[68]

Settlers at the end of empire builds on this foundation, taking into account newly available records in the United Kingdom, South Africa and Zimbabwe as well as employing a transnational approach. Examining South Africa and Rhodesia in the same frame reveals striking similarities. Without overlooking the important differences in the demography and history of these nations, in both cases state policies and migrant practices were shaped by the constraints of a minority settler colonial regime. Looking at the period from 1939 to 1994 also reveals patterns that are not visible with a narrower lens.

Outline

Beginning with the Second World War, Chapter 1 demonstrates the importance of wartime experience to post-war migration and highlights the ways in which the Second World War strengthened connections between the

United Kingdom, South Africa and Southern Rhodesia. The war brought millions of British troops to the region, providing more Britons than ever before with experience of the lifestyle possible for white migrants and motivated many to move after the war. Chapter 2 turns to official planning for post-war migration in the United Kingdom, South Africa and Southern Rhodesia. While many in all three nations sought to use the wartime migration of British children and service personnel to encourage white migration to Southern Rhodesia, South Africa and the other settler colonies of the British Empire, British officials sought to encourage Black service personnel serving in the United Kingdom to return to the Caribbean, reflecting racialised understandings of who was a desirable migrant.

Chapter 3 focuses on the migration policies of Southern Rhodesia and South Africa from the late 1940s to the early 1950s, highlighting the ways in which they reflect the tensions inherent to a minority settler colonial state. Chapter 4 turns to the 1950s, as both South Africa and Southern Rhodesia moved gradually towards more active recruitment of white migrants. In the United Kingdom, although legal restrictions on both emigration and the immigration of Commonwealth migrants of colour were considered, they were rejected as posing a threat to Commonwealth unity and informal measures were implemented instead. Chapter 5 examines the move towards active recruitment of white migrants in the 1960s and 1970s in South Africa and Rhodesia, the motivations of those who moved from the United Kingdom to South Africa and Rhodesia and the implementation in the United Kingdom of legal restrictions on Commonwealth migration that disproportionately impacted migrants of colour.

Chapter 6 turns to the 1970s and 1980s, the final years of Rhodesia and apartheid South Africa. While Rhodesia, subject to UN sanctions and legal bans on advertising, was increasingly unsuccessful in recruiting white migrants from the United Kingdom or elsewhere, white migrants including those from the United Kingdom continued to arrive in high numbers in South Africa up to the early 1980s. At the same time, the United Kingdom saw continued calls for restrictions to be placed on migrants of colour and for those already resident to be removed. Returning to a focus on individual experience, Chapter 7 uses oral histories and memoirs to explore the varied understandings of self and identity in the southern African settler diaspora after decolonisation.

Settlers at the end of empire demonstrates that emigration from the United Kingdom including to South Africa and Rhodesia continued in the decades after the Second World War and significantly, after those nations left the Commonwealth and abandoned all formal political ties with the United Kingdom in the 1960s. These migration flows and networks point to ongoing connections between the United Kingdom, South Africa and

Rhodesia and to the persistence of the ideologies of race that had long underpinned settler colonial and imperial rule.

In reframing the history of decolonisation through this transnational lens, *Settlers at the end of empire* challenges the persistent narrative that sets metropolitan Britain apart from the racism and violence of the settler colonies of southern Africa in the second half of the twentieth century. Just as earlier comparisons to other imperial powers such as Spain and Belgium could cast British imperialism as liberal, by the mid twentieth century Britain increasingly defined itself against the more overt racism in Rhodesia and South Africa and the United States.[69] Part of this comparison has been to emphasise British contributions to the anti-apartheid movement, which has served to obscure both the extent of support for apartheid South Africa and Rhodesia, and the volume of British migration, especially to South Africa. Apartheid and racial segregation in southern Africa as well as racism in Britain were deeply embedded in a longer history of British imperialism, which was always based on a racial hierarchy. Challenging the characterisation of South African republic in 1961 and the Rhodesian Unilateral Declaration of Independence in 1965 as sharp breaks with the United Kingdom, *Settlers at the end of empire* adds to a growing literature complicating the chronology of decolonisation and highlights the entangled histories of these three nations.[70]

Notes

1 Raymond Jackson, *Evening Standard*, 18 January 1969.
2 Jordanna Bailkin, *The Afterlife of Empire* (Berkeley: University of California Press, 2012); Bill Schwarz, *West Indian Intellectuals in Britain* (Manchester: Manchester University Press, 2003); Mike Philips and Trevor Philips, *Windrush: The Irresistible Rise of Multi-Racial Britain* (London: Harper Collins, 1999); Harry Goulbourne, *Ethnicity and Nationalism in Post-Imperial Britain* (Cambridge: Cambridge University Press, 1991); Ceri Peach, *West Indian Migration to Britain: A Social Geography* (Oxford: Oxford University Press, 1968); Louise Ryan and Wendy Webster, *Gendering Migration: Masculinity, Femininity and Ethnicity in Post-war Britain* (Aldershot: Ashgate, 2008); Wendy Webster, *Imagining Home: Gender, 'Race', and National Identity, 1945–64* (London: UCL Press, 1998); Wendy Webster, 'Home, Colonial and Foreign: Europe, Empire and the History of Migration in 20th-century Britain', *History Compass* 7 (2009), 1–19; Kennetta Hammond Perry, *London is the Place for Me: Black Britons, Citizenship, and the Politics of Race* (Oxford: Oxford University Press, 2015); Paul Gilroy, *'There ain't no black in the Union Jack': The Cultural Politics of Race and Nation* (Chicago: University of Chicago Press, 1991); Chris Waters, '"Dark Strangers in Our Midst": Discourses of Race and

Nation in Britain, 1947–1963', *Journal of British Studies*, 36 (1997), 207–38; Centre for Contemporary Cultural Studies, *The Empire Strikes Back: Race and Racism in 70s Britain* (London: Hutchinson, 1982); Paul Gilroy, *After Empire: Melancholia or Convivial Culture* (Abingdon: Routledge, 2004); Clair Wills, *Lovers and Strangers: An Immigrant History of Post-War Britain* (London: Allen Lane, 2017).

3   Exceptions include Kathleen Paul, *Whitewashing Britain: Race and Citizenship in the Postwar Era* (Ithaca: Cornell University Press, 1997), pp. 25–63; A. James Hammerton and Alistair Thomson, *Ten Pound Poms: Australia's Invisible Migrants* (Manchester: Manchester University Press, 2005); A. James Hammerton, '"I'm a citizen of the world": Late Twentieth-Century British Emigration and Global Identities – The End of the "British World"?', in *Empire, Migration and Identity in the British World*, eds Kent Fedorowich and Andrew S. Thompson (Manchester: Manchester University Press, 2013); A. James Hammerton, *Migrants of the British Diaspora Since the 1960s: Stories From Modern Nomads* (Manchester: Manchester University Press, 2017); Jean P. Smith, '"The Women's Branch of the Commonwealth Relations Office": The Society for the Overseas Settlement of British Women and the Long Life of Empire Migration', *Women's History Review* 25:4 (2016), 520–35. Eric Richards' account of emigration since 1600 covers the period up to the 1980s, although its main emphasis is on the nineteenth century, Eric Richards, *Britannia's Children: Emigration from England, Scotland, Wales and Ireland since 1600* (London: Hambledon and London, 2004).

4   Hammerton, *Migrants of the British Diaspora*, pp. 27–8, 57–8.

5   On this point see David Edgerton, *The Rise and Fall of the British Nation: A Twentieth-Century History* (London: Allen Lane, 2018), p. 40. For British emigration before 1945 see James Belich, *Replenishing the Earth: The Settler Revolution and the Rise of the Anglo-World, 1783–1939* (Oxford: Oxford University Press, 2009); Gary B. Magee and Andrew S. Thompson, *Empire and Globalisation: Networks of People, Goods and Capital in the British World, c.1850–1914* (Cambridge: Cambridge University Press, 2010).

6   Looking at migrants with British nationality, my estimate for total departures is 8,334,772 and for departures to the empire and former empire (excluding the United States and Ireland for which there are no clear statistics prior to 1964) is 5,075,962. Data for 1945–64 from the reports of the Oversea Migration Board. Cmnd 2217, Commonwealth Relations Office, *Oversea Migration Board. Statistics for 1962* (London: HMSO, 1963), 7, 12. Cmnd 2861, Commonwealth Relations Office, *Oversea Migration Board. Statistics for 1964* (London: HMSO, 1965), 7. Data for 1964–2000 from Series MN, Office of Population, Censuses and Statistics, *International Migration: Migrants Entering or Leaving the United Kingdom*. Before 1963 the data is based on shipping records and so does not include those travelled by air. From 1963 onwards the data is from the International Passenger Survey, which is based on a random sample of passengers leaving by both air and sea routes. Emigrants are defined as those intending to leave the United Kingdom for more than one

year having lived in the United Kingdom for at least one year. These figures therefore do not take into account people who left or returned sooner than they anticipated, nor for return migration which, of course, varied substantially over time in both directions. For more detail see Jean P. Smith, 'Persistence and Privilege: Mass Migration from Britain to the Commonwealth, 1945–2000', in *The Break-up of Greater Britain*, eds Christian Damm Pederson and Stuart Ward (Manchester: Manchester University Press, 2021). Looking at a slightly different period, 1951–98, Timothy Hatton estimates a figure of 7.3 million emigrants to all non-European destinations. Timothy J. Hatton, 'Emigration from the UK, 1870–1913 and 1950–1998', *European Review of Economic History* 8:2 (2004), 153.

7 The colony of Southern Rhodesia, became Rhodesia after the Unilateral Declaration of Independence in 1965, and Zimbabwe in 1980 at independence. It will be referred to as Southern Rhodesia when the reference is specific to the period before 1965 and as Rhodesia when the reference is either in general terms to the settler regime prior to 1980 or specific to the period between 1965 and 1979.

8 George H. Gallup, ed., *The Gallup International Public Opinion Polls: Great Britain 1937–75* (New York: Random House, 1976), pp. 171, 187, 217, 249, 361, 401, 451, 481, 613, 621, 661, 702, 732, 789, 813, 878, 1036, 1071–2, 1219, 1298, 1441.

9 Eric Richards questions the reliability of such polls as measures of concrete intent to emigrate, however, they certainly reflect awareness of the possibility and an interest in emigration. See Richards, *Britannia's Children*, p. 355, note 15.

10 Ben Jones, *The Working Class in Mid Twentieth-century England: Community, Identity and Social Memory* (Manchester: Manchester University Press, 2012); Florence Sutcliffe-Braithwaite, *Class, Politics, and the Decline of Deference in England, 1968–2000* (Oxford: Oxford University Press, 2018).

11 Simon Gunn, 'Spatial mobility in later twentieth-century Britain', *Contemporary British History* (2021), 1–22.

12 Ibid., 6; Camilla Schofield and Ben Jones, '"Whatever Community Is, This Is Not It": Notting Hill and the Reconstruction of "Race" in Britain after 1958', *The Journal of British Studies* 58:1 (2019), 143–4.

13 On this, see also Hammerton, *Migrants of the British Diaspora*, pp. 7, 83.

14 The data for the line 'British Immigration to South Africa' is based on country of previous permanent residence. Figures for 1939 to 1948, Union of South Africa, *Statistics of Migration 1948* (Pretoria: The Government Printer, 1950), p. 43. Figure for 1949 calculated based on specific data for the years 1945 to 1948 as above and a figure for the period 1945–49 in Republic of South Africa Bureau of Statistics, *Report No. 286: Statistics of Immigrants and Emigrants 1924–1964* (Pretoria: The Government Printer, 1964), 3. Figures for 1950 to 1960, Republic of South Africa Bureau of Statistics, *Report No. 286: Statistics of Immigrants and Emigrants 1924–1964* (Pretoria: The Government Printer, 1964), 4. Figures for 1961 to 1969, Republic of South Africa Department of Statistics, *Report No. 19-01-01, Migration Statistics: Immigrants and Emigrants, 1966 to 1969*

(Pretoria: The Government Printer, 1969), p. 1. Figures for 1970 to 2004, Sally Peberdy, *Selecting Immigrants: National Identity and South Africa's Immigration Policies, 1910–2008* (Johannesburg: Wits University Press, 2009), pp. 276–90.
15 Immigration statistics were not collected systematically for country of previous residence, citizenship or birth in Southern Rhodesia. Figures for 1946 to 1953, Ian Smith Papers, Cory Library, Rhodes University, Grahamstown (hereafter Ian Smith Papers), Deposit No. 1/78/002, Southern Rhodesia Cabinet Memoranda 1953, 'Memorandum on Immigration', 23 July 1953. The Ian Smith Papers were consulted in Grahamstown in 2011, but they have since been returned to Zimbabwe. Figure for 1954, estimate from A.S. Mlambo, *White Immigration into Rhodesia from Occupation to Federation* (Harare: University of Zimbabwe Publications, 2002), p. 8. Figures for 1955 to 1970, Republic of Rhodesia, *Monthly Migration and Tourist Statistics for March 1970* (Salisbury: Central Statistics Office, 1970), p. 1. Figures for the Federation period do not include migration from Northern Rhodesia and Nyasaland. Figures for 1971 to 1979, Josiah Brownell, *The Collapse of Rhodesia: Population Demographics and the Politics of Race* (London: I.B. Taurus, 2011), p. 125.
16 58 per cent of the 500 British migrants to South Africa interviewed by John Stone in 1967 and 1968 stated that the subsidised scheme was a significant reason for choosing South Africa over other destinations. John Stone, *Colonist or Uitlander: A Study of the British Immigrant in South Africa* (Oxford: Clarendon Press, 1973), p. 163.
17 James Hampshire, *Citizenship and Belonging: Immigration and the Politics of Demographic Governance in Postwar Britain* (Basingstoke: Palgrave Macmillan, 2005), pp. 2–9.
18 Paul, *Whitewashing Britain*, pp. 3, 9, 16, 19, 23.
19 Smith, 'Persistence and Privilege'. For more details on this scheme see Chapter 4.
20 Rieko Karatani, *Defining British Citizenship: Empire, Commonwealth and Modern Britain* (London: Frank Cass, 2003), p. 112; Philip Murphy, *The Empire's New Clothes: The Myth of the Commonwealth* (London: Hurst and Company, 2018), p. 24.
21 On the relative weakness of the Race Relations Acts see Bailkin, *Afterlife of Empire*, p. 118.
22 Wendy Webster, *Englishness and Empire, 1939–1965* (Oxford: Oxford University Press, 2005), p. 120; Bill Schwarz, *The White Man's World* (Oxford: Oxford University Press, 2011), pp. 11–12.
23 On the 'local logics' of white nationalism see Daniel Geary, Camilla Schofield, and Jennifer Sutton, 'Introduction: Toward a global history of white nationalism', in *Global White Nationalism: From Apartheid to Trump*, eds Daniel Geary, Camilla Schofield and Jennifer Sutton (Manchester: Manchester University Press, 2020), pp. 7–8.
24 David Kenrick, *Decolonisation, Identity and Nation in Rhodesia, 1964–1979* (London: Palgrave Macmillan, 2019), pp. 244–5; Schwarz, *White Man's World*, pp. 407–10.

25 This draws on Ludwig Wittgenstein's idea of a 'family resemblance', in which 'phenomena have no one thing in common which makes us use the same word for all, but ... they are related to one another in many different ways'. Quoted in Mark R. Beissinger, 'Soviet Empire as "Family Resemblance"', *Slavic Review* 65:2 (2006), 294.

26 John Lambert, '"An Unknown People": Reconstructing British South African Identity', *The Journal of Imperial and Commonwealth History* 37:4 (2009), 599–617; P.S. Thompson, *Natalians First: Separatism in South Africa, 1909–1961* (Johannesburg: Southern Book Publishers, 1990); Donal Lowry, 'Rhodesia 1890–1980: "The Lost Dominion"', in *Settlers and Expatriates: Britons over the Seas*, ed. Robert Bickers (Oxford: Oxford University Press, 2010); David Kenrick, 'Settler Soul-Searching and Sovereign Independence: The Monarchy in Rhodesia, 1965–1970', *Journal of South African Studies* 44:6 (2018), 1077–93.

27 Here the emphasis is on both persistence and evolution. Networks were not 'reified or ossified' but were ever evolving. David Lambert and Alan Lester, 'Introduction: Imperial Spaces, Imperial Subjects', in *Colonial Lives Across the British Empire: Imperial Careering in the Long Nineteenth Century*, eds David Lambert and Alan Lester (Cambridge: Cambridge University Press, 2006), pp. 13, 30.

28 Stephan Daniels and Catherine Nash, 'Lifepaths: Geography and Biography', *Journal of Historical Geography* 30 (2004), 449–58. See also, Lambert and Lester, 'Imperial Spaces', p. 2; Ann Laura Stoler, 'Tense and Tender Ties: The Politics of Comparison in North American History and (Post) Colonial Studies', *The Journal of American History* 88:3 (2001), 862.

29 There is a large literature on the importance of examining metropole and colony in one 'analytic field'. Key works include Frederick Cooper and Ann L. Stoler, 'Introduction: Tensions of Empire: Colonial Control and Visions of Rule', *American Ethnologist* 16:4 (1989), 609–21; Edward Said, *Culture and Imperialism* (New York: Vintage Books, 1994); Edward Said, *Orientalism* (New York: Vintage Books, 2003); Anne McClintock, *Imperial Leather: Race, Gender and Sexuality in the Colonial Contest* (New York and London: Routledge, 1995); Mary Louise Pratt, *Imperial Eyes: Travel Writing and Transculturation* (London: Routledge, 1992). A related literature focuses more closely on colonies of settlement or the 'British World'. For an overview see Carl Bridge and Kent Fedorowich, 'Mapping the British World', in *The British World: Diaspora, Culture, and Identity*, eds Carl Bridge and Kent Fedorowich (London: Frank Cass Publishers, 2003). On the importance of archival rigor and the examination of non-metropolitan archives in imperial history see Dane Kennedy, 'Imperial History and Post-Colonial Theory', *Journal of Imperial and Commonwealth History* 24:3 (1996), 345–63; Richard Price, 'One Big Thing: Britain, Its Empire and Their Imperial Culture', *Journal of British Studies* 45 (2006), 602–27.

30 Ann Laura Stoler, *Along the Archival Grain: Epistemic Anxieties and Colonial Common Sense* (Princeton: Princeton University Press, 2009), pp. 53, 50.

31 Ibid., p. 41.

32 Ibid., pp. 3–4, 35–53.

33 On the use of oral history to gain insight into subjectivity, see Stephan F. Miescher, *Making Men in Ghana* (Bloomington and Indianapolis: Indiana University Press, 2003), p. 14; A. Portelli, 'What Makes Oral History Different', in *The Oral History Reader*, eds Robert Perks and Alistair Thomson (New York: Routledge, 2006), pp. 32–42. On the impact of migration on identity see Lambert and Lester, 'Imperial Spaces', p. 26.
34 For more on the importance of phrasing questions see Valerie Raleigh Yow, *Recording Oral History* (Lanham, MD: Altamira Press, 2005), pp. 72–4.
35 On the difficulties of anonymity see Ibid., pp. 134–5.
36 Ronald Hyam and Peter Henshaw, *The Lion and the Springbok: British and South Africa since the Boer War* (Cambridge: Cambridge University Press, 2003).
37 Dick Hoerder provides a compelling discussion of these myriad motivations for migration, comprising what he refers to as the 'holistic material-emotional approach'. Dick Hoerder, *Cultures in Contact: World Migrations in the Second Millennium* (Durham and London: Duke University Press, 2002), p. 20. See also, a similar discussion in relation to British emigration in general and to Australia in the decades after the Second World War, Richards, *Britannia's Children*, p. 288; Hammerton and Thomson, *Ten Pound Poms*, pp. 28–78.
38 Lorenzo Veracini, *Settler Colonialism: A Theoretical Overview* (London: Palgrave Macmillan, 2010), pp. 3, 12; Lorenzo Veracini, *The Settler Colonial Present* (London: Palgrave Macmillan, 2015), pp. 1–5; Lorenzo Veracini, 'Introduction: Settler colonialism as a distinct mode of domination', in *The Routledge Handbook of the History of Settler Colonialism*, eds Edward Cavanaugh and Lorenzo Veracini (Abingdon: Routledge, 2017), pp. 2–4.
39 J. Kehaulani Kauanui and Patrick Wolfe, 'Settler Colonialism Then and Now: A Conversation Between J. Kehaulani Kauanui and Patrick Wolfe', *Politica & Società* 2 (2012), 248–9. For an insightful critique of Wolfe's definition of settler colonialism as 'eliminationist' in relation to South Africa see Edward Cavanaugh, 'Settler Colonialism in South Africa: Land, Labour and Transformation, 1880–2015', in *The Routledge Handbook of the History of Settler Colonialism*, eds Edward Cavanaugh and Lorenzo Veracini (Abingdon: Routledge, 2017), pp. 291–309.
40 Stoler, 'Tense and Tender Ties', pp. 858–9; Jeremy Seekings, '"Not a Single White Person Should Be Allowed to Go Under": *Swartgevaar* and the Origins of South Africa's Welfare State, 1924–1929', *The Journal of African History* 48:3 (2007); Duncan Money and Danelle van Zyl-Hermann, 'Introduction: Rethinking White Societies in Southern Africa, 1930s–1990s', in *Rethinking White Societies in Southern Africa, 1930s–1990s*, eds Duncan Money and Danelle van Zyl-Hermann (London: Routledge, 2020), pp. 9–10, 15.
41 Smith, 'Persistence and Privilege'.
42 Marilyn Lake and Henry Reynolds, *Drawing the Global Colour Line: White Men's Countries and the International Challenge of Racial Equality* (Cambridge: Cambridge University Press, 2008), p. 5; Radhika Viyas Mongia, 'Race, Nationality, Mobility: A History of the Passport', in *After the Imperial*

Turn: Thinking with and through the Nation, ed. Antoinette Burton (Durham: Duke University Press, 2003), pp. 196–214.

43 Jean P. Smith, 'From Promising Settler to Undesirable Immigrant: The Deportation of British-born Migrants from Mental Hospitals in Interwar Australia and South Africa', The Journal of Imperial and Commonwealth History 46:3 (2018), 502–23; Alison Bashford, Imperial Hygiene: A Critical History of Colonialism, Nationalism and Public Health (Basingstoke: Palgrave Macmillan, 2003), pp. 137–63; Jane Carey, 'White Anxieties and the Articulation of Race: The Women's Movement and the Making of White Australia, 1910s–1930s', in Creating White Australia, eds Jane Carey and Claire McLisky (Sydney: Sydney University Press, 2009), p. 199; Alison Bashford, 'At the Border: Contagion, Immigration, Nation', Australian Historical Studies 33:120 (2002), 344–58.

44 There were earlier restrictions including the Aliens Acts of 1793, 1826 and 1848, but these were largely short-lived emergency measures aimed at European revolutionaries. Karatani, Defining British Citizenship, pp. 53, 86.

45 Ibid., pp. 116, 127–8; Paul, Whitewashing Britain, pp. 111–30; Randall Hansen, Citizenship and Immigration in Post-war Britain: The Institutional Origins of a Multicultural Nation (Oxford: Oxford University Press, 2000), pp. 36, 49, 53, 56–7; Ann Dummett and Andrew Nicol, Subjects, Citizens, Aliens and Others: Nationality and Immigration Law (London: Weidenfeld and Nicolson, 1990), pp. 177–8.

46 Karatani, Defining British Citizenship, pp. 116–26; Paul, Whitewashing Britain, pp. 9–24; Hansen, Citizenship and Immigration, pp. 35–56.

47 Smith, 'Persistence and Privilege'. On the ways in which whiteness and white privilege have often been overlooked or taken for granted in scholarship on British emigration see Daniel Conway and Pauline Leonard, Migration, Space and Transnational Identities: The British in South Africa (Basingstoke: Palgrave Macmillan, 2014), pp. 28, 54–8.

48 Stuart Ward, 'Introduction', in British Culture and the End of Empire, ed. Stuart Ward (Manchester: Manchester University Press, 2001), p. 1.

49 Fedorowich and Thompson place a particular emphasis on a transnational approach. Kent Fedorowich and Andrew Thompson, eds, Empire, Migration and Identity in the British World (Manchester: Manchester University Press, 2013); Robert Bickers, ed., Settlers and Expatriates: Britons over the Seas (Oxford: Oxford University Press, 2010); Marjory Harper and Stephen Constantine, Migration and Empire (Oxford: Oxford University Press, 2010).

50 The most comprehensive is Richards, Britannia's Children.

51 Howard L. Malchow, Population Pressures: Emigration and Government in Late Nineteenth-Century Britain (Palo Alto: Society for the Promotion of Science and Scholarship, 1979).

52 A. James Hammerton, Emigrant Gentlewomen: Genteel Poverty and Female Emigration, 1830–1914 (London: Croom Helm, 1979). See also A. James Hammerton's reflections on how this earlier work might be improved by greater attention to the lower-middle class. A. James Hammerton, '"Out of their Natural Station": Empire and Empowerment in the Emigration of

Lower-Middle-Class Women', in *Imperial Objects: Essays on Victorian Women's Emigration and the Unauthorized Imperial Experience*, ed. Rita S. Kranidis (New York: Twayne Publishers, 1998), pp. 143–69; Julia Bush, '"The Right Sort of Woman": Female Emigrators and the Emigration to the British Empire, 1890–1910', *Women's History Review* 3:3 (1994), 385–409; Lisa Chilton, 'A New Class of Women for the Colonies: *The Imperial Colonist* and the Construction of Empire', *The Journal of Imperial and Commonwealth History* 31:2 (2003), 36–56; Lisa Chilton, *Agents of Empire: British Female Migration to Canada and Australia, 1860s–1930* (Toronto: University of Toronto Press, 2007); Cecilie Swaisland, *Servants and Gentlewomen to the Golden Land: The Emigration of Single Women from Britain to Southern Africa, 1820–1939* (Oxford: Berg, 1993); Rita S. Kranidis, *The Victorian Spinster and Colonial Emigration: Contested Subjects* (New York: St. Martin's Press, 1999); Katie Pickles, 'Empire Settlement and Single British Women as New Zealand Domestic Servants during the 1920s', *New Zealand Journal of History* 35:1 (2001), 22–44; Katie Pickles, 'Pink Cheeked and Surplus: Single British Women's Inter-war Migration to New Zealand', in *Shifting Centres: Women and Migration in New Zealand History*, eds Lyndon Fraser and Katie Pickles (Otago: Otago University Press, 2002), pp. 63–80; Jean Jacques Van-Helten and Keith Williams, '"The Crying Need of South Africa": The Emigration of Single British Women to the Transvaal, 1901–1910', *Journal of South African Studies* 10:1 (October 1983), 17–38; Brian L. Blakely, 'Women and Imperialism: The Colonial Office and Female Emigration to South Africa, 1901–1910', *Albion: A Quarterly Journal Concerned with British Studies* 13:2 (1981), 131–49; B.W. Higman, 'Testing the Boundaries of White Australia: Domestic Servants and Immigration Policy, 1901–45', *Immigrants and Minorities* 22:1 (2003), 1–21.

53 John M. Robson, *Marriage or Celibacy? The Daily Telegraph on a Victorian Dilemma* (Toronto: University of Toronto Press, 1995).

54 Ellen Boucher, *Empire's Children: Child Emigration. Welfare, and the Decline of the British World, 1869–1967* (Cambridge: Cambridge University Press, 2014); Philip Bean and Joy Melville, *Lost Children of the Empire* (London: Unwin Hyman Limited, 1989); Roger Kershaw and Janet Sacks, *New Lives for Old: The Story of Britain's Child Migrants* (Kew: The National Archives, 2008); Richards, *Britannia's Children*; Geoffrey Sherington and Chris Jeffery, *Fairbridge: Empire and Child Migration* (London: Woburn Press, 1998); Gillian Wagner, *Children of the Empire* (London: Weidenfeld and Nicolson, 1982).

55 Lynne Bowen, *Muddling Through: The Remarkable Story of the Barr Colonists* (Vancouver: Douglas & McIntyre, 1992); Jean G. Kristiansen, *Brother Officers on the Sheep's Back: An Account of the Indian Army Officers' Settlement in Victoria in the 1920s* (Camperdown: J.G. Kristiansen, 1993); C.E. Wetton, *The Promised Land: The Story of the Barr Colonists* (Lloydminster: Lloydminster Times, 1955); Marilyn Barber and Murray Watson, *Invisible Immigrants: The English in Canada since 1945* (Winnipeg: University of Manitoba Press, 2015); Anthony Richmond, *Post-War Immigrants in Canada* (Toronto: University of Toronto Press, 1967); Ninette Kelley and Michael Trebilcock, *The Making of*

the Mosaic: A History of Canadian Immigration Policy (Toronto: University of Toronto Press, 2010).
56 Megan Hutching, Long Journey for Sevenpence: An Oral History of Assisted Immigration to New Zealand from the United Kingdom, 1947–1975 (Wellington: Victoria University Press, 1999).
57 Reg Appleyard, The Ten Pound Immigrants (London: Boxtree Limited, 1988); Peter Black, Poms in the Sun (London: The Travel Book Club, 1965); Stephen Constantine, 'Waving Goodbye? Australia, Assisted Passages, and the Empire and Commonwealth Settlement Acts, 1945–72', Journal of Imperial and Commonwealth History 26:2 (1998), 176–95; Stephen Constantine, 'The British Government, Child Welfare, and Child Migration to Australia after 1945', Journal of Imperial and Commonwealth History. 30:1 (2002), 99–132; Hammerton and Thomson, Ten Pound Poms; James Jupp, The English in Australia (Cambridge and New York: Cambridge University Press, 2004); Michael Roe, Australia, Britain, and Migration, 1915–1940: A Study of Desperate Hopes (Cambridge: Cambridge University Press, 2002); Sarah Wills, '"When Good Neighbours Become Good Friends": The Australian Embrace of its Millionth Migrant', Australian Historical Studies 35:124 (2004), 332–54; A.C. Palfreeman, The Administration of the White Australia Policy (Melbourne: Melbourne University Press, 1967); James Jupp, From White Australia to Woomera: The Story of Australian Immigration (Cambridge: Cambridge University Press, 2002).
58 Mlambo, White Immigration; Brownell, Collapse of Rhodesia.
59 Edna Bradlow, 'Immigration into the Union, 1910–1948: Policies and Attitudes' (PhD dissertation, University of Cape Town, 1978); Edna Bradlow, 'Empire Settlement and South African Immigration Policy, 1910–1948', in Emigrants and Empire: British Settlement in the Dominions Between the Wars, ed. Stephen Constantine (Manchester: Manchester University Press, 1990); F. G. Brownell, British Immigration to South Africa, 1946–1970 (Pretoria: The Government Printer, 1985); Esme Bull, Aided Immigration from Britain to South Africa, 1857–1867 (Pretoria: Human Sciences Research Council, 1991); John M. MacKenzie with Nigel R. Dalziel, The Scots in South Africa: Ethnicity, Identity, Gender and Race, 1772–1914 (Manchester: Manchester University Press, 2007); Stone, Colonist or Uitlander; Swaisland, Servants and Gentlewomen; Peberdy, Selecting Immigrants.
60 Kent Fedorowich, Unfit for Heroes: Reconstruction and Soldier Settlement in the Empire between the Wars (Manchester: Manchester University Press, 1995); Angela McCarthy, Personal Narratives of Irish and Scottish Migration, 1921–65 (Manchester: Manchester University Press, 2007); Philip Payton, The Cornish Overseas: The Epic Story of Cornwall's 'Great Emigration' (Exeter: University of Exeter Press, 2020); Belich, Replenishing the Earth; Magee and Thompson, Empire and Globalisation; Hammerton, Migrants of the British Diaspora.
61 Constantine is careful to state that this essay is 'highly speculative' and that the date provided of 1940 might be 'premature' and might be different in the case of each receiving country. Stephen Constantine, 'British Emigration to the

Empire-Commonwealth since 1880: From Overseas Settlement to Diaspora?', *Journal of Imperial and Commonwealth History*. 31:2 (2003), 19, 25, 31.
62 Mlambo, *White Immigration*.
63 Brownell, *Collapse of Rhodesia*; Kenrick, *Decolonisation, Identity and Nation*, pp. 28–37.
64 An exception is the recent work of George Bishi. George Bishi, 'Immigration and Settlement of "undesirable" whites in Southern Rhodesia, c.1940s–1960s', in *Rethinking White Societies in Southern Africa, 1930s–1990s*, eds Duncan Money and Danelle van Zyl-Hermann (London: Routledge, 2020), pp. 59–77.
65 Bradlow, 'Empire Settlement'; Bradlow, 'Immigration into the Union'.
66 Brownell, *British Immigration to South Africa*.
67 Peberdy, *Selecting Immigrants*.
68 Stone, *Colonist or Uitlander*; Conway and Leonard, *Migration, Space*.
69 Webster, *Englishness and Empire*, pp. 165, 179.
70 Bailkin, *Afterlife of Empire*; Stephen Howe, 'Internal Decolonization? British Politics since Thatcher as Post-colonial Trauma', *Twentieth Century British History* 14:3 (2003), 286–304; A. G. Hopkins, 'Rethinking Decolonization', *Past and Present* 200:1 (2008), 211–47.

1

'The height of my ambition is to become a Springbok': Wartime travel to southern Africa, race and the discourse of opportunity

Penny Salter, an English army nurse, stopped in Durban, South Africa on her way to serve in Burma and India during the Second World War. Like millions of Allied service men and women, Salter received a warm welcome in a sunny port city with miles of golden sand beaches. Her stay in South Africa, far removed from the dangers and discomforts of life on both the British home front and the battlefront stands out in Salter's memoir as a stark contrast to wartime austerity. At Stuttafords, a well-stocked department store, she was able to buy 'white kid shoes and pure silk stockings and … luxury goods and cosmetics we had forgotten existed'. As well as rejoicing over the availability of consumer goods, Salter described the mood of wartime patriotism and hospitality in Durban:

> We certainly did have a wonderful week … the races at Clairmont, bathing in shark infested waters of the Indian Ocean and the Valley of a Thousand Hills, well into the interior, where hills rolled upon hills for miles unceasingly over the horizon. Then it was the south coast, amid the sugar canes, that blew in waves so violently onto the silver shores of the Indian Ocean itself. Apart from our daytime entertainment, we danced the nights away under the starry sky, mostly at the Athlone Gardens night club, where here, even the baby monkeys cavorted and frolicked as they laughingly peered at us through the trees. Then, all too soon, it was like a dream, this inconceivable week had come to an end.[1]

Influenced by her wartime experience, Salter moved to southern Africa after the war. She described her return to Britain as 'an anti-climax', and after securing a nursing contract in Southern Rhodesia through a surgeon she had met during the war, she returned in 1947. Aboard the RMMV *Cape Town Castle* she found herself among 'a venturesome crowd of mostly ex-service men and women, now thoroughly sick and tired of the gloom and dreary atmosphere, rations and restrictions of post-war Britain … running away to make a new life for themselves in sunnier climes'.[2] Her narrative speaks to the appeal of the settler colonies of southern Africa to British migrants in the 1940s: the contrast to austerity in Britain, the climate, the sense of opportunity and the lifestyle available to a privileged racial minority. It also suggests a largely unexamined consequence of the Second World War, that more Britons than ever before had direct experience of the empire.

While restrictions and the dangers of travel meant that formal emigration rates were low during the conflict, the global reach of the war prompted both military and civilian movement on an enormous scale.[3] In the case of Britain, studies of wartime migration have largely focused on internal evacuation, especially of children, from urban areas to the countryside, and exile communities in the United Kingdom.[4] However, the global scale of the war led many Britons to travel more widely than they would have in peacetime. As well as the well-documented Anglo-American relationship, the war also brought many into contact with colonial and Dominion troops and civilians, not only in the United Kingdom, but throughout the Empire–Commonwealth.[5]

This chapter traces the impact of the unprecedented scale of British travel to two imperial sites, South Africa and Southern Rhodesia, and argues that this led to an increase in post-war migration to the region. As well as leading to the formation of relationships, wartime experience contributed to South Africa and Southern Rhodesia's place in the British imaginary as desirable locations to live. Though rarely articulated explicitly, the opportunities available to British migrants were based on the racial logic of these settler colonial regimes.[6]

In investigating the consequences of such large numbers of Britons spending time in southern Africa during the war, this chapter contributes to a growing literature on the British Empire during the Second World War.[7] This work has served both to complicate the resilient story of Britain's isolation as a besieged island nation, and to stress the importance of the war in former colonies, where it has often been overlooked or addressed only as a 'prelude to nationalist movements in the post-war era'.[8] In this vein, work on Southern Rhodesia during the war has focused on industrialisation, urbanisation and the introduction of conscription for agricultural labour as factors contributing to the anti-colonial movement.[9] As well as similar arguments regarding wartime industrial development, scholarship on South Africa during the war has focused on Afrikaner nationalist calls for neutrality and the close parliamentary vote which ultimately overruled them.[10] This attention to the neutrality crisis as a harbinger for the eventual triumph of Afrikaner nationalism and republicanism has overshadowed the important role that South Africa played in the war.

Though removed from fields of battle, South Africa and its neighbour, Southern Rhodesia, became another home front for Allied soldiers, sailors, airmen and civilians, a transport hub, a base for military training and an industrial centre manufacturing war materials.[11] Because of the dangers of the route through the Mediterranean, most Allied ships travelled around the Cape of Good Hope to North Africa, South Asia and the Pacific for the first three years of the war. South African ports became important bases for repairing and resupplying Allied vessels. Service men convalesced in South Africa and were sent to South Africa and Southern Rhodesia for training. Officials and businessmen relocated to support the war effort, children were evacuated from Britain, and refugees fleeing the Pacific, India and East Africa travelled to southern Africa. Millions of Allied service men and women and close to 300,000 civilians spent time in southern Africa during the war.[12]

Such contact did not end with the war. Immediately thereafter, a large number of people moved from Britain to South Africa and Southern Rhodesia, more than 70,000, or 20 per cent of emigrants leaving the United Kingdom from 1945 to 1948.[13] More British people moved to South Africa than Australia in 1947.[14] Though immigration rates levelled out from this post-war surge by the early 1950s, British migrants continued to arrive in southern Africa in the decades after the war, and immigration rates rose again dramatically in the 1960s and 1970s, as discussed in later chapters.[15]

This post-war surge in British migration to southern Africa has not yet been fully explained. Most scholars have focused on the more open approach to British immigration under Jan Smuts' United Party coalition, contrasting this with the more restrictive approach taken by the National Party government, which came to power in 1948.[16] However, neither the Smuts government in South Africa nor the Huggins government in Southern Rhodesia implemented assisted migration schemes as did the other main receiving countries of British migrants in this period: Australia, Canada and New Zealand. As described in more detail in Chapter 3, the Southern Rhodesian government, despite initial plans to offer subsidies, instead implemented strict controls as migrants, predominantly from Britain and South Africa, arrived in large numbers. Wartime experience of South Africa and Southern Rhodesia, this chapter argues, played an important, though previously overlooked, role in this migration.

The war brought more Britons to southern Africa than ever before and many formed new relationships, both personal and professional. The wartime experience of the lifestyle available in the temperate, settler colonial societies of southern Africa convinced many to move permanently after the war. The heightened experience of war, the sense of normal business in suspension, the excitement and exhilaration that often accompanied the terror and tedium also had an impact. The bleak reality of post-war Britain made migration even more appealing to many. Experience in southern Africa made the decision to move there easier, as did its promise of the exotic tempered by familiar language, food and cultural institutions.

Assessments of the relationship between Britain and the settler colonies of southern Africa in the post-war period have focused primarily on the political divisions made final by the declaration of South African Republic in 1961 and the Rhodesian Unilateral Declaration of Independence in 1965. Emphasis on the neutrality crisis and Afrikaner nationalist opposition to the war effort as precedents to this split has obscured the history of wartime imperial patriotism in the region and the long-standing cultural, economic and personal connections that persisted with the United Kingdom.[17]

By looking at contemporary understandings of the settler colonies of southern Africa in the late 1940s rather than reading backwards from the political separations of the 1960s, this chapter also contributes to a growing literature examining the continued resonance of empire in post-1945 Britain. It takes seriously Jordanna Bailkin's recent call to examine critically the 'post war' and especially its relationship to the 'post imperial'.[18] Similarly, Bill Schwarz has persuasively argued that the circulation of 'people, goods, and stories' between Britain and the empire has meant that the 'imagined geographies of empires' and especially those of settler societies had a strong resonance in the metropole.[19] Wendy Webster's examination of print media, radio and films also supports this conclusion, especially her discussion of the depiction of the 'people's empire' in the immediate post-war period.[20] This chapter explores a particular instance of the traffic between Britain and the empire, mass wartime travel to southern Africa and the ways in which these exchanges contributed to metropolitan understandings of these imperial sites.

It draws on sources that shed light on the British experience of wartime southern Africa and its appeal for prospective immigrants: memoirs and the enquiry letters of would-be migrants to the South African government.[21] The records of the Department of the Interior and the Director General of Demobilisation in the National Archives of South Africa contain material representing 680 letters, covering the period from 1943 to 1950.[22] While many are straightforward enquiries, others provide pages of personal details and in a few cases photographs. Recurring themes in the letters are further elaborated in memoirs of those who spent time in southern Africa during the war. Memoirs, largely from the Imperial War Museum collection in London, include those of service men and women and overseas child evacuees.[23] They provide a sense of what it was like to travel to southern Africa during the war and, though they are by no means a representative survey, they add depth and texture to the more abbreviated material from the letters.

These sources describe time spent in South Africa and Southern Rhodesia and the attractions of the privileged lifestyle of the ruling white minority. Many explicitly address the motivations of aspiring migrants. Some sought new opportunities, others had married or hoped to marry South Africans or Rhodesians, or were motivated by the climate and standard of living. Many mention the sense of welcome they felt and the friendships and business relationships they had forged. They often emphasise the hospitality provided by the white community including encouragement to move to the region.[24] These snapshots of a particular moment in the lives of ordinary people are useful in two ways. One is to evaluate general trends based on quantitative analysis of these letters, for example, how many mention time in wartime southern Africa or marriage. The second is qualitative, aiming to shed light on the 'social worlds' of these ordinary Britons, their motivations for moving and their understandings of South Africa, Southern Rhodesia, Britain and empire in this period.[25]

'I fell in love with the place whilst on convoy to the Middle East': Wartime travel and the formation of personal networks

Wartime travel led to the formation of new relationships and strengthened existing networks between the United Kingdom and southern Africa. This section outlines the scope of wartime travel to southern Africa, the volume of interest in immigration there and the importance of personal relationships, especially marriage, in the decision to relocate. For three years, after the closure of the Mediterranean to Allied shipping in 1940 with the entry of Italy into the war, the route around the Cape was more important than it had been since the opening of the Suez Canal in 1869.[26] Allied naval and merchant vessels used the Cape route to transport Lend-Lease goods to the Soviet Union by way of the Persian Gulf and troops and supplies to the Middle Eastern, Asian and Pacific theatres of war and during the war close to 50,000 Allied ships passed through South African ports.[27] Durban was the base for the Allied invasion of Vichy-held Madagascar in May 1942 and South African ports served as repair stations for Allied ships, especially after the loss of Singapore, repairing more than 13,000.[28]

More than 400 troop convoys carrying millions of troops passed through South African ports. Many were the 'WS' or 'Winston's Specials' who transported British service men between the United Kingdom, North Africa, the Middle East, South Asia and South-east Asia.[29] Allied service men also went to southern Africa for training. More than 33,500 airmen prepared for active service in South Africa, the largest number after Canada, and more than 10,000 received air training in Southern Rhodesia.[30] Naval training operations were also based in South Africa at the HMS *Assegai* camp near Durban.[31]

Many of these service men and women expressed interest in moving to South Africa and Southern Rhodesia after the war. There was a precedent for this in the soldier settlement schemes after the First World War, which provided subsidised passages to the Dominions for ex-service men. Knowledge of these schemes is reflected in service men's enquiries as to whether they would be repeated after the Second World War.[32] A number of British and South African officials wrote to the South African Ministry of the Interior asking how they should handle the numerous queries they received about post-war immigration, indicating wide interest. As early as 1941, the commander of an air school near Oudtshoorn wrote to the Governor-General of South Africa, Sir Patrick Duncan, proposing a government scheme to resettle Royal Air Force personnel in South Africa.[33] In 1943, Lieutenant-Colonel E.G. Malherbe, the South Africa Director of Military Intelligence and Chief of Army Educational Services, sought further information about immigration because 'at all air stations where Information Officers come into contact with RAF Personnel this matter continually crops up'.[34] In May 1945, *The Patriot*, the South African Special Operations Executive journal forwarded a request for information about post-war immigration from A.F. Eccles, serving with the RAF in South Africa, noting the 'scores of men who are making the same enquiry'.[35]

Such requests also came from South African officials serving with British troops abroad. The South African Consul in Egypt asked for information about immigration to South Africa for publication in a local newsletter, *Gen*, in response to all the enquiries he had received from British service men.[36] Similar requests came from South African officials in India and East Africa.[37] As the end of the war appeared imminent, the Army Education section of the South African Defence Force again noted the number of queries from British service men about demobilisation in the Union.[38] So did the Chief of the General Staff, citing correspondence from the public relations officer in the Middle East: 'Numerous enquiries being made post-war immigration to South Africa. Can you obtain official statement for wide publication among Allied Forces?'[39] That these enquiries continued throughout and after the war indicates that many service men and women were considering the possibility of migration to South Africa as they planned for demobilisation.[40]

These requests from South African officials reveal both the extent of interest in migration and the concerns of would-be immigrants. These included the prospects of post-war employment, the formalities of immigration and whether it would be possible to demobilise in the Union, particularly in the case of those who had married South Africans. Many of these themes were further developed in individual letters of enquiry, which often provided details of the authors' personal circumstances and reasons for migration.

These letters must be read with a critical eye, as their authors clearly intended to persuade officials that they would make worthy immigrants. Even so, what they assumed might help their case is of interest. Many framed their requests in terms of their affection for South Africa based on time spent there and often emphasised relationships they had formed with South Africans. Of the 409 letters regarding service men surveyed, close to half, 176, mentioned time they had spent in South Africa, usually during the war.[41] It is likely than an even higher proportion had visited the Union, given that many letters were straightforward enquiries about immigration procedures and offered no personal information.

These letters often emphasised relationships between would-be migrants and South Africans, highlighting the importance of personal relationships in motivating migration.[42] The most frequent relationship given as a reason for migration was marriage.[43] Eighty-one of the letters surveyed mentioned marriage and twenty-three mentioned engagement to a South African as a reason for migration, almost a quarter of the total.[44] These included the letter of Robert Smith, who had worked for the British Overseas Airways Corporation on an overseas contract in South Africa for four and a half years. In this time, Smith had married a South African and hoped to stay in South Africa after the war.[45] Another example is the letter of Mrs P.M. Norton, who in her enquiry about her husband mentioned the 'many other girls who have married men from England who intend to reside here permanently'.[46] Relationships could also begin in Britain and set in motion chain migration. A memorandum from November 1945 noted that '350 wives and 83 children of U.D.F. [Union Defence Force] service personnel' were in the United Kingdom waiting for passages to South Africa, and requested that they be allocated priority passages.[47] Another example is Harold Robson, who went to Southern Rhodesia in 1947 to join his sister, who had married a Rhodesian pilot she had met in Britain during the war.[48]

Though marriage to a South African woman did not make any legal difference in terms of immigration, it is frequently mentioned in these letters. Under South African law women took on the nationality of their husband upon marriage. Most British service men, however, could obtain entry as immigrants in their own right. South Africa gave priority to 'natural-born British subjects' (natural-born a clear euphemism for white), provided they were free of infectious diseases, had no criminal record and could prove the ability to support themselves.[49]

Other personal relationships were also frequently cited, with sixty letters mentioning friends in South Africa, and forty mentioning relatives.[50] Captain A. G. Ross wrote to enquire about the possibilities of migration on behalf of several other officers: 'We have friends and relatives in the country and our brief visit, en route for India confirmed our wish to settle here.'[51] A.E. Pratt, serving in the RAF in India wrote to the Ministry of the Interior in May 1944 asking to be demobilised in South Africa. As he put it, 'during the three months I spent in the Union last year I made many friends, also made up my mind to return, just as soon as possible ... I have adopted S. Africa as my new country – will you help me to come home to it?'[52] Flight-Lieutenant Jan Witthoft also emphasised his connections to South Africa, writing: 'I am English with relations residing in Johannesburg, Pilgrims Rest and Durban. It was my great privilege to spend six months in South Africa last year, during which time I made innumerable friends, grew to look upon the Union with great affection, and upon its people, English and Africaners [sic] with the highest esteem.'[53] Though he makes no explicit mention of race, Witthoft's vision of South Africa is restricted to its white population and his letter stresses his connection with Afrikaners as well as English South Africans, suggesting a kind of racial solidarity. Although it is unclear whether this was a genuine sentiment, or an attempt to portray himself as a desirable immigrant who would integrate well with the white South African population, it speaks to the growing importance of racial solidarity or 'white South Africanism' in this period.[54]

This correspondence with the South African Department of the Interior makes visible the personal networks that existed between Britain and the settler colonies of southern Africa. Not only are such connections referred to in the letters, but many were written on behalf of would-be migrants by fiancées, wives, friends, employers and family members in South Africa. Though some of these connections predated the war, many were forged through wartime circumstances. As well as leading to personal connections that might factor into a decision to move to the region, time in southern Africa during the war also exposed Britons to the lifestyle and opportunities available to the privileged ruling white minority.

'Lights, unlimited bread and huge tins of Koo melon and lemon jam': Abundance and pleasure in wartime Southern Africa

Wartime recollections reflect the contrast between the abundance of southern Africa and the hardship and austerity of both the battlefront and the British home front. Domestic consumption in South Africa was among the least restricted in the wartime empire because Smuts, fearing the incitement of further opposition to South Africa's participation in the war and to his government, did not impose strict rationing, higher taxation or conscription on the white population, even as Black African workers, as in much of the continent, were subjected to an increasingly interventionist regime. South Africa saw occasional shortages, for example of meat and maize in 1942 and 1943, and restrictions placed on items such as paper, white flour and petrol.[55] There were more shortages in Southern Rhodesia, where maize was rationed from 1942, however, for the most part in both places a wider variety of food was available than in the United Kingdom.[56] Shipping shortages meant that some locally produced foodstuffs, such as fresh fruit, which were scarce in the United Kingdom, were more readily available to the domestic market than before the war.[57]

The variety of food available in southern Africa reflected the realities of wartime political economy but it also drew on long-standing ideas about the region. People expected fruit and sunshine and they found both.[58] Service men and women again and again remembered eating fruit and jam. Such recollections became a kind of shorthand for the abundance and climate of southern Africa. Penny Salter mentioned her excitement at the fruit bowls on tables on board the ship to South Africa during the war.[59] Derek Wilkins, sent from Liverpool on the SS *Orbita* for air training in Southern Rhodesia in December 1943, described the sharp difference between life in wartime Britain and aboard the crowded, ill-provisioned troop ship and the abundance in South Africa, a paradise with 'lights, unlimited bread and huge tins of Koo melon and lemon jam'.[60] Fred Dane wrote about his time in Durban:

> After the austerity of wartime Britain we couldn't have landed in a more beautiful place than Durban ... It was warm, sunny, and Durban was an attractive city, spotlessly clean and crammed with an abundance of the most delicious foods. There were enormous oranges, bananas, tomatoes, and melons, things that we had not seen in England since the war started.[61]

K.A.C. Melvin, travelling to Southern Rhodesia for air training, wrote at length about his excitement at being able to buy tinned peaches on the ship to South Africa and pooling his money with a friend to buy as many cans as possible.[62] Melvin also described the food available at the transit camp outside Durban, emphasising the unlimited amount of jam available:

> Every four feet or so down the centre of each scrubbed wooden table was a 7 lb tin of jam ... Between each tin was a loaf of bread and a knife. The colourful tins told us of fruits, some of which we had never heard, and of course us young lads just had to try them all. One of them was mango and pineapple jam and another pawpaw.

The enormous tins of jam signified the abundance of South Africa and served as a metaphor for its appeal as a place both familiar and exotic. Jam was a comfortingly British staple, yet the tropical fruit added an unfamiliar and exciting novelty. Sugar was rationed early in the war, making jam a rare treat in Britain and a nostalgic symbol of life before the war.[63]

The quantity of food available was appealing, although perhaps more important was its quality and variety. Melvin described a visit to a restaurant in Durban, the Victoria Club, where he and some friends were so excited about the food available that they ate dinner twice:

> We were all entranced at the display of goodies! Having left Blighty's meagre fare followed by the troopship 'galley grub', the sight of people eating beautifully cooked mixed grills with eggs, bacon, sausage and all that goes on such a plate, was just too much. We all had the same followed by what was called a banana split – and I had never seen one of these before! A large oval plate with banana and other fruits all smothered in jelly and cream. I do not know what our waitress thought as when that was finished, we declined coffee and ordered the same again! It took us the whole evening but we did it! Yes, we made pigs of ourselves and thoroughly enjoyed the experience![64]

Though few are as vivid as this description, detailed accounts of meals and food appear frequently in wartime memoirs. This focus on food is not surprising given wartime conditions in Britain. This was not necessarily a question of quantity. Rationing and wartime employment meant that many had access to more food than in the 1930s.[65] Food was, however, often less palatable due to shortages of ingredients such as onions, lemons and anchovies that provided flavour.[66] The focus on food also reflected the low quality of military food especially in the early years of the war when the Cape route saw the most traffic before the creation of the more professional Army Catering Corps and the introduction of the composite ration.[67]

Along with abundant food, soldiers described South African hospitality.[68] Durban particularly stood out in recollections of wartime South Africa, with its golden beaches on the warm Indian Ocean. Its large Anglo-South African population welcomed British troops with an outpouring of imperial patriotism and hospitality.[69] This was symbolised by Perla Gibson, the 'Lady in White', who sang to greet each troop ship through a megaphone.[70] Dressed in her trademark billowing white dress with either a striking red felt or a straw hat, Gibson, who was also known as 'Ma' or 'Nightingale' reputedly sang to more than 5,000 ships during the war, varying her repertoire depending on the ship.[71] Gibson became so famous among British service men that that she was invited to the United Kingdom several times to perform after the war, appearing on the BBC in 1955 and at the Royal Albert Hall in 1964. As late as 1970 Gibson performed in Plymouth as the guest of the HMS *Devonshire* Survivors Association. Her continuing resonance with British veterans as a symbol of their time in South Africa is demonstrated by the reissue of her autobiography in 1991 and the organisation of a tour to South Africa for British veterans in 1992 including a performance by a Gibson impersonator.[72] A statue of Gibson, also funded by British veterans, was unveiled by Queen Elizabeth II in 1995 in Durban harbour and was displayed there until it was temporarily relocated in 2016 to the Port Natal Maritime Museum.[73]

As well as the patriotic greetings of the 'Lady in White', service men recalled the hospitality offered to them once ashore. W.J. Malone described his time in Durban. Beginning in a bar in West Street, they moved on to the Victoria League Club 'full of service men enjoying cooked meals and being served by young ladies'. After 'selecting' dates at the Club, Malone and his friends,

> drove out to the Round-house outside Durban and relaxed over a drink under a starry sky and a panoramic view of the city. We danced until after midnight before seeing the girls home and returning to camp. The following evening, Pat, the girl I had partnered, invited me home to meet her family who lived near the Botanical Gardens. My recollection of their hospitality and their Zulu servant who they got to speak his native tongue remains today.[74]

As well as the hospitality offered by Pat and her friends, Malone's specific mention of the 'Zulu servant' and his language performance shows an awareness of both the possibility of enjoying a privilege available only to the wealthy in the United Kingdom, domestic servants, and the exotic allure of the landscape of South Africa and its indigenous people. African people appear rarely in these wartime memoirs, and if they do it is usually as servants or signifiers of the exotic setting.[75]

The letters of would-be immigrants also frequently emphasise the welcome the authors received in South Africa and Southern Rhodesia. Of the time he spent in Cape Town en route to India, T.J. Weddell of the RAF recalled, 'the hospitality we received was the finest I have ever seen. In fact, words fail me to describe it.'[76] John Weighill wrote about the 'overwhelming hospitality' he experienced in Durban: 'The family I met there subsequently proved to be the most loyal friends and correspondents and throughout my service sent me constant reminders of their affection in the shape of parcels of cigarettes, sweets, etc.'[77] The provision of often extravagant hospitality for Allied troops can be understood in a number of ways: as support for the war effort, as a demonstration of patriotism or even just as an enjoyable diversion.[78]

Orchestrating much of this welcome was the South African Women's Auxiliary Service (SAWAS) and its Rhodesian equivalent, the Women's National Service League. Between 1939 and 1947 when it ceased operations after the royal visit of that year, SAWAS coordinated 65,000 volunteers, 'the Universal Aunts of South Africa', who organised dances and other activities, and ran clubs and canteens, where food was available at cheap rates to troops.[79] Operating on a smaller scale, the Women's

National Service League in Rhodesia also ran canteens and childcare facilities that enabled mothers to undertake war work, and organised care packages to be sent to men on active service.[80] Though SAWAS was active throughout South Africa, much of its work focused on the 'WS' convoys as they passed through South African ports en route to the Middle East, the Pacific and Burma.[81] SAWAS organised drivers to take troops on excursions and deliver 'comforts'. As E.A.S. Bailey described it, 'a fleet of cars would be waiting at the dock gates at that hour to take the troops swimming, shopping, or for a tour in the country, and "up-homers" for a smashing meal – the like of which they had not sampled since before the war – if ever!' Bailey cites one service man's recollection of his arrival in Cape Town, a 'transformation to paradise' with a 'line of cars stretched for three miles'. This welcome also extended beyond the docks: 'When we went into shops, whatever we tried to buy was wrapped up and given to us! Everywhere we went we were welcomed with open arms.'[82] SAWAS organised food parcels and news to be sent to family back in Britain. They paid for two-week holidays for the crews of warships that were refitting in South African ports and provided these for more than 50,000 men in the port of Simon's Town alone. These activities served as a respite between time spent in war-torn Britain and on the battlefront and further cemented the image of South Africa's thriving consumer culture with food, shops and leisure readily available.

Those who spent time in Southern Rhodesia also emphasised the hospitality they received. Aside from a few rural bases, such as Guinea Fowl and Thornhill, near present-day Gweru, most of the air training bases were clustered around the two major urban centres, Bulawayo and Salisbury (present-day Harare). A member of the RAF wrote to the newspaper thanking 'the large number of hosts and hostesses in Mashonaland who have opened their homes and extended their hospitality to officers and airmen of all ranks in the R.A.F. during the recent Christmas break'.[83] Service men interviewed by John Golley reminisced about the drinking establishments of Salisbury, such as the Bodega Bar, the cheap alcohol and cigarettes, and the hospitality of Rhodesians, who entertained cadets in their homes.[84] Many spent holidays in places like Victoria Falls and a particular favourite, Durban on the South African coast.[85] T.S. Kilpatrick described how he would take the train down to Durban and after a week's seaside holiday fly back to Southern Rhodesia in a newly assembled Harvard aircraft. Kilpatrick made this journey nineteen times while posted to Southern Rhodesia and fondly remembered his stays at the Mayfair Hotel 'at the cost of a mere 11 shillings a day, which provided a jolly good room and private bath plus four marvellous meals daily. Even a Flying Officer's pay of 18s 12d a day contrived to cater for that!' He also recalled the affordable price of South African wine and brandy, which he would purchase in bulk and fly back to the mess.[86] Life in southern Africa, with cheap wine and jaunts to the coast stood in stark contrast to wartime Britain and to the often difficult conditions of service in Europe, North Africa or Asia.

W.J. Malone, who, after training in Southern Rhodesia travelled through South Africa, stopping in Pretoria to visit a friend's family, articulated this contrast and the consequent attractions of emigration:

> With no nightly black-outs, air raid warnings and food shortages, life in South Africa was far removed from the war, and I could not help contrasting this pleasant interlude with the hardships of families and friends back home. Many of the people I met hoped we would come and settle in South Africa after the war but such thoughts could not be entertained with the enormous task that lay before us.[87]

Malone's account highlights the way that the war exacerbated the differences between the United Kingdom and South Africa to the latter's advantage even as the events of the conflict brought more Britons to the region than ever before. Though he felt unable to consider moving while engaged in his military duties, his memoir highlights the welcome he received not only as a visitor but as a potential migrant.

Wartime experience could also influence a decision to move long after the war. Mark Dawson described his father's motivation to move to South Africa from Britain in 1963 as influenced by his time in the navy during the war when he visited a number of countries including South Africa.[88] Sandra Conway moved to South Africa in the 1970s in part because of the stories her father had told her about his wartime experiences.[89] Similarly John Stone's sociological survey of British migrants to South Africa in the late 1960s found that many had visited the region during the war.[90] Bringing millions of Britons to southern Africa, the war exposed them to hospitality, abundance and the opportunities and lifestyle available to a privileged racial minority.

While most of the descriptions emphasise Rhodesians' and South Africans' hospitality, some do recall conflict or the threat of conflict from those who were opposed to South African participation in the war. Officers warned Melvin, in the region for air training, about the OBs, members of the Ossewabrandwag (The Ox-wagon Sentinel) an Afrikaner nationalist organisation which had attacked some RAF personnel, but he never had any trouble himself.[91] Moira Mackie, a British girl evacuated to Cape Town, described an incident when her victory badge was torn off her blazer on a train and thrown out the window by an opponent of South African participation in the war.[92] Clearly, those who did experience such hostility might also be less likely to wish to move to South Africa and such instances are therefore unlikely to appear in the letters of would-be migrants. There were also those who disagreed with the racism and segregation of South African society. Alun Lewis, a Welsh poet who visited South Africa while serving in the British Army for instance wrote, 'I don't agree with those of my friends who say they'd like to settle in South Africa after the war,' citing his concerns about the suppression of South Africans of colour.[93]

Nonetheless, the overwhelming tone in both the letters and the memoirs was of welcome and hospitality and not only in the English-dominated coastal cities. W.J. Malone, for example, mentions being greeted by a festive tea for service men when his train stopped at the small, largely Afrikaner town of Zeerust, en route to air training in Southern Rhodesia.[94] Without underplaying the activities of the Ossewabrandwag, which included sabotage and the harassment of service men, particularly those from South Africa, these letters and memoirs demonstrate an alternative experience of wartime South Africa, that of imperial patriotism and hospitality.[95]

'A future, room to expand': Perceived opportunity and racial privilege

The welcome offered to Allied troops as visitors and as potential migrants, and their inclusion into a group defined by racial privilege, presented an opportunity for social mobility for many. This sense of opportunity, though fundamentally rooted in the racially based system of settler colonialism, was also tied to the climate and the perception of wide-open space, and the idea of South Africa and Southern Rhodesia as new nations, free of the class hierarchy of Britain.[96] These perceptions of modernity and opportunity also drew on the romance of the frontier and nineteenth-century pioneers who symbolised the relatively recent history of development. This proved appealing to many, especially to those who sought to reinvent themselves and make a dramatic change after their wartime experiences.

The shock on returning to Britain was a common theme. Bernard Lloyd's response was typical: 'Oh God this is a dowdy place – it is all so small and dirty. Everyone is so grey and tired looking ... The houses are unpainted and in need of repair. And the roads are unkempt.'[97] Like Lloyd, Alfred Blacking was originally a child evacuee. Blacking had joined the South African Air Force at the age of seventeen, over his parents' objections and returned to Britain in 1946. In his view, 'Britain seemed a very grey peace on my return in 1946. The weather (having come from a S. African summer to a British winter) seemed most depressing.'[98] As well as the obvious contrast in the weather and shock at the extent of the bomb damage, these narratives also convey the notion of the United Kingdom as old-fashioned.[99] Many felt constrained both by the physical conditions and social attitudes they encountered in post-war Britain.

Southern Africa for many seemed not only sunnier than grey Britain, but a place of opportunity with a higher standard of living. Many had encountered new employment prospects during the war. A.I. Haskell, serving in the British Army Film and Photographic Unit hoped to go into business with a South African from Johannesburg.[100] Correspondence between the South African Army Education department and the Ministry of the Interior also included several cases where men serving in the RAF in South Africa had been offered jobs by local employers.[101] Others wrote of their belief in the possibility of upward social mobility in the region. Charles Wright, for example, who had worked as the head steward for a West End club before the war, wrote of his ambition to open his own hotel in South Africa.[102]

Such possibilities for advancement were linked to perceptions of South Africa and Southern Rhodesia as young countries, free of the class hierarchies that beset an 'old' nation like Britain. Edward Coventry, who stopped in Cape Town for four days on the way to North Africa, praised the 'apparent size and roominess of South Africa', contrasting it to crowded Britain, which lacked the 'scope ... for getting on'. He hoped to 'live a fuller life in a bigger and newer country like South Africa'.[103] Here he connected the space and modernity of South Africa with the possibility of self-improvement. Hetty Heist of Lancashire wrote about her son's disillusionment after returning from the camaraderie and excitement of his war service to his previous job, with 'no chance of anything better'. She hoped he could return to South Africa, which had 'a future, room to expand' unlike England where 'we live in the Past'.[104] Her letter's emphasis on the absence of a class hierarchy in South Africa elided the presence of one based on race.

Though it was often implicit, the basis for this kind of advancement in the southern African context was racial privilege. Stephen Hughes, a child evacuee to South Africa, reflected that he was able to experience a very different way of life:

> The standard of living was very much higher in South Africa. I came to accept that servants doing the menial tasks were a fact of life. There were far more opportunities open to me, both academically and athletically. Travel was open to me, and now miles were counted in thousands not hundreds. I was treated as a member of a higher class from whence I came. I did have the opportunity to stay in South Africa and join my host in his successful surveying practice, and I have no doubt that this would have been successful for me. However, at that time (1945) the war in Europe was almost over, and I wanted to see my parents and enlist in the forces, so I decided to return.[105]

Though Hughes and others reflecting on the lifestyle available, rarely mentioned race explicitly, the social mobility they describe was based on the racial privilege available to the ruling minority in a settler colonial regime. Hughes' description of his class elevation was based on his race, including the academic and professional opportunities open to him and the lifestyle enabled by the employment of servants.

Perceptions of Africans and the African landscape also drew on imagery and ideas that had circulated in fiction, educational materials and travel accounts since the nineteenth century.[106] This is clear in the account of Fred Dane, a trainee in the RAF:

> I shall always remember Rhodesia with great affection, when I was there it was an untamed, free, peaceful and beautiful country. On the few occasions when I was alone in the bush, I could easily imagine the crack of the bull whip and the moan of the oxen as the early pioneers pushed their wagons further and further into the unexplored heart of Africa, with the heat and the dust and ever constant danger from predatory animals and from the proud and warlike Zulu warriors.[107]

Dane imagined Southern Rhodesia as wild and romantic, open and unpopulated, employing the well-worn tropes of colonial fantasy. The influence of adventure fiction and the mythology surrounding the nineteenth century British settlement of southern Africa is clear in his writing. He imagines himself as a successor to these pioneers, who appear as heroic figures. Though in the end his desire to see combat meant that Dane turned down an offer to stay on in Africa, his narrative reflects the foundational myth of the settler colony, that of brave pioneers exploring and ultimately claiming and developing an untamed land.

This sense of the wide-open spaces in South Africa and Southern Rhodesia was tied into the perceptions of the opportunities available there. The contrast between sunny, modern, southern Africa and grey, damp and old-fashioned Britain evoked in letters and memoirs, though based in part on objective measures such as climate, also rested on racial privilege. Presenting the opportunities available as inherent to the landscape or the relatively recent European settlement of South Africa and Southern Rhodesia rendered invisible the racial discrimination and dispossession underpinning the promise of upward social mobility for British immigrants to the region.

Conclusion

Illustrating the continuing resonance of white settler societies in post-war Britain, these letters and memoirs highlight the way in which the assumed privileges of whiteness were implicitly accepted, but rarely articulated in this period. The language of wide-open colonial territory, empty and ripe for development, shows continuity with long-standing imperial ideas. What was new was that the war meant that more Britons than ever before had first-hand experiences of such places.[108]

Experience in southern Africa and relationships forged there made the decision to move easier, as did its promise of the exotic tempered by the familiar in such things as language, food and cultural institutions. Wartime travel to the region, therefore, contributed to the high rates of migration in the immediate post-war years. And even for those who did not decide to relocate, time spent in the region deepened awareness of the British Empire. Such experience, and the memories and impressions of South Africa and Rhodesia they created, continued to circulate in Britain in the decades after the war and contributed to the ongoing resonance of empire in post-war British society and culture.

Notes

1 Imperial War Museum, London, United Kingdom (hereafter IWM), 11/35/1, Personal Papers of P. Salter, pp. 18–19.
2 IWM, 11/35/1, Personal Papers of P. Salter, pp. 18–19.
3 Pertti Ahonen et al., *People on the Move: Forced Population Movements in Europe in the Second World War and Its Aftermath* (Oxford: Berg, 2008); Tara Zahra, *The Lost Children: Reconstructing Europe's Families after World War II* (Cambridge: Harvard University Press, 2011).
4 John Welshman, *Churchill's Children: The Evacuee Experience in Wartime Britain* (Oxford: Oxford University Press, 2010); Martin Conway and José Gotovich, eds, *Europe in Exile: European Exile Communities in Britain 1940–45* (Oxford: Berghahn Books, 2001).
5 Wendy Webster has written about this contact within the United Kingdom, not only with people from the empire, but also from Europe. Wendy Webster, *Mixing It: Diversity in World War Two Britain* (Oxford: Oxford University Press, 2018).
6 On the ways in which race and particularly whiteness 'rarely needed to be made explicit' in the context of empire see Schwarz, *White Man's World*, p. 10. See also Stoler, *Along the Archival Grain*, p. 3.
7 On the crucial role of troops and resources from the Empire–Commonwealth to the war effort see Ashley Jackson, *The British Empire and the Second World War* (New York: Hambledon Continuum, 2006), pp. 1–10; Ashley Jackson, *Distant Drums: The Role of Colonies in British Imperial Warfare* (Brighton: Sussex Academic Press, 2010); David Killingray and Martin Plaut, *Fighting for Britain: African Soldiers in the Second World War* (Suffolk: James Currey, 2010); David Killingray and Richard Rathbone, eds, *Africa and*

the Second World War (Basingstoke: Macmillan, 1986); Jonathan Fennell, *Combat and Morale in the North African Campaign: The Eighth Army and the Path to El Alamein* (Cambridge: Cambridge University Press, 2011); Jonathan Fennell, *Fighting the People's War: The British and Commonwealth Armies and the Second World War* (Cambridge: Cambridge University Press, 2019); Iain Johnston-White, *The British Commonwealth and Victory in the Second World War* (London: Palgrave Macmillan, 2017). On the social and cultural impact of the war see Ashley Jackson, Yasmin Khan and Gajendra Singh, eds, *An Imperial World at War: Aspects of the British Empire's War Experience, 1939–1945* (London: Routledge, 2017); Sonya Rose, *Which People's War?: National Identity and Citizenship in Britain 1939–1945* (Oxford: Oxford University Press, 2003); Yasmin Khan, 'Sex in an Imperial War Zone: Transnational Encounters in Second World War India', *History Workshop Journal* 73:1 (2012), 240–58; Yasmin Khan, *The Raj at War: A People's History of India's Second World War* (London: The Bodley Head, 2015); Mark J. Crowley and Sandra Trudgen Dawson, eds, *Home Fronts: Britain and the Empire at War, 1939–1945* (Woodbridge: The Boydell Press, 2017).

8 Judith A. Byfield, 'Preface', in *Africa and World War II*, eds Judith A. Byfield, Carolyn A. Brown and Timothy Parsons (Cambridge: Cambridge University Press, 2015), p. xviii. On the cases of India, South Africa and Southern Rhodesia respectively see Khan, *The Raj at War*, p. xiii; Bill Nasson, *South Africa at War: 1939–1945* (Auckland Park: Jacana, 2012), pp. 20–3; Jackson, *The British Empire*, p. 228.

9 See more detail on this in Chapter 2 and Jackson, *The British Empire*, pp. 228–32; David Johnson, 'Settler Farmers and Coerced African Labour in Southern Rhodesia, 1936–46', *The Journal of African History* 33:1 (1992), 111–28; Kenneth P. Vickery, 'The Second World War Revival of Forced Labour in the Rhodesias', *The International Journal of African Historical Studies* 22:3 (1989), 423–37.

10 See, for example, Andrew Stewart, 'The British Government and the South African Neutrality Crisis, 1938–39', *English Historical Review* 123:503 (2008), 947–72.

11 For a general overview see Nasson, *South Africa at War*. For a political and economic overview of the war see H.J. Martin and Neil D. Orpen, *South Africa at War: Military and Industrial Organization and Operations in Connection with the Conduct of the War, 1939–1945* (Cape Town: Purnell, 1979). For popular accounts of the South African home front see Jennifer Crwys-Williams, *A Country at War 1939–1945: The Mood of a Nation* (Rivonia: Ashanti Publishing, 1992); Margot Bryant, *As We Were: South Africa 1939–1941* (Johannesburg: Keartland Publishers, 1974).

12 Ashley Jackson estimates that 6 million Allied service men passed through South African ports during the war. Jackson, *The British Empire*, p. 176. The number of foreign visitors to South Africa (not including military personnel) was 289,744 for the years 1939 to 1945. Republic of South Africa Department

of Statistics, *Report No. 19–01–01, Migration Statistics: Immigrants and Emigrants, 1966 to 1969* (Pretoria, 1969), p. 1.
13 From 1946 to 1948, 341,545 emigrants left the United Kingdom; 53,588 immigrants to South Africa listed their previous country of residence as the United Kingdom; 18,221 immigrants to Southern Rhodesia listed their place of birth as the United Kingdom (Southern Rhodesia did not keep records by previous country of residence). Union of South Africa, *Statistics of Migration 1948* (Pretoria: The Government Printer, 1950), 43; Commonwealth Relations Office, *Oversea Migration Statistics 1955* (London, HMSO, 1956), 5, 13, 14.
14 Australia received 13,012 immigrants from Britain in 1947, compared to 20,614 who came to South Africa. Union of South Africa, *Statistics of Migration 1948*, 43; Commonwealth Relations Office, *Oversea Migration Statistics 1955*, 8.
15 Figures for 1950 to 1960, Republic of South Africa Bureau of Statistics, *Report No. 286: Statistics of Immigrants and Emigrants 1924–1964* (Pretoria, 1964), 4. Figures for 1961 to 1969, Republic of South Africa Department of Statistics, *Report No. 19–01–01, Migration Statistics: Immigrants and Emigrants, 1966 to 1969* (Pretoria: The Government Printer, 1969), p. 1. Figures for 1970 to 2004, Peberdy, *Selecting Immigrants*, pp. 276–90.
16 Peberdy, *Selecting Immigrants*, pp. 97–101; Brownell, *British Immigration to South Africa*, p. 34.
17 On the persistence of military and economic connections see Hyam and Henshaw, *The Lion and the Springbok*.
18 Bailkin, *Afterlife of Empire*, p. 2.
19 Schwarz, *White Man's World*, p. 10.
20 Webster, *Englishness and Empire*, pp. 7, 19–91.
21 Due to the difficulties of obtaining a research permit for foreigners in Zimbabwe, I was only able to visit the National Archives of Zimbabwe for three days in 2011 and did not find comparable enquiry letters. Many of the memoirs consulted, from the Imperial War Museum and elsewhere, however, do describe wartime Southern Rhodesia.
22 National Archives of South Africa (hereafter NASA), Pretoria. BNS 1/1/401, Ref. 301/74, Vols 1–3, Post-war Immigration of British and Allied Soldiers, 1942–45; BNS 1/1/402, Ref. 301/74, Vols 4–7, Post-war Immigration of British and Allied Soldiers, 1945–46; DGD Vol. 195, Ref. 57/3, Immigration. Post War Enquiries from members of the Allied Forces, 1944 to 1948; BNS, 1/1/410, Ref. 336/74, Vol. A, Immigration of British Subjects to South Africa, 1946; BNS 1/1/411, Ref. 336/74, Vols B–D, Immigration of British Subjects to South Africa, 1946–47; BNS 1/1/412, Ref. 336/74, Vol. E, Immigration of British Subjects to South Africa, 1948–50.
23 The memoirs of evacuee children come in the form of a 1990 survey conducted by Patricia Lin. IWM, 91/33/2, Private Papers of Miss P.Y. Lin, Questionnaires of Overseas Evacuees. See also Patricia Y. Lin, 'National Identity and Social Mobility: Class, Empire and the British Government Overseas Evacuation of Children during the Second World War', *Twentieth Century British History* 7:3 (1996), 310–44.

24 John Lambert, '"Their Finest Hour?" English-speaking South Africans and World War II', *South African Historical Journal* 60 (2008), 60–84.
25 Clare Anderson, *Subaltern Lives: Biographies of Colonialism in the Indian Ocean World, 1790–1920* (Cambridge: Cambridge University Press, 2012), pp. 6–7. See also McCarthy, *Personal Narratives*, pp. 7–12.
26 David Killingray and Richard Rathbone, 'Introduction', in *Africa and the Second World War*, eds David Killingray and Richard Rathbone (Basingstoke: Macmillan, 1986), p. 9; Michael Crowder, 'The Second World War: Prelude to Decolonisation in Africa', in *The Cambridge History of Africa, Vol. 8, From c.1940 to c.1975*, ed. Michael Crowder (Cambridge: Cambridge University Press, 1984), p. 16.
27 Lambert, 'Their Finest Hour?', p. 80. Jonathan Hyslop has argued that South Africa's ports were the Union's most important contribution to the war effort. Jonathan Hyslop, 'The Lady in White: British Imperial Loyalism and Women's Volunteerism in Second World War Durban', *Journal of Natal and Zulu History* 32:1 (2018), 40–1.
28 Jackson, *The British Empire*, p. 245.
29 Archive Munro estimates that a million service personnel embarked from the United Kingdom from 1940 to 1943 via the Cape route. Archie Munro, *The Winston Specials: Troopships via the Cape, 1940–3* (Liskeard: Martime Books, 2006); Jackson, *The British Empire*, pp. 175–6, 245.
30 Jackson, *The British Empire*, p. 241; John Golley, *Aircrew Unlimited: The Commonwealth Air Training Plan During World War Two* (Sparkford: Patrick Stephens, 1993), pp. 16, 150, 173, 36.
31 National Archives of the United Kingdom (hereafter TNA), ADM 1/11778, Naval Training, *HMS Assegai*, 1942–43.
32 Fedorowich, *Unfit for Heroes*.
33 NASA, GG 1313, Ref. 36.390, Enquiries regarding a scheme of immigration to South Africa: possibility of settling men of RAF in S.A. after the war, 15 January 1941.
34 NASA, BNS 1/1/401, Ref. 301/74, Vol. 1, Lt. Col. E.G. Malherbe, 'Post-war Settlement of Imperial (RAF) Personnel in the Union', 21 September 1943. For more on Malherbe see his memoir, E.G. Malherbe, *Never a Dull Moment* (Cape Town: Howard Timmins, 1981).
35 South African Military Archives Depot, Pretoria (hereafter SAMAD), AG (3) 154, Box 132, Ref. 1158, A.G. White to The Adjutant General, Union Defence Force, 19 May 1945.
36 NASA, BNS 1/1/401, Ref. 301/74, Vol. 1, Consul for the Union of South Africa, Egypt to the Minister of the Interior, 14 January 1943.
37 NASA, BNS 1/1/401, Ref. 301/74, Vol. 2, C.D. Baldwin to the Trade Commissioner for South Africa, Bombay, 'The Emigration of British Service personnel of His Majesty's Forces to Dominions, Colonies and Crown Possessions', 30 September 1944; N. Wilson to Secretary for External Affairs, 8 September 1944.

38 NASA, BNS 1/1/401, Ref. 301/74, Vol. 1, D.C.S. (Army Education) to Secretary for Defence, 7 December 1944.
39 NASA, BNS 1/1/401, Ref. 301/74, Vol. 2, Chief of the General Staff to Secretary of the Interior, 28 October 1944.
40 NASA, BNS 1/1/401, Ref. 301/74, Vol. 3, Major Fuller to Dr Steyn, 10 August 1945; SAMAD, AG 3 154, Box 57, Ref. AG (3) 154X/591, A.M. Van Wyck to Minister of the Interior, 11 June 1945; Telegram from Commissioner, Nairobi to Secretary for External Affairs, 18 June 1945; 'Immigration Policy, 1943'. This interest in emigration after demobilisation was widespread, see Alan Allport, *Demobbed: Coming Home After World War Two* (New Haven: Yale University Press, 2009), pp. 212–13.
41 A lower, but still significant proportion of the enquiries filed under British subjects rather than service men also mentioned time spent in South Africa, 67 out of 271. NASA, BNS 1/1/410–412.
42 Hammerton and Thomson found a similar connection between migration and existing relationships with Australians, many forged during the war. Hammerton and Thomson, *Ten Pound Poms*, p. 42.
43 The war led to many such international marriages, the best known of which are probably the British women who married American service men, although many marriages between Britons and Dominion nationals also occurred. For Canada see Melynda Jarratt, *War Brides: The Stories of the Women Who Left Everything Behind to Follow the Men They Loved* (Stroud: Tempus, 2007). For South Africa see Jean P. Smith, '"Young blood" and "the blackout": Love, Sex and Marriage on the South African Home Front', in *Home Fronts: Britain and the Empire at War, 1939–45*, eds Mark J. Crowley and Sandra Trudgen Dawson (Woodbridge: The Boydell Press, 2017).
44 The number was reduced for the more general files on the enquiries of British subjects, 29 mention marriage and 8 engagement out of 271. NASA, BNS 1/1/410–412.
45 NASA, BNS 1/1/401, Ref. 301/74, Vol. 1, Robert Smith to Minister of the Interior, August 1944.
46 NASA, BNS 1/1/401, Ref. 301/74, Vol. 1, P.M. Norton to Sir Edward Thornton, 25 January 1944.
47 SAMAD, WR Box 242, File 124/3, Repatriation of Wives of Service Men and Evacuation of Fiancées, 1945–47.
48 Interview with Harold Robson, Santa Barbara, USA, 3 October 2009. At the interviewee's request, this name is a pseudonym.
49 On the implicit racial connation of the phrase 'natural-born British subject' see Alison Bashford, 'Immigration restriction: rethinking period and place from settler colonies to postcolonial nations', *Journal of Global History* 9:1 (2014), 45.
50 Here the files concerning British subjects from 1946 to 1950 include a higher proportion mentioning friends or relatives in South Africa, out of 271, 35 mention friends and 52 mention relatives. One possible explanation is the beginning of chain migration as immediate post-war migrants (including those

who married South Africans during the war) began to petition for the relatives to move. NASA, BNS 1/1/410–412.
51 NASA, BNS 1/1/401, Ref. 301/74, Vol. 1, Capt A.G. Ross to the Governor-General, 18 November 1943.
52 NASA, BNS 1/1/401, Ref. 301/74, Vol.1, A.E. Pratt to Secretary for the Interior, 7 May 1944.
53 NASA, BNS 1/1/401, Ref. 301/74, Vol. 1, Jan Witthoft to Minister for the Interior, 24 June 1943.
54 Saul Dubow, 'How British was the British World? The Case of South Africa', *The Journal of Imperial and Commonwealth History* 37:1 (2009), 14.
55 Nasson, *South Africa at War*, p. 68.
56 Johnson, 'Settler Farmers', pp. 188–9; Nhamo Samasuwo, 'Food Production and War Supplies: Rhodesia's Beef Industry during the Second World War, 1939–1945', *Journal of Southern African Studies* 29:2 (2003).
57 J.M. Tinley, *South African Food and Agriculture in World War II* (Stanford: Stanford University Press, 1954), pp. 3–4, 116; Lizzie Collingham, *The Taste of War: World War Two and the Battle for Food* (London: Allen Lane, 2011), pp. 8, 66–7; David Edgerton, *Britain's War Machine: Weapons, Resources and Experts in the Second World War* (London: Allen Lane, 2011), pp. 158, 160, 172.
58 South African fruit was well known in Britain, in part as a result of the Empire Marketing Board in the interwar years. Stephen Constantine, '"Bringing the Empire alive": the Empire Marketing Board and imperial propaganda, 1926–33', in *Imperialism and Popular Culture*, ed. John M. MacKenzie (Manchester: Manchester University Press, 1986).
59 IWM, 11/35/1, Personal Papers of P. Salter, p. 16.
60 Golley, *Aircrew Unlimited*, p. 42.
61 IWM, 11/13/1, Personal Papers of F. Dane, p. 21.
62 IWM, 03/33/1, Personal Papers of K.A.C. Melvin, p. 13.
63 Ina Zweiniger-Bargielowska, *Austerity in Britain: Rationing, Controls, and Consumption, 1939–1955* (Oxford: Oxford University Press, 2000), p. 18; Collingham, *Taste of War*, p. 361.
64 IWM, 03/33/1, Personal Papers of K.A.C. Melvin, p. 28.
65 Edgerton, *Britain's War Machine*, pp. 169–70.
66 Collingham, *Taste of War*, p. 392.
67 Ibid., pp. 399–411; Edgerton, *Britain's War Machine*, pp. 170–2; Fennell, *Combat and Morale*, pp. 130–42.
68 For more on wartime hospitality in South Africa, tensions over relationships between visiting service men and local women and the experience of visiting service personnel of colour see Smith, 'Young blood', pp. 93–110; Jean P. Smith, 'Race and hospitality: Allied troops of colour on the South African home front during the Second World War', *War and Society* 39:3 (2020).
69 John Lambert, '"The Last Outpost": The Natalians, South Africa, and the British Empire', in *Settlers and Expatriates: Britons over the Seas*, ed. Robert Bickers (Oxford: Oxford University Press, 2010), pp. 171–2.

70 Nasson, *South Africa at War*, pp. 77–9; Hyslop, 'Lady in White'.
71 Gibson is mentioned in many troop memoirs, see IWM, 03/33/1, Personal Papers of K.A.C. Melvin, p. 16; Hyslop, 'Lady in White'.
72 Perla Siedle Gibson, *Durban's Lady in White: An Autobiography* (Northaw: Aedificamus Press, 1991), pp. 7–8; Sam Morley, *Back to Durban ... 50 years on!: The 'Lady in White' Memorial Visit of March '92* (Northaw: Aedificamus Press, 1992), p. 55.
73 Hyslop, 'Lady in White', p. 53. '"Lady in White" statue to be relocated', *Northglen News*, 1 July 2016, https://northglennews.co.za/86449/lady-in-white-statue-to-be-relocated/ (accessed 9 April 2018).
74 IWM, 08/29/1, Personal Papers of W.J. Malone, pp. 11–12.
75 This is long-running trope in European writing about southern Africa. See, for example, Pratt, *Imperial Eyes*, pp. 59–61; J. M. Coetzee, *White Writing: On the Culture of Letters in South Africa* (New Haven: Yale University Press, 1988), pp. 9, 177; Kenneth Parker, 'Fertile land, romantic spaces, uncivilized peoples: English travel-writing about the Cape of Good Hope, 1800–1850', in Bill Schwarz (ed.) *The Expansion of England: Race, Ethnicity and Cultural History* (London: Routledge, 1996), pp. 198–231. On the portrayal of Zulu people see Kathryn Castle, *Britannia's Children: Reading Colonialism through Children's Books and Magazines* (Manchester: Manchester University Press, 1996), pp. 72–3.
76 NASA, BNS 1/1/401, Ref. 301/74, Vol. 2, T.J. Weddell to Ministry of the Interior, 12 February 1945.
77 NASA, BNS 1/1/402, Ref. 301/74, Vol. 4, John Weighill to General Smuts, 19 March 1946.
78 Lambert, 'Their Finest Hour?', pp. 61–3; Smith, 'Race and hospitality', p. 159.
79 Bryant, *As We Were*, pp. 59–160.
80 J.F. MacDonald, *The War History of Southern Rhodesia, 1939–45*, Vol. I (Salisbury: Government of Rhodesia, 1947), pp. 5–6, 46–7, 100, 240.
81 For an overview of SAWAS, especially their activities in Cape Town see Vivian Bickford-Smith, Elizabeth Van Heyningen and Nigel Worden, *Cape Town in the Twentieth Century: An Illustrated Social History* (Claremont: David Philip Publishers, 1999), pp. 96–8; E.A.S. Bailey, ed., *SAWAS 1938–1947: Book of Thanks* (Edinburgh: Macdonald Printers, 1981); Crwys-Williams, *Country at War*, pp. 43–9; Gwen Hewitt, *Womanhood at War: The Story of the SAWAS* (Johannesburg: Frier and Munro, 1947); Martin and Orpen, *South Africa at War*, pp. 288–93.See also the memoir of one its founders, Lucy Bean, *Strangers in our Midst* (Cape Town: Howard Timmins, 1970).
82 Bailey, *SAWAS*, p. 16. Similar sentiments were also reflected in the collection of letters sent to Bailey as he compiled this publication. IWM, Item 1375, Misc. 92, Letters concerning the South African Women's Auxiliary Services during the Second World War.
83 J.F. Macdonald, *The War History of Southern Rhodesia, 1939–45*, Vol. II (Salisbury: Government of Southern Rhodesia, 1950), p. 609.
84 Golley, *Aircrew Unlimited*, pp. 40, 42.

85 G.M. Ball noted that they were given discounts at tourist attractions as service men, mentioning specifically staying at the grand hotel at Victoria Falls for a half price rate. IWM, 85/19/1, Personal Papers of G.M. Ball, p. 255.
86 Golley, *Aircrew Unlimited*, p. 40.
87 IWM, 08/29/1, Personal Papers of W.J. Malone, p. 10, 12.
88 National Archives of Zimbabwe, Harare (hereafter NAZ), ORAL/232, Interview of Mark Edward Dawson, by I.J. Johnstone, London, 1983, p. 3.
89 Conway and Leonard, *Migration, Space*, p. 5.
90 Stone, *Colonist or Uitlander*, p. 167.
91 IWM, 03/33/1, Personal Papers of K.A.C. Melvin, p. 28.
92 IWM, 91/33/2, Questionnaires of Overseas Evacuees, No. 96, Moira Mackie.
93 Quoted in Hyslop, 'Lady in White', p. 50.
94 IWM, 08/29/1, Personal Papers of W.J. Malone, p. 9.
95 Christoph Marx, *Oxwagon Sentinel: Radical Afrikaner Nationalism and the History of the Ossewabrandwag*, trans. Sheila Gordon-Schröder (Pretoria: University of South Africa Press, 2008), pp. 353–62, 521–5; Patrick Furlong, *Between Crown and Swastika: The Impact of the Radical Right on the Afrikaner Nationalist Movement in the Fascist Era* (Middletown: Wesleyan University Press, 1991), pp. 138–60.
96 On the idea of Rhodesia as egalitarian and its limits see Lowry, 'Rhodesia 1890–1980: "The Lost Dominion"', pp. 135–9.
97 IWM, 91/33/2, Questionnaires of Overseas Evacuees, No. 114 Bernard Lloyd.
98 IWM, 91/33/2, Questionnaires of Overseas Evacuees, No. 103, Alfred Blacking.
99 See, for instance, Laura Wynn and Hendry Henderson, discussed in more detail in Chapter 7. IWM, 91/33/2, Questionnaires of Overseas Evacuees, No. 111, Laura Wynn; No. 113, Henry Henderson.
100 NASA, BNS 1/1/401, Ref. 301/74, Vol.1, A. I. Haskell, to the Minister for the Interior, 29 June 1943.
101 NASA, BNS 1/1/401, Ref. 301/74, Vol. 2, D.C.S. (Army Education) to Secretary for Defence, 7 December 1944.
102 NASA, BNS 1/1/401, Ref. 301/74, Vol. 2, Charles N. Wright to General Smuts, 21 February 1945.
103 NASA, BNS 1/1/402, Ref. 301/74, Vol. 5, Edward A. Coventry to J.C. Smuts, 18 August 1946.
104 NASA, BNS 1/1/402, Ref. 301/74, Vol. 6, Hetty Heist to Jan Smuts, date illegible, 1946. Such disillusionment was a common response for demobilised service men, many of whom sought a new beginning after the war. See Allport, *Demobbed*, pp. 141–58, 165–9.
105 IWM, 91/33/2, Questionnaires of Overseas Evacuees, No. 92, Stephen Hughes.
106 John MacKenzie argues that racial stereotypes persisted in British history and geography textbooks until at least the 1960s. John M. MacKenzie, *Propaganda and Empire: The Manipulation of British Public Opinion, 1880–1960* (Manchester: Manchester University Press, 1984), p. 193. See also Castle, *Britannia's Children*; Robert H. MacDonald, *The Language of Empire: Myths and Metaphors of Popular Imperialism, 1880–1918* (Manchester: Manchester

University Press, 1994); J.A. Mangan, ed., *The Imperial Curriculum: Racial Images and Education in the British Colonial Experience* (London: Routledge, 1993); Jeffrey Richards, ed., *Imperialism and Juvenile Literature* (Manchester: Manchester University Press, 1989).
107 IWM, 11/13/1, Personal Papers of F. Dane, p. 34.
108 Gunn, 'Spatial mobility in later twentieth-century Britain', p. 4.

2

'We want new settlers of British stock': Planning for post-war migration

White British service men and women were not alone in moving to a place where they had spent time during the Second World War. Among the passengers arriving on the HMT *Empire Windrush* and its lesser known predecessors the SS *Ormonde* and SS *Almanzora* were many returning ex-service men, such as Sam King and Alford Gardner who had served in the RAF.[1] Like white British service men and women who spent time in southern Africa during the war, Black service personnel from the Caribbean who spent time in the United Kingdom had married or formed relationships with local men and women and their previous experience made the prospect of a move easier.[2]

Like white British migrants to other parts of the Empire–Commonwealth, migrants coming to the United Kingdom from the British Caribbean colonies could expect similar cultural institutions and the same language. In many ways the experience of war, the physical mobility it engendered and the exposure to media that stressed participation in a joint endeavour had strengthened connections between the United Kingdom and the Caribbean.[3] The war, as it did for so many people, seemed an opportunity to change one's life, to do something different, to improve one's circumstances. It also provided the practical means to move, as many migrants from the Caribbean either stayed on in the United Kingdom or used their ex-service gratuity to pay for their passage.[4]

There are striking differences, however, between the experiences of veterans who moved from the Caribbean to the United Kingdom and those that moved from the United Kingdom to southern Africa in the immediate post-war years. Rather than leaving the grey, cold and austere United Kingdom for sunny southern Africa, migrants from the Caribbean made the reverse journey from sunshine to rain and fog. Black British service personnel, including famously the cricketer Learie Constantine, had faced racism and discrimination in wartime Britain and not only from white American GIs.[5] By contrast, while some British service personnel who spent time in South Africa mentioned encountering anti-British sentiment from Afrikaner nationalists, the overwhelming experience, as described in Chapter 1, was one of welcome, hospitality and abundance. While white British migrants were likely to experience social mobility in South Africa and Southern Rhodesia as members of a privileged racial minority, Black migrants to the United Kingdom were more likely to experience the reverse due to racial discrimination in housing and employment.[6]

In official terms too, these migrations were considered very differently. The migration of white Britons was posed as the solution to a wide range of potential post-war problems from a shortage of housing to Britain's falling geopolitical position. By contrast, despite the long-standing rhetoric of universal British subjecthood, and its codification in the British Nationality Act of 1948, the migration of British subjects of colour was largely perceived as both a problem in itself and the cause of other problems including racial tension, violence and crime. While the vital wartime contributions of service personnel and civilian workers of colour were officially praised, as Wendy Webster has shown, the often limited welcome they received was largely just for the duration.[7] Even before the end of the war, British officials sought to limit the number of service men and women of colour from the Caribbean staying on in the United Kingdom and to discourage them from returning.

Despite rhetoric about imperial unity and pressure to avoid the appearance of racism, therefore, many officials in the United Kingdom were opposed to the presence of Black British subjects in the United Kingdom well before the arrival of the *Empire Windrush*. By contrast, many, both in Britain and southern Africa saw the circumstances of the war as a tremendous opportunity to encourage white British migration to South Africa and Southern Rhodesia. South African and Rhodesian promoters largely sought migrants to shore up the white population in their minority-ruled nations, while those in the United Kingdom primarily saw British migration to Rhodesia and South Africa as well as the other Dominions as a way to strengthen imperial ties.

Although general migration schemes were proposed, many focused specifically on children or ex-service men. The evacuation of children to the Dominions, a wartime exigency, was recast as an opportunity to promote migration. As after the First World War, migration schemes were proposed to smooth the difficulties of demobilisation and reinforce imperial connections.[8] In South Africa and Southern Rhodesia efforts to recruit migrants were often focused on the same groups, ex-service men and children. Importing skilled workers, from Britain (and Europe more generally) was seen as necessary for the continued growth of the industrial economy catalysed by the war and many promotors of migration sought to capitalise on the wartime presence of British service men in the region, many of whom had technical skills gained from their military service. Others focused their efforts on children, as they were thought to be more easily assimilated and would not immediately enter the labour market providing competition to returning South African and Rhodesian service men, but would increase the white population in the long run.

Such efforts to promote white British migration to southern Africa and elsewhere in the Empire–Commonwealth were not uncontested. In Britain, opponents of migration raised the labour shortage and the possibility that Britain might lose its many of its most productive citizens. Similarly, in Southern Rhodesia and South Africa, many advised caution about the recruitment of too many new migrants, concerned that they might compete with returning soldiers for housing and employment. Behind much of this concern was the spectre of the 'poor white', the tensions between increasing the white population and providing the resources to ensure that all white residents had access to the appropriate lifestyle for the ruling white minority. In South Africa, many Afrikaner nationalists also opposed too large an influx, especially of British migrants, fearing that this might hamper their chances of establishing an independent republic. This chapter's focus is on plans proposed during and after the war, both those intended to encourage migration and those to discourage it, regardless of whether they were implemented. Such plans, even those that never came to fruition, provide insight into how their promoters envisioned the post-war interests of their nations and how they understood them in terms of race.

'There is ... only one solution; and that is, repatriation': Returning Black service personnel to the Caribbean

In contrast to the support provided for the post-war migration of white British service men, British officials expressed concern about the demobilisation of British service personnel of colour in the United Kingdom early in the war. While acknowledging in a 1942 report that as British subjects, 'coloured' service personnel from the Empire–Commonwealth could neither be 'refused admission' or 'deported if they prove to be undesirable citizens', the War Cabinet expressed concern over the 'serious social consequences which might arise from the demobilisation in this country of any appreciable numbers of certain classes of coloured men who are serving in His Majesty's Forces'. Pointing to the 1919 riots targeting Black and other minority ethnic communities in British port cities as an example of the kind of trouble that might result from an 'influx' of service personnel of colour, the War Cabinet recommended 'very strongly' that everything possible should be done to minimise their demobilisation in the United Kingdom.[9] Given that any 'apparent discrimination in the nature of a "colour bar"' was not possible, the War Cabinet advocated 'administrative actions' to prevent the demobilisation of service personnel of colour in the United Kingdom such as their 'concentration' in particular units, the restriction of their service to theatres abroad and their repatriation 'in complete units'.[10] However, this proved difficult to execute in practice as illustrated by the case of Black RAF personnel.

Correspondence on the repatriation of Black RAF personnel to the Caribbean highlights the contrast between the assumptions made about white British migrants and migrants of colour from the British Empire. While the assumption was that white British ex-service men and women would be economic assets and contribute to the development of Commonwealth countries, the skill and potential of Black service men and women, often with similar experience, was not recognised. Rather, their presence was understood as the cause of the discrimination and violence that they faced. As discussed below, members of the RAF associated with the air training scheme in Southern Rhodesia were considered particularly desirable migrants due to their technical skills. Although it is not stated explicitly, military service with the implications of physical fitness and discipline likely also contributed to the assumption that they would be desirable migrants in terms of eugenic ideas of racial fitness. By contrast, British military officials pushed for the quick return of Black personnel serving in the RAF to the Caribbean.

In correspondence between the Air Ministry and the Colonial Office from 1945 to 1947, military officials consistently advocated the prompt return of Black airmen to the Caribbean, citing violent clashes between them and white service men including a riot in Manchester. The specific circumstances of these clashes or who instigated them is rarely mentioned and does not appear to have been a consideration. Rather, the very 'presence of these coloured airmen' was posited by Air Marshal Sir Grahame Donald as an obstacle to keeping order. Donald also mentions the role of a 'certain class of white airmen and airwomen' in these conflicts, conforming to the common trope of blaming the racist white working class. In the end, Donald concluded, 'There is ... only one solution; and that is, repatriation.'[11] The correspondence also draws on stereotypes of Black criminality and sexuality. There are frequent although often vague references to stabbing and other forms of knife crime in the correspondence and also the suggestion that if Black service men could not be repatriated quickly, 'concentrating' them at a station where no members of the Women's Auxiliary Air Force were based might be an alternate solution.[12] The main concern of Colonial Office officials was how to manage this 'repatriation' without the appearance of racial discrimination, but they did not object to the basic premise that Black service men should return.

Racist assumptions about the capabilities and ambition of Black service men are also evident from the correspondence. It had been anticipated that no more than 10 per cent of West Indian RAF personnel would be accepted on Ministry of Labour training courses offered as part of demobilisation, but 60 per cent applied and 50 per cent were accepted. In stark contrast to the discussions in South Africa and Southern Rhodesia about how to convince white British service men to remain, the number of Black service personnel staying to enrol on these courses was a matter of official concern. The courses ranged from six months to two years, and most of the airmen concerned had enrolled on a course of nine months. Limited by the need to avoid the appearance of racial discrimination, officials could not stop these airmen from enrolling on the courses to which they had been accepted, so instead emphasised the importance that at the conclusion of the course they be recalled and sent back as service personnel.[13] Finally, it is worth mentioning that all of this concern was over a relatively small number of people, roughly 5,500 in total. By July 1947, the number remaining in the United Kingdom was 1,839, the majority of whom were engaged in training courses, with only 10 who had been 'released in the UK' and 21 with pending applications to do so.[14]

The level of concern about so few service personnel of colour settling in the United Kingdom presaged the similar reaction, discussed in Chapter 4, to the arrival of the *Windrush* and the less well-known ships who preceded it, the *Ormonde* and the *Almanzora* as did the discussions of how to discourage Black British subjects from settling in the United Kingdom without the appearance of racial discrimination. The explicit discussions of how to implement a racist policy without the appearance of racism signal the extent to which ideologies of race influenced those who sought to shape post-war population movements, whether through the encouragement of white Britons to move to South Africa, Southern Rhodesia or the other settler colonies of the British Empire or the discouragement of service personnel of colour from remaining in the United Kingdom.

'The redistribution of population within the Empire': The promotion of white emigration in the United Kingdom

While the post-war presence of service personnel of colour in the United Kingdom was considered by British officials to be a problem, British migration to the Commonwealth including to South Africa and Southern Rhodesia was posited as solution to the problem of the United Kingdom's diminishing economic and geopolitical position as well as projected post-war problems such as the housing shortage and food dependence. The economic impact of the war led to attempts to make imperial rule in Africa more profitable, the 'second colonial occupation'.[15] Building on precedents in the interwar period, colonial policy in Africa during and after the war accelerated the shift from indirect rule to more direct state intervention and an increased emphasis on industry and 'scientific' agriculture such as large-scale irrigation projects. Such initiatives, including the Colonial Development and Welfare Acts of 1940 and 1945 and the foundation of the Colonial Development Corporation in 1947, though cast in the language of modernisation and the promotion of colonial self-sufficiency, were also efforts to shore up Britain's faltering economy and currency and amounted, despite the rhetoric, to a renewed imperialism in Africa.[16] Part of this renewed imperialism was the promotion of British migration, which was cast as an important contribution to the development of the African colonies thought to be suitable for European habitation: South Africa, Southern Rhodesia and Kenya, whose majority indigenous populations, following a long-standing justification for colonisation, were seen as either unable or not yet ready to develop the vast resources of these regions themselves.

At the same time as they redoubled their efforts in Africa, British policy-makers aimed to bolster British power through reinforcing links with the Commonwealth and particularly the former colonies of settlement. They saw the migration of what they often termed 'British stock' as a way to maintain the loyalty and 'Britishness' of Australia, New Zealand, Canada, South Africa, and Southern Rhodesia as these countries increasingly developed their own national identities and pursued their own national interests.

The wartime government scheme to evacuate children to the Dominions, the Children's Overseas Reception Board (CORB), was one site of efforts to promote migration. British and South African officials, private individuals and organisations used the evacuation of children, ostensibly a temporary wartime measure, to promote permanent migration from Britain to the empire. Organisations dedicated to promoting migration to the empire were involved in the CORB Advisory Council from the beginning. These included the 1820 Memorial Settlers' Association and the Society for the Overseas Settlement of British Women (SOSBW) that had long promoted British migration to southern Africa. Strong support for migration is also evident in the public statements and private writings of the first chairman of the CORB Board, Sir Geoffrey Shakespeare, a long-standing advocate of imperial migration.

Though more than 211,000 applications were received over the course of just a few weeks, and more than 24,000 were approved, in the end CORB administered the evacuation of only 3,000 children to Canada, Australia, New Zealand and South Africa because the scheme was halted in October 1940 after a German submarine sank the ocean liner, *City of Benares*, with ninety CORB children aboard.[17] Although the scheme sent no more children abroad after this tragedy, CORB operations continued until after the war, overseeing the care of the children already overseas.

Shakespeare and other promoters of migration hoped to take advantage of the imperial unity engendered by the war to promote migration. In the receiving countries many hosts saw taking in British children as a patriotic act that signified their allegiance to the United Kingdom. As Patricia Lin has argued, the overseas evacuation of children differed from its domestic counterpart. While the internal evacuation to the countryside in the United Kingdom was marked by class conflict and often unwilling hosts, the CORB children were generally associated with their national rather than class identity upon arrival in the Dominions and often lived with wealthy, professional families who opened their homes in a show of British patriotism.[18]

Shakespeare envisioned CORB and the post-war migration he hoped it would spur as the beginning of a reinvigorated chapter in imperial history. In a 1941 speech to the Victoria League, Shakespeare declared that the Dominions' offer to take in child evacuees reflected the 'inherent unity of the Empire'.[19] For Shakespeare, imperial unity was firmly based on the idea that Britons and the white residents of the Dominions shared a common ethnic and cultural background and indeed a familial relationship.[20] Although he acknowledged that the primary purpose of CORB was the safety of the children, for Shakespeare 'an almost more important aspect of this scheme' was the 'strengthening of the ties between the country of evacuation and the countries of reception'. Shakespeare cited letters he had received from the parents of CORB children as evidence of the role that evacuees could play in promoting imperial unity. One letter writer saw his son as playing a role in bringing the empire closer together: 'We are pleased to believe that the temporary absence of our son constitutes an invisible export for this country in that it has been the means of still further fostering the happy relations between His Majesty's subjects in this country and in our great Dominion.'[21] The ostensibly temporary movement of British children, under the duress of war, was cast as a way to increase imperial ties and forge new permanent connections.

From the inception of the scheme, the question of its use to facilitate the permanent post-war migration of the evacuee children and their families was actively discussed and promoted by the Advisory Council.[22] Long an advocate of what he termed in his memoir 'the redistribution of population within the Empire', Shakespeare was optimistic that the scheme would lead to post-war migration.[23] Shakespeare frequently mentioned CORB children who wished to stay in the Dominions, careful to emphasise that their parents encouraged these ambitions and often hoped to join them after the war.[24] In 1942 he cited a parent's letter, which focused on the opportunities available to his children in Canada and looked to the possibility of moving there after the war to join them, because 'the young rascals absolutely refuse to come home'.[25] Although Shakespeare clearly believed that CORB had helped to safeguard children from the Blitz, he also sought to use the scheme to further his long-standing promotion of migration to the very end of his term as CORB chairman.[26]

Despite the promotion of migration undertaken by Shakespeare and others officially involved in the scheme, the government was also at pains to set CORB apart from other child migration schemes, which often removed children without parental consent.[27] The organisers of CORB placed the evacuees in private homes, rather than the large and often impersonal institutions of previous schemes. Foster parents would not receive compensation for their hospitality in another attempt to separate CORB from earlier, notorious 'baby-farming' schemes. Officials in the Dominions Office also stressed the temporary nature of the scheme, even as they hoped it would lead to the post-war migration of the children's families.

Most of the evacuees returned to Britain. Of the 355 who went to South Africa, 80 per cent (284) had returned by early 1946. But some remained in South Africa or returned after the war. In 1946, one had withdrawn from the scheme to marry, nine had been joined in South Africa by their parents, three evacuees' parents were making their own arrangements, sixteen remained 'temporarily to complete course of training or until fit to travel', four were 'settling irrespective of parents' plans', fourteen were 'settling if joined by parents', and twenty-four were serving in the Dominion Forces.[28] Others returned to Britain after the war and then returned to South Africa.[29] Regardless of how many evacuees ultimately left Britain permanently, however, these attempts to encourage migration reflect one strand of official thinking at this time that saw British migration to South Africa and the other Dominions as a way to strengthen imperial ties based on racial and cultural affinity.

Promoters of migration in the United Kingdom also targeted those serving in the armed forces. As after the First World War, supporters of migration proposed that a subsidised move to the Dominions might be part of the demobilisation process for those veterans interested.[30] Given that veterans would already be facing a transition back to civilian life, they might be more willing to make such a drastic change and as explored in Chapter 1, many had served in South Africa and Southern Rhodesia during the war and had contacts there that could help them to settle.

One such scheme was suggested by Lieutenant Eric Simmonds in 1943. Prior to the war, Simmonds had spent twenty years in South Africa and Southern Rhodesia. Modelling his plan on the Civilian Conservation Corps in the United States, Simmonds suggested that rather than demobilising soldiers in the UK, they could be sent to the Dominions to work on various engineering, agricultural or infrastructure projects. After a year they could choose whether to stay (and have their dependants sent out at government expense) or return to the United Kingdom for demobilisation. Simmonds also suggested other incentives such as a free return journey to visit family in the United Kingdom and argued that because ex-service men would have the chance to experience life in the Dominions before deciding whether to move permanently and would have the continuing companionship and camaraderie of their army battalion, they would be more likely to move.[31]

The same year Major Henry Forrester submitted plans for a migration scheme to the Dominions Office. Anticipating concerns that large-scale emigration would take away the workforce needed for rebuilding in the United Kingdom, Forester argued that migration to the 'under populated' Dominions would address unemployment in Britain and the inevitable financial crisis as the United Kingdom repaid money borrowed for the war effort. At the same time the Dominions would benefit from skilled workers for their nascent industrial sectors. In terms of publicity, Forrester proposed that officers should visit military units and factories promoting the advantages of emigration to the Dominions.[32] Neither of these schemes was implemented, but they reflect the wide interest in post-war migration as part of the process of demobilisation.

Post-war migration to the Dominions was also discussed in the House of Lords during the war. Supporters of migration pointed to interwar precedents for their planned schemes and emphasised the role that migration could play in promoting imperial unity.[33] These included the soldier settlement schemes after the First World War and the Overseas Settlement Board, which administered the Empire Settlement Acts of the interwar period.[34] The wartime travel of service men to the Dominions and the connections and relationships many had made were also identified as a means of promoting and facilitating post-war migration.[35]

The question of the settlement of demobilised soldiers in the Dominions was considered by the Inter-Departmental Committee on Migration set up by the War Cabinet. A report on this subject was approved in February 1943 and circulated to the Dominions and Southern Rhodesia. In their responses, Canada, New Zealand and South Africa emphasised that their priority would be to assist their own returning veterans to settle back into civilian life. Australia stated that plans for a free passage scheme for veterans and an assisted passage scheme for civilians in collaboration with the British were underway and would soon be announced. This was the programme that would become known as the 'Ten Pound Pom' scheme. The South African response emphasised that due to the racial labour hierarchy, they were interested only in skilled British migrants and could not 'embark on any big migration scheme' but they would consider applications from the British Forces, especially those in the RAF who had received training in South Africa and married South African nationals. Southern Rhodesia announced an agreement reached with the British government for a migration scheme for ex-service personnel.[36] As discussed in Chapter 3, however, this scheme was never implemented due to the high rates of migration before it had even begun.

The promotion of British migration to the Dominions continued after the war. A newsreel covering the 1948 Commonwealth Prime Ministers' conference posed the 'redistribution' of British population to the Dominions and Southern Rhodesia as the greatest problem facing the Commonwealth.[37] It drew on long-running imperial tropes, depicting Canada, Australia, South Africa and Southern Rhodesia as empty and under-utilised lands, in need of skilled British workers to make proper use of their vast resources. Britain is depicted as overcrowded, its inhabitants described as 'restricted', ignoring housing shortages in the Dominions. Emigration was posed as a solution to the post-war housing shortage and to concerns about Britain's ability to feed its own population.

All of this planning, whether it aimed to promote white British migration to the settler colonies of the British Empire or to ensure the return of service personnel of colour to the Caribbean, was premised on imperial ideologies of race. The idea that the migration of 'British stock' to the Dominions and Southern Rhodesia would strengthen imperial ties, assumed racial affinity and that white British migrants would contribute to and be welcome in those countries. The idea that the presence of Black migrants from the Caribbean in the United Kingdom would lead not to the strengthening of ties but to conflict, also speaks to underlying assumptions about the racial hierarchies that had long underpinned the British Empire. The concern of British officials not to appear racist even as they engineered discrimination by covert means also foreshadowed the approach that would continue into the late 1940s and 1950s.

'White people of a type more urgently needed here': Debating migration in South Africa and Southern Rhodesia

The Second World War also shaped planning for post-war migration in South Africa and Southern Rhodesia. Many argued that white migration was crucial to continue the industrial development spurred by the war. This was tied to arguments for increasing white migration as a demographic defence of minority rule, against a background of the growth of African labour and anti-colonial activism and increased African migration to cities spurred by the war. However, opponents, particularly of subsidised migration schemes raised concerns about the potential threat they might pose to local white employment, especially of returning veterans. Long-running fears about the threat of 'poor whites' to racial prestige dictated that any migration policy implemented would be selective. In South Africa, child migration emerged as a compromise position; while increasing the white population in the long run, children were assumed to be more easily assimilated than adults and would not come into competition with returning veterans for employment. In Southern Rhodesia, the main focus of migration advocates was the air training scheme, highlighting the sharp distinction between the way white RAF personnel were treated in this context and the way in which Black RAF personnel in the United Kingdom were treated.

In both South Africa and Southern Rhodesia, wartime demand led to economic growth, especially in the industrial and manufacturing sectors, but also in agriculture, which in Southern Rhodesia involved the use of forced African labour.[38] This meant a shift in recruitment efforts away from their previous emphasis on 'gentleman' farmers with capital to include professionals and the skilled and semi-skilled workforce. At the same time, in both nations, increasing rates of African urbanisation, population growth and both labour and anti-colonial protest, heightened by the war, led many to promote the migration of Europeans (including Britons) as a way to maintain racially based minority rule.[39]

As in Britain, the CORB children became a focus for such promotion in South Africa.[40] Support for CORB in South Africa was widespread, although not all supporters viewed the scheme in the same terms. Some focused on CORB as part of the war effort, others emphasised its possibilities for permanent migration, and some believed it would serve both purposes. Committees to coordinate the reception and placement of children were formed, even in small towns. Although in many cases these towns did not actually receive any evacuees, they set up committees, held meetings and received applications from prospective foster parents.[41] This suggests that had CORB not ceased to send children overseas after the *City of Benares* disaster, South Africa would have been willing to host many more evacuees. Some of the committees were in predominantly Afrikaans-speaking towns and the records show that the meetings were conducted in Afrikaans suggesting that support for evacuation was not limited to English-speaking South Africans.[42]

There was also support for child migration from Europe more broadly. Several Afrikaner families offered homes to refugee children from the Netherlands or Belgium.[43] In 1940 Harry Lawrence, the Minister of the Interior, proposed an adoption scheme for children from all Allied countries. Unlike CORB this would be a scheme of 'permanent adoption'.[44] By expanding their plans for child migration beyond Britain, Lawrence and other United Party MPs sought to counter criticism from Afrikaner nationalists that they supported British migration for their own political ends, on the assumption that British immigrants would support the United Party.

Child migration evaded the most frequent criticism of a large-scale immigration scheme in this period, that they would make finding employment and housing for demobilised white South African soldiers more difficult. Labour MP Duncan Burnside recommended the delay of a mass immigration scheme for six years so as to avoid competition with returning veterans but argued that a scheme for the adoption of the 'literally thousands and thousands' and 'perhaps millions' of orphans from Europe could be implemented immediately after the war. This would have the effect of increasing the birth rate of white South Africans and simultaneously contribute to the post-war reconstruction of Europe he argued. Cecil Miles-Cadman echoed his colleague, arguing that 200,000 orphans should be adopted, who 'would be brought up as South Africans' in this 'sunny country of ours, this empty country that wants the laughter of children and the growth and strength of youth'.[45] Both emphasised that the children would easily assimilate to white South African culture.[46]

The 1820 Memorial Settlers' Association and Mr R. Haldane Murray, a prosperous South African sheep farmer and philanthropist, were even more active in using the war to promote child migration to South Africa. Unsatisfied with the CORB rule that children be at least five years old, Murray set up his own scheme focusing on the evacuation of younger children. The Murray scheme was much more overt in its settlement agenda than CORB. Murray's proposals to the South African government describe the scheme in terms of aiding the Allied war effort but his migration agenda is a clear subtext, including the adoption of children and the migration of refugees or wounded service personnel from across Europe.[47]

The Murray scheme caused concern in the CORB office and among other government agencies both in Britain and in South Africa. Edith Thompson, of the British High Commission in Pretoria, described the Murrays as 'fanatics on the subject of settlement and the importance of introducing good English or Scottish stock into this country'.[48] A note from a CORB employee, S.S. Nichole, described a phone call with Murray's sister and representative of the Murray scheme in Britain, who was 'anxious to arrange for adoption when possible in order to secure more white population for South Africa'.[49] This focus on increasing the white population demonstrates that the scheme was not purely focused on aiding the war effort or helping refugees. Letters from the National Society for the Prevention of Cruelty to Children and the Social Welfare Department sent to CORB enquiring about the Murray scheme indicate wider concern about Murray's activities. Although he corresponded with government agencies in both South Africa and Britain, the Department of Social Welfare in South Africa and British High Commissioner's Office claimed to have no knowledge of Murray's activities and had not given them official sanction.[50] Murray intended to bring 100 children to South Africa, and at least eleven had gone by 1941 including one 'infant in arms'.[51]

Murray also worked with the 1820 Memorial Settlers' Association, an organisation devoted to the promotion of British migration to South Africa and named after the first official scheme to encourage British settlement in the Cape Colony in the early nineteenth century. The Association was inspired by Murray's efforts and wanted to use his plan as a model for a post-war migration scheme. The Association was involved in the CORB Advisory Council and corresponded with the Dominions Office about the possibility of extending the scheme after the war. In March 1941, the Association sent a series of memos to the Dominions Office proposing a scheme for child migration. Admitting that due to shipping difficulties, the implementation of the scheme would probably be delayed until after the war, the proposal advocated fundraising during the war because wartime patriotism would have a 'greater pulling effect'. The proposed plan, like Murray's, focused on the migration of young children assuming they would be easier to assimilate. The memo concluded with the hope that such a scheme would have the dual purpose of furthering 'sound European settlement' in South Africa and assisting with post-war reconstruction.[52] A later memo argued that the most efficient use of their funds was to send orphans and provide assistance to artisans who wished to settle in South Africa and could pay part of the passage since these would be 'men with large families of just the type most likely to help South Africa'.[53] Here the focus on enlarging the white population of South Africa and thereby entrenching its rule is clear. As this statement also suggests, within this goal, there was also a focus on recruiting the right 'type' of immigrant.

The tension between encouraging immigrants of the 'right sort' and protecting the employment prospects of returning soldiers was evident in the debates of the South African Senate. In March 1944, National Party senators pressed Charles Clarkson, the Minister of the Interior on the government's policy on immigration, expressing concern that returning South African soldiers should be the priority in terms of employment. They were careful to state that the National Party was not opposed to immigration but only to the arrival of people who might be become a burden on the state and who would not be easily assimilated.[54] This emphasis on the ability of the immigrant to adapt reflects the long-running concern of many Afrikaner nationalists that their culture and political influence might be threatened by immigration, especially from Britain.

In response, Clarkson argued that South Africa could easily find work for both new European immigrants and returning service men as it would need artisans to work in the building industry, 'We ought to encourage 30,000, 40,000, 50,000 skilled artisans to help us develop South Africa without injury to any of our own people.'[55] Clarkson, aware of the competition South Africa might face with the other Dominions or the United States for immigrants from Britain, also pointed to the presence of British service men in the country as an opportunity to recruit desirable immigrants: 'We have to-day 30,000 of these fine RAF boys training in South Africa. They have been living in the sunshine for a number of years and they want to come back here.'[56] Clarkson and the Smuts government supported selective migration, but as discussed in more detail in Chapter 3, did not support mass immigration or subsidised migration schemes.

As a result, the government also received pressure and criticism from advocates of migration, who argued that the government's hedging meant that they were missing the valuable opportunities that the war provided for recruiting new immigrants.[57] Others saw immigration from Europe as the best way to continue the development and industrialisation caused by the war. Senator Hyman Basner argued that immigration from Europe and the development that it would bring combined with the end of the colour bar was the best solution to both the problem of 'poor whites' and of the racial tension caused by fear of the African majority. A similar argument was made by Senator George Richards.[58]

This debate resumed on much the same lines in 1945 with almost the same protagonists. National Party senators argued against immigration schemes subsidised by the government, describing the ideal immigrant as one who could make his own way to South Africa.[59] Richards extended the argument of taking advantage of wartime circumstances beyond the recruitment of Allied service men and women to the evacuees and refugees brought there by the war. Urging the government to take a 'broad statesman-like vision in regard to the future' and to take 'fullest advantage' of the situation of war to recruit new immigrants, Richards described evacuees brought to South Africa by the war as 'white people of a type more urgently needed here than perhaps in other parts of the world'.[60] The debate on immigration in the Legislative Assembly took on much the same form, though also included long speeches from E.H. Louw, the MP for Beaufort West, against Jewish immigration.[61]

Private citizens and organisations also suggested migration schemes. The South African Boy Scouts Association proposed to recruit Scouters and Senior Scouts in the United Kingdom who might be interested in moving to

South Africa, who would then be assisted by the South African Association in finding employment and accommodation. The original letter argued that 'men trained in the ideals and aims' of Scouting 'would make most desirable immigrants'.[62] This was ambiguous as it could refer to the imperial ethos of Scouting but also to its emphasis on self-reliance and an outdoor lifestyle. Clarkson replied with characteristic support: 'I ... am very pleased that your Organisation is going into the question of encouraging British Scoutmasters and senior Scouts to settle in South Africa after the war. There is no question that we need suitable immigrants in this country.'[63] Here again, the emphasis is on 'suitable' migrants. Mr Lazarus of Durban, a businessman involved in manufacturing, wrote in 1943 requesting support from the government for the establishment of an information office for prospective immigrants in London. While agreeing in principle that such information should be available to intending immigrants, Douglas Forsyth, the Secretary for External Affairs, declined to support the scheme on the grounds that such information should be provided by South Africa House and other official government channels.[64] The Rotary Club of Randfontein, a mining town near Johannesburg wrote to the government concerning the 'immigration and settlement of RAF and British service men in particular'.[65] As in was the case with the Boy Scouts Association, the implication was that military veterans would make good migrants, drawing on long-running ideas of settler masculinity.

In Southern Rhodesia, the primary focus of migration promoters was the air training scheme. As in South Africa, advocates argued that such migration would not harm the prospects of returned Rhodesian soldiers and would contribute to industrial development. There was also a similar emphasis on the importance of selective migration. In October of 1943, for instance, Frank Harris, the Minister of Land and Agriculture, asserted that there was 'room for all if they are of the right type'.[66] Later that month Edward Noaks, the MP for Mazoe, posited the RAF scheme and especially the technical expertise of RAF mechanics in the country as a great opportunity for industrial development and to increase the white population.[67] By 1944 it was agreed with the imperial government that RAF men stationed in Southern Rhodesia could seek their discharge there if they met immigration regulations.[68]

By June 1945, as many RAF personnel in Southern Rhodesia began planning for demobilisation, there were increasing calls for the government to take more decisive action to recruit them and other white migrants. William Leggate, MP for Hartley, argued for European immigration as the only way that Southern Rhodesia might reach the 'honoured position' of a fully self-governing Dominion and cited the presence of so many RAF personnel in the country as an opportunity to implement the colony's long-running goal of increasing its European population. Citing the large volume of immigration applications received by the High Commissioner, Leggate argued that more immigration would help the development of the country and therefore the prospects of returning Rhodesian soldiers. Leggate cited the cases of three RAF personnel seeking immigration permits to stay on in Southern Rhodesia that had been featured in the Bulawayo paper, *The Sunday News*, arguing that 'officialdom has run riot'. By allowing the RAF men to be demobilised in Southern Rhodesia, the colony would gain immigrants and the British government would even pay the cost of sending out their dependants. Leggate concluded, 'These are very valuable men – perhaps the most valuable we have ever had an opportunity of securing in our history. It seems deplorable that men who wish to stay here should be sent out of the country.'[69] From Leggate's perspective, an important aspect of the value of these men, aside from whatever skills they might possess, was their Britishness alongside their whiteness. This is clear in the promotional literature drafted to attract British migrants after the war, which proclaimed 'we want new settlers of British stock'.[70] This open emphasis on the Britishness of the ideal settler differentiated Southern Rhodesia from South Africa, although beyond this, the debate over post-war migration and the idea type of migrant proceeded in both nations on very similar lines.

Even though some supporters of migration in southern Africa saw it as a way to strengthen imperial ties or to promote development, most supporters of migration were primarily concerned with its potential to increase the white population and so contribute to both the economic development of South Africa and Rhodesia and the entrenchment of their white minority regimes. Opponents to subsidised or unselective migration also framed their arguments in terms of what would be best for these settler colonial nations.

Conclusion

Supporters of migration in both the United Kingdom and southern Africa, including government officials, private citizens and voluntary organisations, used the circumstances of the war to advance their agenda. Though South African and Rhodesian promoters largely sought migrants to shore up the white population in their minority regimes, officials in London primarily saw British migration to the Dominions as a way to strengthen imperial ties and ensure the unity and loyalty of the emerging Commonwealth. Regardless of these differing motivations, the promotion of British or broader European migration was ultimately aimed at the reinforcement of settler colonial rule in South Africa and Southern Rhodesia, whether as part of the British Empire, or Commonwealth or as an independent state.

Planning for post-war migration 67

By looking at the way promoters of migration justified and explained its benefits, it is possible to get a sense of the concerns and expectations of the immediate post-war era. Though many of these migration schemes were unsuccessful or never implemented, the discussion surrounding them shows the ways in which British policymakers and others sought to reverse Britain's diminished economic and geopolitical position after the Second World War. And for many, the migration of 'British stock' to the Dominions and Southern Rhodesia seemed the best way to encourage development there, which would bolster the British economy and reinforce British influence in the Commonwealth and thus her global position in the days of the early Cold War. By contrast, the free migration of British subjects of colour to the United Kingdom, such as the Black RAF personnel discussed above, was perceived by policymakers as destabilising, an inversion of the long-running racial hierarchy of empire, causing rather than solving the problems faced by Britain in the immediate post-war period. Both the promotion of white British migration to the settler colonies and attempts to ensure the return of Black service personnel to the Caribbean after the war can be viewed as attempts to reinforce the long-running imperial order in the face of increasing challenges.

Notes

1 Clair Wills describes this as a 'delayed demobilisation' noting that 110 passengers on the SS *Ormonde* and 495 passengers on the HMT *Windrush* were ex-service men. Wills, *Lovers and Strangers*, p. 10.
2 For instance, Hazel Carby's father, Carl, from Jamaica, had served in the RAF during the war, married her Welsh mother, Iris, in England where they settled. Hazel V. Carby, *Imperial Intimacies: A Tale of Two Islands* (London: Verso, 2019).
3 Wills, *Lovers and Strangers*, p. 8; Anne Spry Rush, *Bonds of Empire: West Indians and Britishness from Victoria to Decolonization* (Oxford: Oxford University Press, 2011), pp. 128–47, 157–65.
4 Lydia Lindsey, 'Halting the Tide: Responses to West Indian Immigration to Britain, 1946–1952', *The Journal of Caribbean History* 26:1 (1992), 74–5.
5 Peter Fryer, *Staying Power: The History of Black People in Britain* (London: Pluto Books, 1984), pp. 358–66.
6 Colin Grant writes about this in relation to his mother, Ethlyn, who left a middle-class upbringing with servants in Jamaica, 'not even knowing how to boil an egg' and ended up working a factory job at Vauxhall Motors. Colin Grant, *Home Coming: Voices of the Windrush Generation* (London: Jonathan Cape, 2019), p. 112.
7 Webster, *Mixing It*, pp. 16, 19.
8 Fedorowich, *Unfit for Heroes*.

9 These riots saw racially motivated attacks on communities of colour across nine ports in the United Kingdom. Jacqueline Jenkinson, *Black 1919: Riots, Racism and Resistance in Imperial Britain* (Liverpool: Liverpool University Press, 2009).
10 TNA, CAB 66/30/28, War Cabinet, R.P. (42) 33, 'Committee on Reconstruction Problems. Interdepartmental Committee on the Machinery of Demobilisation. Final Report', 9 October 1942, p. 27.
11 TNA, AIR 20/9051, Sir Grahame Donald to Sir John Slessor, 30 November 1945.
12 TNA, AIR 20/9051, Air Chief Marshal Sir John Slessor to Air Marshal Sir James Robb, 21 January 1946.
13 TNA, AIR 20/9051, 'West Indian Ground Personnel' 12 October 1946.
14 TNA, AIR 20/9051, 'Repatriation of West Indian Airmen', 18 July 1947.
15 D.A. Low and J.M. Lonsdale, 'Introduction: Towards the New Order 1945–1963', in *History of East Africa: Volume 3*, eds D.A. Low and Alison Smith (Oxford: Clarendon Press, 1976), p. 12; D.A. Low, *Eclipse of Empire* (Cambridge: Cambridge University Press, 1991), p. 238.
16 P.J. Cain and A.G. Hopkins, *British Imperialism: Crisis and Deconstruction 1914–1990* (London and New York: Longman, 1993), pp. 278–81.
17 1,532 children were sent to Canada in nine parties; 577 children sent to Australia in three parties; 353 children were sent to South Africa in two parties; 202 children were sent to New Zealand in two parties. TNA, DO 131/43, M. Maxse, 'History of the Children's Overseas Reception Board', 1940–44, pp. 6, 7, 10. Much of the work on the evacuation tends to be focused on Canada where the majority of evacuees went and there are few sustained scholarly discussions of the evacuation. Perhaps the most scholarly discussion, focused on the social history of the evacuation is Carlton Jackson, *Who Will Take Our Children?* (London: Methuen, 1985). On Canada see Geoffrey Bilson, *The Guest Children: The Story of the British Child Evacuees Sent to Canada During World War II* (Saskatoon: Fifth House, 1988). For accounts of the scheme written by former evacuees see Jessica Mann, *Out of Harm's Way: The Wartime Evacuation of Children from Britain* (St. Ives: Headline, 2005); Michael Fethney, *The Absurd and the Brave: CORB – The True Account of the British Government's World War II Evacuation of Children Overseas* (Sussex: The Book Guild Ltd, 1990).
18 Lin, 'National Identity'. For more on the evacuation of children within Britain see Robert Mackay, *Half the Battle: Civilian Morale in Britain during the Second World War* (Manchester: Manchester University Press, 2002), pp. 3–9; Rose, *Which People's War?*, pp. 56–62; Welshman, *Churchill's Children*.
19 TNA, DO 131/28, 'The Operation of the Children's Overseas Reception Scheme', 15 July 1941, pp. 11–12. Shakespeare likely found a sympathetic audience in the Victoria League, an organisation founded in 1901 to promote imperial unity based on a sense of shared British identity. Katie Pickles, '"A link in the great chain of Empire friendship": The Victoria League in New Zealand', *Journal of Imperial and Commonwealth History* 33:1 (2005).
20 TNA, DO 131/28, 'A New Imperial Policy', undated pp. 2, 4.

21 TNA, DO 131/28, Speech to be made by Geoffrey Shakespeare at the Kinsman Luncheon, 17 February 1942, pp. 1–2.
22 TNA, DO 131/4, Minutes of the Advisory Council to the Children's Overseas Reception Board, 19 June 1940.
23 Geoffrey Shakespeare, *Let Candles be Brought In* (London: MacDonald, 1949), p. 244.
24 TNA, DO 131/28, 'The Operation of the Children's Overseas Reception Scheme', 15 July 1941, p. 9.
25 TNA, DO 131/28, Speech to be made by Geoffrey Shakespeare at the Kinsman Luncheon, 17 February 1942, p. 2.
26 TNA, DO 131/28, Geoffrey Shakespeare, Farewell letter, 12 March 1942.
27 Lin, 'National Identity', pp. 310–11. The Dominions Office also sought to differentiate British child evacuees from refugees from continental Europe as demonstrated by the controversy over the name of the administrative apparatus set up to receive the children in South Africa. The initial name of the organisation in South Africa was the 'Child Refugee Committee' but the British government objected to the use of the term refugee. The name was subsequently changed to the 'Overseas Children's Reception Administration' but officials and prospective foster parents in South Africa continued to use the term 'refugee' interchangeably with 'evacuee' and 'child-guest' in their correspondence. Western Cape Archival Repository, Cape Town (hereafter KAB), 3/ELN Vol. 893, Ref. 1975/3, 'Refugee and Evacuee Children from Overseas Refugee Camps', 1940–49. By contrast, the term 'evacuee' was consistently used in British government records. The British government insisted on differentiating between British child evacuees, who had left their homes as a temporary expedient, and refugees from continental Europe, many of whom had made their way to Britain. This conflict over language demonstrates both different understandings and the varying intentions of supporters of wartime child evacuation in South Africa and in Britain, as well as an underlying racial anxiety, that British children should not be lumped in the same category as European, and particularly Jewish, refugees.
28 TNA, DO 131/43, 'Children's Overseas Reception Scheme, Position at 14 Feb 1946'.
29 See Chapter 7 for a discussion of several such post-independence trajectories.
30 Fedorowich, *Unfit for Heroes*, p. 1.
31 TNA, DO 35/1133, E. Simmonds to Cranbourne, 3 October 1943.
32 TNA, DO 35/1133, 'Proposals for Emigration from U.K. after the War to the Dominions', undated.
33 *Parliamentary Debates, Lords*, 5th Ser., Vol. 129, 22 September 1943, Col. 67.
34 For more on the interwar soldier settlement schemes see Fedorowich, *Unfit for Heroes*.
35 *Parliamentary Debates, Lords*, 5th Ser., Vol. 129, 22 September 1943, Cols 70, 72.
36 Cmd 6658, *Migration with the British Commonwealth. Statement by His Majesty's Government in the United Kingdom* (London: HMSO, 1945), 3–5.
37 'Should 20 Million Emigrate?', Pathé Newsreel, Issued 18 October 1948.

38 Killingray and Rathbone, 'Introduction', p. 13; Jackson, *The British Empire*, pp. 231–2, 252–3; Ian Phimister, 'Zimbabwe: The Path of Capitalist Development', in *History of Central Africa Vol. 2*, eds David Birmingham and Phyllis Martin (London: Longman, 1983), p. 285; L.H. Gann, *Huggins of Rhodesia the Man and His Country* (London: George Allen & Unwin Ltd, 1964), pp. 152–3; Johnson, 'Settler Farmers'; Vickery, 'Revival of Forced Labour'.

39 B. Davidson, 'South Africa and The Second World War', in *Africa and the Second World War: Symposium: Papers and Report*, ed. Unesco (Paris), p. 108. On the connection between urbanisation and anti-colonial nationalism see Crowder, 'The Second World War', p. 35. During the war there were protests against the pass laws that restricted African movements and employment in 1943 and 1944, the foundation of the more militant ANC Youth League in 1944, a bus boycott in Alexandria in 1944, a strike at Durban's ports near the end of the war, and the 1946 Mine Strike. Cherry Gertzel, 'East and Central Africa', in *The Cambridge History of Africa*, ed. Michael Crowder (Cambridge: Cambridge University Press, 1984), p. 390; Jackson, *The British Empire*, p. 251; Davidson, 'South Africa', pp. 116–19; Francis Wilson, 'Southern Africa', in *The Cambridge History of Africa*, ed. Michael Crowder (Cambridge: Cambridge University Press, 1984), p. 282; Phimister, 'Zimbabwe: The Path of Capitalist Development', p. 287.

40 Southern Rhodesia offered to host British children but was not included in the scheme due to transportation difficulties. Four children with relatives in Southern Rhodesia were sent there from South Africa, however. TNA, DO 131/6, 'Reception Arrangements – Southern Rhodesia'.

41 KAB, 1/CT Vol. 420, Cape Town National Child Refugee Administration; 1/MDB Vol. 73, Middelburg National Child Refugee Administration; 1/NKE Vol. 38, Nqamakwe National Child Refugee Administration; 1/PKB Vol. 32, Piquetburg National Child Refugee Administration, 1/PTA Vol. 13, Port Alfred National Child Refugee Administration; 1/STG Vol. 10, Steynburg National Child Refugee Administration; 1/RMD Vol. 31, Richmond National Child Refugee Administration; 1/IWE Vol. 4/1/25, Ingwe National Child Refugee Administration; 1/LSM Vol. 50, Ladismith The Overseas Children's Reception Administration; 1/LBG Vol. 38, Laingsburg The Overseas Children's Reception Administration; 1/BW Vol. 12/36, Beaufort West The Overseas Children's Reception Administration; 1/BIZ Vol. 6/46, Bizana The Overseas Children's Reception Administration. For committees which never hosted any children see KAB, 1/LSK Vol. 66, Lusikisiki National Child Refugee Administration; 1/KNT Vol. 95, Kentani National Child Refugee Administration; 1/HFD Vol. 7/1/13, Hopefield National Child Refugee Administration, 1/KNY Vol. 8/25, Knysna National Child Refugee Administration.

42 KAB, 1/MDB Vol. 73, Middelburg National Child Refugee Administration.

43 KAB, 3/ELN Vol. 893 Ref. 1975/3 Refugee and Evacuee Children from Overseas Refugee Camps, 1940–49; 1/WIL Vol. 4/6 Ref. 33/1/2/3, Evacuee Child Williston. There was also some concern from the Dominions Office that the children coming to South Africa would be placed in British homes, rather than Afrikaner ones although many children seem to have gone to Afrikaner homes

for holidays. Similarly, there was also a debate over whether the British evacuees would be required to learn Afrikaans like all other South African schoolchildren. See KAB, PAE Vol. E806 Ref. Z/709, 1940, Evacuee Children from Overseas.
44 Union of South Africa, *Debates of the House of Assembly*, Vol. 39 (Cape Town: Unie Volkspers BPK, 1940), Col. 1537.
45 Union of South Africa, *Debates of the House of Assembly*, Vol. 47 (Cape Town: Unie Volkspers BPK, 1944), Cols 2192–9.
46 Similar arguments were made in the South African Senate. See The Senate of South Africa, *Debates (Official Report) 1944* (Cape Town: Nasionale Pers Beperk, 1944), Col. 321. The Senate of South Africa, *Debates (Official Report) 1945* (Cape Town: Nasionale Pers Beperk, 1945), Col. 167.
47 TNA, DO 131/50, R. Haldane Murray to H.C. Lawrence, Minister of the Interior, Union of South Africa 'Re: Importation of 100 War Stricken Children into Graaf Reinet and District', 1 June 1940; R. Murray to E. Thompson of the High Commissioner's Office (Pretoria), 4 July 1941.
48 TNA, DO 131/50, E. Thompson, 'Dispatch No. 21: Mr. Haldane Murray's Scheme for the evacuation of young children'.
49 TNA, DO 131/50, S.S. Nichole to M. Maxse, 26 November 1940.
50 TNA, DO 131/50, S.S. Nichole to M. Maxse, 26 November 1940.
51 TNA, DO 131/50, E. Thompson, 'Dispatch No. 19: Mr. Haldane Murray's Scheme'.
52 TNA, DO 131/36, 'Child Settlement in South Africa: A Scheme for the Settlement of Children in South Africa on the lines of the Haldane Murray Scheme with which the 1820 Settler's Association was associated', 15 March 1941, pp. 4, 7.
53 TNA, DO 131/36, Brendan Quinn to Paul Emrys Evans, 13 April 1943.
54 The Senate of South Africa, *Debates*, 1944, Cols 312–13.
55 The Senate of South Africa, *Debates*, 1944, Col. 694.
56 The Senate of South Africa, *Debates*, 1944, Col 695.
57 The Senate of South Africa, *Debates*, 1944, Col. 322.
58 The Senate of South Africa, *Debates, 1944*, Cols 332–3, 518–19. Basner was the representative of the Orange Free State and Transvaal Africans and a former member of the South African Communist Party and opponent of the segregationist policies of South Africa. Miriam Basner and Hymnan Basner, *Am I an African? The Political Memoirs of H.M. Basner* (Johannesburg: Witwatersrand University Press, 1993).
59 The Senate of South Africa, *Debates, 1945*, Col. 149.
60 The Senate of South Africa, *Debates, 1945*, Col. 166.
61 See, for example, Union of South Africa, *Debates of the House of Assembly*, Vol. 39 (Cape Town: Unie: Volkspers BPK, 1940), Cols 7469–73.
62 NASA, BNS 1/1/401, Ref. 301/74, Vol. 1, G.E. Fish to C.E. Clarkson, 21 March 1944.
63 NASA, BNS 1/1/401, Ref. 301/74, Vol. 1, C.E. Clarkson to G. Fish, 28 March 1944. There had been similar schemes in the interwar era, see Richard A. Voeltz, 'The British Boy Scout migration plan 1922–1932', *The Social Science Journal* 40:1 (2003).

64 NASA, BTS Ref. 59/6, Vol. 51, Info Office for Immigrants in London 1944.
65 NASA, BNS 1/1/401, Ref. 301/74, Vol.1, Secretary of the Rotary Club of Randfontein to the Minister of the Interior, 10 November 1943.
66 Southern Rhodesia, *Debates of the Legislative Assembly 1943*, Vol. 23 (Salisbury: Rhodesian Printing and Publishing Co. Ltd, 1944), Cols 2363–4.
67 Southern Rhodesia, *Debates of the Legislative Assembly 1943*, Vol. 23, Cols 2515, 2518–19.
68 Southern Rhodesia, *Debates of the Legislative Assembly 1944*, Vol. 24, Col. 2235.
69 Southern Rhodesia. *Debates of the Legislative Assembly 1946*, Vol. 25, Cols 2000–8.
70 TNA, DO 35/1135, Public Relations Department of Southern Rhodesia, *Southern Rhodesia: Facts and Figures for the Immigrant*, undated.

3

'Immigration on a Selective Basis': The competing imperatives of minority settler colonialism, 1945–53

In late January 1947 King George VI and his family set off on a two-month tour of southern Africa, the first royal state visit after the Second World War. In a speech to the South African Senate, the Prime Minister, Jan Smuts, spoke of the honour it was to be chosen as the location for the first post-war royal tour and the favourable, worldwide publicity that the visit would garner. This, he asserted, would build on the events of the war, which had caused 'the name of South Africa to be spread throughout the world'.[1] The images of Smuts and his wife hosting the royal family further cemented his reputation as an imperial statesman. The media coverage of the royal tour in the United Kingdom created an enticing portrait of a sun-drenched paradise that might have seemed especially appealing to Britons who had just shivered through one of the coldest winters on record.[2] The royals were not alone in making their way to southern Africa. In the immediate aftermath of the war, a great many Britons chose to rebuild their lives in South Africa and Southern Rhodesia.

Close to 20 per cent of emigrants leaving the United Kingdom, approximately 90,000 in total, came to South Africa and Southern Rhodesia in the late 1940s.[3] As discussed in Chapter 1, many were influenced by their wartime experience in the region and attracted by the climate and the promise of social mobility.[4] This surge in migration, like the royal tour, which attracted huge crowds, reveals and contributed to economic, social and cultural connections between the United Kingdom and South Africa and Southern Rhodesia in the immediate post-war period.[5] In the case of South Africa, these continued connections have been overshadowed by the 1948 National Party electoral victory that set South Africa on the road to apartheid and by 1961 republic and political separation from Britain.[6]

At first glance, it seems that the political shift of 1948 was mirrored by a drop in both overall European immigration and the proportion of British immigrants after 1948, as illustrated in Table 3.1. Previous studies have attributed the immediate post-war increase to pro-British immigration policies pursued by the United Party government under Smuts from 1945 to 1948 and the subsequent decrease in immigration to the less welcoming policies of the post-1948 National Party government under D.F. Malan.[7] It seems intuitive that the United Party led by General Smuts, the imperial statesman, would encourage British immigration, while the Afrikaner nationalist Malan government would adopt a more cautious approach. The rhetoric of the National Party also supports this interpretation as the new administration sought to distance itself from the policies of its predecessor.

However, despite a clear difference in rhetoric and public statements regarding British migration, an analysis of the implementation of policy under both the Smuts and Malan administrations and in neighbouring Southern Rhodesia demonstrates that all three governments pursued a similar, cautious approach to immigration. While the change in government likely contributed to the decline in British migrants after 1948 in South Africa, it was not the only or even the most important factor. Rather than a dramatic break, this chapter argues for continuity between the Smuts and Malan governments' approach to immigration in the decade after the Second World War. Just as scholars have found continuity between the implementation of formal apartheid in 1948 and long-standing intellectual and legal

Table 3.1 British migration to South Africa and Southern Rhodesia, 1946–54

Year	Migration from the United Kingdom to South Africa[i]	Percentage of total migration to South Africa from the United Kingdom	British-born migrants to Southern Rhodesia[ii]	Percentage of total migrants to Southern Rhodesia born in Britain[iii]
1946	7,471	66.37	3,360	37.65
1947	20,604	71.44	6,287	48.52
1948	25,513	71.60	8,574	58.75
1949	9,629	65.15	5,908	47.56
1950	5,094	39.79	4,750	32.72
1951	5,903	38.73	6,130	38.96
1952	6,491	35.14	6,808	54.37
1953	5,416	33.31	5,290	51.33
1954	4,629	28.20	4,089	41.82

[i] South African immigration figures for 1946 to 1948, Union of South Africa, *Statistics of Migration 1948*, p. 43. Figure for 1949 calculated based on specific data for the years 1945 to 1948 as above and a figure for the period 1945–49 in Republic of South Africa Bureau of Statistics, *Report No. 286: Statistics of Immigrants and Emigrants 1924–1964*, p. 3. Figures for 1950–54, Republic of South Africa Department of Statistics, *Report No. 19–01–01, Migration Statistics: Immigrants and Emigrants, 1966 to 1969* (Pretoria: Government Printer, 1969), p. 4.
[ii] Commonwealth Relations Office, *Oversea Migration Statistics 1955*, 14.
[iii] These figures reflect the influence of new restrictions placed on British and other migrants in 1948 and quotas implemented starting in 1952 as described in this chapter.

traditions and discriminatory practice, immigration policy as implemented was largely consistent.[8] Even though the Malan government made minor changes in administration, and its rhetoric signalled a completely different approach, in essence the policy remained the same. The practicalities of how to increase the European population while maintaining the privileged lifestyle thought to be appropriate for the white minority defined immigration policy under both the United Party and the National Party alike and a similar dilemma faced the Southern Rhodesian government.[9]

The Smuts government supported limited British immigration as part of a wider push for immigration from Europe. Unlike Australia, New Zealand and Canada, South Africa did not offer subsidised passages or loans in the immediate post-war years. The Smuts government sought to recruit migrants from many European countries, not only the United Kingdom. They enacted limited measures such as an agreement with the Union-Castle shipping company in response to the post-war shipping shortage and the establishment of the Immigration Council to coordinate immigration and provide information to would-be immigrants. This did not amount to an unqualified support for immigration from Britain or elsewhere. Concerns over both the numbers and perceived character of immigrants, particularly from Britain, were frequently raised by the Smuts administration. The conclusion of the Union-Castle agreement and stricter enforcement of immigration regulations for British immigrants though implemented under Malan, were initially decided under Smuts.

The National Party government under Malan did make small policy changes when they came to power in 1948 and employed a different rhetoric regarding immigration. However, in practice, both Smuts and Malan promoted limited European immigration, while promising that the housing and employment of white South Africans, especially ex-service men, would be their priority. The Malan administration disbanded the Immigration Council but replaced it with the Inter-departmental Advisory Council Concerning Immigration Matters. Both administrations pursued child immigration (albeit with limited success) as a compromise position that would not threaten the employment of returning service personnel. There was also no change to immigration law for those with British nationality under Malan. The Aliens Control Act of 1937, which made immigration to South Africa easier for 'natural-born' (a clear euphemism for white) British subjects than other migrants, remained in place throughout the 1950s.[10]

Comparison with Southern Rhodesia also reveals the flaws in a simple correlation between the drop in immigration rates and the policies of the new Malan government. Though not a Dominion, Southern Rhodesia had obtained internal self-government in 1923, making it the closest equivalent to South Africa as a minority settler colony. There are clear differences in terms of both the demographic and political contexts between Rhodesia, with its smaller, majority British white population, and South Africa, with its politically and numerically powerful Afrikaner community. However, both were minority settler colonies whose very existence depended on the perpetuation of racial privilege and power. This demographic difference, that settlers remained a minority in Southern Rhodesia and South Africa, resulted in a racial labour hierarchy that had implications for immigration policy. As well as restrictions placed on African workers this hierarchy also dictated that white settlers should not undertake work considered to be appropriate only for Africans such as unskilled or manual labour. This meant that European immigrants without skills or capital who might become 'a charge upon the state' had long been discouraged.[11]

Though initially there was more public and official support for European and particularly British immigration than in South Africa, the Southern Rhodesian government took a similarly cautious and reactive approach to that of its neighbour. Concerns about the number of immigrants that could be absorbed by the existing infrastructure led to the imposition of immigration restrictions in Southern Rhodesia beginning in 1948.[12] By 1952 Southern Rhodesia's quota-based policy was far more restrictive than that of South Africa. These restrictions were put in place in response to the post-war surge in immigration, which led to the doubling of the European population between 1941 and 1951.[13] This rapid increase led to fears about the provision of housing and employment thought to be appropriate for Europeans. Such anxieties had diminished by the mid 1950s, by which time both the Southern Rhodesian and the South African governments began a cautious promotion of immigration. A close examination of South African immigration policy across the Smuts and Malan administrations and alongside the contemporary policies of neighbouring Southern Rhodesia reveal a shared pragmatic and reactive approach to immigration, despite differences in ideology and political rhetoric.

'The prior claims of the settled population': The implementation of South African immigration policy across the Smuts and Malan administrations

After the Second World War, there was a surge in migration to South Africa from Europe and particularly from the United Kingdom. More than 11,000 immigrants categorised as European arrived in South Africa in 1946, nearly 29,000 in 1947 and 35,000 in 1948. In 1949 the number declined to just less than 15,000.[14] Whether classified by country of previous residence (an average of 65.78 per cent), birth (67.89 per cent) or citizenship

(84.56 per cent), British immigrants made up the clear majority of those coming to South Africa in the years immediately after the war.[15] These high rates were in part caused by the six-year wartime hiatus in normal patterns.

Despite the Smuts government's attempts to attract immigrants from continental Europe as well as the United Kingdom, it was largely Britons who moved to South Africa. In part, this was because those from the United Kingdom were able to migrate freely in this period. While other European governments restricted their populations' ability to emigrate, the British government not only allowed but encouraged emigration to the Commonwealth, hoping that this would cement ties with the United Kingdom. As discussed in Chapter 1, the impact of wartime experience was also crucial. Pre-war understandings of empire, wartime experiences and the British government's efforts to encourage emigration to the Commonwealth all shaped this post-war movement.

Though the Smuts government presided over the post-war surge and many in the United Party approved of it, it was not primarily driven by government policy, which did not subsidise passages as the governments of Australia and New Zealand did or offer loans as the government of Canada did in this period. As mentioned above, the Smuts government set up an Immigration Council in December 1946, which played a limited role in coordinating immigration. The Council sent officials overseas to provide information to prospective immigrants and to provide advice on the completion of the required forms upon landing.[16] It set up temporary accommodation in three former military camps, Westlake near Cape Town, Milner Park in Johannesburg and Wentworth in Durban, though the camps never operated at capacity. Immigrants were required to pay for accommodation and food and generally didn't stay long. At Westlake, for example, the average stay was 5.641 days and the camp, which operated from April 1947 to December 1948, had only served 1,217 immigrants by March 1948.[17] Furthermore, rather than providing subsidised accommodation, it was intended that the camps be funded by fees charged to immigrants for lodging and meals. This was never successful, however, partly because the required capacity was overestimated, and the camps ran at an estimated loss of £200 per month. These financial difficulties were a continual point of contention, which eventually led to the closure of the camps.[18]

The Council also coordinated the activities of voluntary immigration and employment committees in Cape Town, Pretoria, Johannesburg, Bloemfontein, Durban, Port Elizabeth and East London, which included representatives of commerce and industry, who were to help new immigrants on arrival with employment and housing. Netherlands immigration committees also operated in many of these locations. The Council established offices in London, the Hague and Rome, demonstrating the efforts undertaken to recruit migrants from continental Europe as well as the United Kingdom. In London, a selection committee was established, with the remit of assigning priority passages to immigrants whose skills were most in demand.[19]

In response to the post-war shipping shortage, the South African government entered into an agreement with the Union-Castle shipping line, which ran the mail service between the United Kingdom and South Africa. Union-Castle agreed to delay the refurbishing of several ships which had served as troop ships. This provided more passages, though it meant less comfortable accommodation. Three ships were involved: the *Carnarvon Castle*, the *Winchester Castle* and the *Arundel Castle*. Eighty-five per cent of the berths were allocated to those purchasing a special immigration fare at a reduced rate. These priority passages were intended for 'skilled artisans in respect of which there is a shortage in the Union'.[20] The government did not provide direct financial assistance either to immigrants, who were responsible for paying their own fares, or to Union-Castle, although it did guarantee that they would make up the difference if ships returned to Europe with fewer than a third of berths occupied. This arrangement began in June 1947 and was originally intended to last for one year, though this was subsequently extended because of the continuing shipping shortage and delays in the reconditioning of former troop ships.[21]

These were limited steps rather than a wholesale endorsement of mass immigration. The Smuts government always emphasised that support for immigration was a second priority after the welfare of white South Africans, particularly ex-service men. As Saul Dubow has argued, by this time 'South Africanism' was the dominant political discourse and support for immigration and other policies were framed in terms of the benefit that white South Africa, broadly understood, would receive.[22] Though the South African government smoothed the path for some immigrants, it did not directly subsidise immigration or implement policies which would prioritise British over other European migrants. The Smuts government did not, for instance, provide funding to the 1820 Memorial Settlers' Association, an organisation devoted to the promotion of British migration to South Africa, despite repeated requests.[23]

The Smuts government also applied a more selective policy to British immigrants than scholars have recognised. Sally Peberdy has argued that the Smuts government employed an 'open door policy' and that South African officials in London were instructed to 'waive the means test and relax other rules for British immigrants'.[24] However, the memo she cites was not a blanket policy to waive the means test. Rather it specified that it was only in certain cases that the means test should be 'practically waived'.[25] Such cases were described in a letter enclosing the memorandum as those with 'substantial financial resources', those interested in establishing businesses (though not those who 'propose merely to open small fruit and green grocery stores, tea-rooms and the like'), those with experience in farming and in the skilled trades.[26] Such instructions show a selective rather than open-door policy in operation for British immigrants. They also demonstrate that the Smuts government required potential immigrants to either meet financial criteria or possess qualifications or skills in occupations in demand in South Africa.

There is also evidence that the Smuts administration aimed to exclude British-born immigrants they deemed undesirable by working closely with the Union-Castle line and other shipping companies to screen passengers before they departed. The procedure was that the shipping company would ask anyone who applied for a passage whether they intended to move to South Africa permanently. If so, they would be required to fill in documentation which would then be scrutinised by the London committee who had the ability to recommend against the granting of a priority passage. It was hoped that 'in this way the majority of undesirables would be deterred from emigrating to South Africa'.[27] As these efforts underline, rather than offering an open-door policy, the Smuts government aimed to be selective about the British immigrants it received.

The high proportion of British immigrants in the years immediately after the war was largely due to factors beyond the Smuts government's control. As discussed in Chapter 1, the wartime experience of South Africa, a major base of Allied operations in the region, led many Britons to return after the war based on their personal experience or relationships they had formed, regardless of official policy. Because the British government aimed to strengthen links with the Empire, increasingly rebranded as the Commonwealth, they did not limit emigration in the immediate post-war years as did many other continental European governments, including the Netherlands.

The Smuts government tried to recruit continental Europeans, but difficulties with shipping and restrictions on emigration stymied such efforts. For example, the Dutch government initially forbade the immigration of those who might aid with the reconstruction effort and later limited the capital that could be removed from the Netherlands to the equivalent of £10 or £15. As well as acting as a disincentive in itself, this restricted would-be Dutch immigrants to Dutch ships, on which there were very few passages available, and meant that the Smuts government was unable to divert a Union-Castle ship to the Netherlands to transport would-be immigrants as they had hoped.[28]

Dutch restrictions on emigration were revoked in 1948, just as the National Party came to power and emigration rates from the Netherlands, including to South Africa, subsequently soared. Reversing their previous policy, the Dutch government actively promoted emigration from 1949. Though most Dutch emigrants went to Canada and Australia, approximately 12 per cent went to South Africa in this period, slightly less than the third most popular destination, the United States.[29] This was one external factor in explaining the lower proportion of British immigrants from 1950 onwards. Though much more difficult to measure, another potential factor was that the election of the National Party may have made South Africa a less attractive destination for many British immigrants.

Despite their limited scope, the Smuts government's policies came under criticism from both sides in Parliament, echoing the wartime debates detailed in Chapter 2. Supporters of a more proactive immigration policy asserted that the post-war situation provided a unique opportunity to increase the white population and that South Africa should provide incentives to attract the best immigrants. They also argued that the recruitment of new skilled immigrants to work in the growing manufacturing and industrial sector would benefit the economy, providing employment for South African ex-service men, and ameliorating the so-called 'poor white' problem. Opponents argued that any government-backed recruitment would bring people who would compete with white South Africans for jobs and might not easily assimilate into South African society. Though the government did not offer subsidies to immigrants, opponents frequently termed even the limited measures undertaken by the Smuts government as 'state-aided' immigration, which they argued was a sure way to get the 'wrong sort' of immigrants, rather than those who could pay their way.[30]

Seeking a political compromise between these viewpoints led the Smuts and later the Malan governments to pursue child migration schemes, as children would serve to build up the white population of South Africa without competing with veterans.[31] They were also thought to be more easily assimilated into white South African society than adults. In November 1945, the South African government announced a scheme for the immigration of white war orphans from Europe.[32] Though the scheme was not implemented, its planning reveals official thinking on immigration at this juncture and shows how it sought to assimilate and balance the ethnic groups that constituted the white population of South Africa. As the original intention was to find orphans from northern European countries and to limit the number of Jewish and Catholic children, the scheme reveals religious and national dimensions at play within the notion of whiteness.

The plans showed a clear preference for children from northern Europe, claiming that they aimed to engineer a balance in the countries of origin of the children to reflect the various constituencies within white South Africa.[33] The initial idea was that children would be drawn from Britain,

France, Belgium, the Netherlands and Scandinavia reflecting in broad strokes the planners' perceptions of the origins of the settler population of South Africa. Further, the committee recommended that the number of Jewish children in the scheme should be limited to 'maintain the existing proportion of persons of Jewish race' in South Africa and that pre-existing ratios of Protestants and Catholics should likewise be maintained. Though it seemed necessary to house the children in an institution when they first arrived, the committee believed that adoption by families would assist with assimilation. Though the aim was for children to be adopted into private homes, the committee planned for some children to remain in government-run institutions for up to three years at a cost of £100 per child per year and a total cost of £150,000 the first year including the cost of transportation and converting a former military camp. Anticipating a shortage of nurses and nursery nurses, the committee also recommended that they should be recruited in Europe and given the opportunity to become Union nationals after three years.[34]

Set up to administer the scheme in early 1946, an interdepartmental committee began investigating several military camps in search of one with facilities for 1,000 children and 139 staff. The children would be between two and seven, up to the age of ten if coming with a younger sibling. They would be orphans or free to be adopted and 'healthy', excluding children with mental or physical disabilities. The committee specified that Union nationals, 'preferably high-ranking Union officials' should be charged with the selection of children and 'great care' should be taken in the process. These conditions on the scheme, the young age and the lack of family connections, reflected the intention that these children would be easily assimilated into their new families and into South African culture. The health and nationality criteria reflect the eugenic thinking behind the scheme.[35]

In 1946, the South African government wrote to the United Kingdom, France, Belgium, the Netherlands, Norway, Denmark and Greece offering a home for war orphans. Greece was later added to the initial plans because it was thought to have many such orphans. All of these states, except the United Kingdom and Greece rejected this offer.[36] Greece expressed interest, particularly in the adoption of Jewish orphans but stated that until a law preventing the adoption of children by overseas parties was revoked the scheme would be impossible.[37] The United Kingdom declined to participate but did refer the committee to correspond with private institutions such as orphanages with whom they might be able to cooperate.[38]

Though they had not secured any orphans, the committee began making preparations to convert a former military camp in Durban to house 1,000 children.[39] The Department of Social Welfare also began the process of evaluating prospective adoptive parents, with local representatives of the department and private social welfare organisations submitting reports on their finances, character, employment, religion and housing situation.[40] There was broad public interest in the scheme, which was covered extensively in the South African press, with articles appearing in *Die Burger*, *The Cape Times*, the *Cape Argus*, the *Pretoria News*, *The Star*, *The Natal Mercury* and *Die Volkstem*, and also the British paper, the *Daily Mail*. The Sons of England offered to care for orphans in a 'cottage home' on their property until they could be adopted.[41] The scheme also attracted the support of the 1820 Memorial Settlers' Association, which had long advocated for the adoption of war orphans. Numerous private individuals wrote in offering to adopt child migrants, many of them specifying the nationality, age and sex they would prefer. Some families attempted to use the proposed child migration scheme to engineer the migration of family members from Europe, by offering to adopt relatives, who were often children but sometimes in their late teens.[42] In the end the official government scheme was never implemented, although the government did grant permission for a scheme for 400 Jewish orphans, run by South African Jewish charities, which had brought over 250 children by 1947 and later supported a private child migration scheme, Dietse Kinderfonds or the 'Teutonic Children's League'.[43]

Debates over government policy towards Dietse Kinderfonds shows continuity between the Smuts and Malan administrations. As originally conceived after the war, Dietse Kinderfonds planned to support the immigration of 10,000 orphans from Belgium, Holland, Germany, Austria and the Scandinavian countries.[44] The Dutch Reformed Church supported Dietse Kinderfonds, as did many prominent Afrikaner nationalists, including D.F. Malan, the future prime minister and architect of apartheid.[45] Belgium, Holland and the Scandinavian countries were disinclined to allow orphans to emigrate, however, and Dietse Kinderfonds soon began to focus on Germany. German orphans had not been included originally due to concerns that the children might face 'hostility' in the immediate aftermath of the war. Officials expressed a preference that if German children (at this stage classified as enemy aliens and therefore not able to gain entry as migrants) were permitted to come it should be under the government scheme, which had not yet been abandoned.[46]

However, soon reversing course, in 1947, the Smuts administration stated a willingness to finance the passages, though not the maintenance, of German orphans arriving under the auspices of Dietse Kinderfonds. A memorandum from the Secretary for Social Welfare in January 1947 positioned this shift as necessary to maintain balance within the population, again showing the prejudice towards northern Europe within the broader rubric of 'European':

In view of the fact that very few, if any, children will be coming from Great Britain or Allied countries in North Eastern Europe, the pertinent question now arises whether it will not be wise to offset the predominance of Greek, Polish, and Jewish children by increasing the number of children of Teutonic stock. This can only be done by including German and Austria [sic] children.

The memorandum goes on to highlight the plight of many German civilians and argues for the decision not to include Germany the previous year to be reviewed given that the United Kingdom, France, the United States and other Allied countries were now aiding German civilians including taking in orphans. In August 1947, the Smuts administration set aside £5,500 to pay for the transport of 100 orphans and seven escorts from Germany, though it mandated that Dietse Kinderfonds would be responsible for the maintenance of the children once they arrived.[47] Though the first Dietse Kinderfonds migrants arrived after the change of government in 1948, planning and support for the immigration of German children began before the Malan government came into office, signalling continuity in policy across administrations.

Though Malan and the National Party accused Smuts of favouring British immigration, the Malan government largely continued Smuts' policies. Indeed, both contemporary perceptions of Smuts immigration policy as pro-British and those of historians have been coloured by politically motivated attacks on Smuts and the United Party. Even Fred Brownell, who largely recognises this point, still cast the Smuts plan as 'subsidised immigration' and Malan's policy as 'unassisted immigration' in his overview and chapter headings.[48] Peberdy's study is even more emphatic, arguing that the Malan government's 'new exclusionary procedures and practices targeted British immigrants', while encouraging other European immigration.[49] Yet this assessment is largely based on an analysis of the contrasting political rhetoric of the Smuts and Malan administration rather than the legal and administrative workings of their immigration policies. Both contemporary critics and historians of the Smuts scheme often overlooked its selective criteria, including financial and employment qualifications for potential immigrants including those from Britain, and have not acknowledged attempts by Smuts government to recruit immigrants from continental Europe, largely because they were unsuccessful. The term 'subsidised' overstates the support for immigration from 1945 to 1948, implying subsidised passages rather than the modest organisational apparatus that the Smuts government put in place.

The changes implemented by the Malan government were more in form than in substance. The new Minister of the Interior, Eben Donges, announced the termination of the agreement with the Union-Castle shipping line soon after taking office. But movement to towards the ending of the agreement had already begun under the Smuts government. A cable from Pretoria to South African representatives in London in April 1948, before the May election, stated the government's intention to terminate the agreement.[50] Prior to this, arrangements had already been made to 'tighten up' the granting of priority passages and for the phasing out of the *Winchester Castle*, the *Carnarvon Castle* and the *Arundel Castle* on September 1948, December 1948 and March 1949 respectively.[51] The original agreement was largely a response to the post-war shipping shortage and was always intended as a temporary expedient.

The Malan government disbanded the Immigration Council and voluntary committees, however this was largely an administrative reshuffling in which responsibility for immigration moved from the Department of External Affairs to the Department of the Interior. The Immigration Council was replaced by the Inter-departmental Advisory Council Concerning Immigration Matters. Enquiries from prospective immigrants and South African employers were now to be handled by the Department of Labour. The press statement outlining the reorganisation noted that the 'Department of Labour and other Departments concerned will give all possible assistance in arrangement of transport, accommodation and the provision of employment' but would not accept financial responsibility, continuing the Smuts approach of facilitating but not subsidising immigration.[52]

Furthermore, the Malan government did not make any substantive changes to immigration law. From the time that the National Party took office in 1948 up until the declaration of republic in 1961, it remained easier for British subjects, classified by the South African state as 'European', to migrate to South Africa than any other group as they entered under the 1913 Immigrants' Regulation Act, which provided that 'natural-born' (i.e. white) British subjects could enter, provided they met health and financial criteria.[53] All others were subject to the 1937 Aliens Control Act, and more stringent requirements that they prove their physical and mental health, character, stable financial state, skills or potential for employment in a trade, and a clean criminal record.[54]

To account for this legal inaction, Peberdy argues that though British nationals had no legal obligation to undergo screening by the Immigrants Selection Committee in London before embarking, the Malan government enforced existing immigration regulations more strictly and set up de facto measures to restrict the immigration of British nationals.[55] This initiative predated the Malan government, however. Minutes from 16 March 1948, more than two months before the May election, demonstrate that the Immigration Council under Smuts favoured a policy requiring British passengers on the Union-Castle and other shipping companies to gain approval by the London committee. According to the March minutes, shipping companies were not to 'recognize those who have applied for cabin- or tourist-class accommodation as potential passengers in so far as a priority passage is concerned until the form has been duly approved by the London committee of the Immigration Council'.[56] Though this policy had not yet come into effect by the election, it suggests, that even if the United Party had remained in power it would have taken a similar approach.

European migrants, including those from Britain, continued to arrive in South Africa after 1948 in historically high numbers. Though it would not be until the 1960s that rates of immigration matched and then exceeded the immediate post-war rates, throughout the 1950s they remained substantially higher (at least double and sometimes triple) the rate during the inter-war period.[57] After dropping by more than half in 1949 to 14,780, from the high of 35,681 in 1948, rates of European migration continued to drop in 1950 to 12,803, but then began to increase again in 1951, reaching 15,243 and then 18,473 in 1952. From 1953 to 1955, rates held steady at around 16,000, dropping slightly to between 14,500 and 15,000 from 1956 to 1958. Due, probably, to uncertainty over the declaration of republic, 1959 and 1960 saw a decrease, followed by a dramatic increase from 1963.[58]

The decrease in European immigration generally and the smaller percentage of British immigrants to South Africa after 1948 cannot be attributed solely to a change in policy by the Malan government. A drop-off in immigration after 1948 would have been likely had the Smuts government remained in power as the build-up of would-be immigrants who had been unable to get passages during or immediately after the war was reduced. Though the National Party restructured the immigration administrative apparatus set up by the Smuts government, it did not implement a fundamental change in policy and throughout the 1950s it was easier for white immigrants from the United Kingdom and the wider Commonwealth to enter South Africa than any other group, including immigrants from continental Europe.

The Malan government's approach was founded on the same dilemma as that of the Smuts government and the Rhodesian government, discussed below, how to increase the minority population while maintaining its character and privilege. This is reflected in *Immigration on a Selective Basis*, a 1948 leaflet expressing the new government's immigration policy, which recognised the need to increase the number of Europeans in order that 'this great experiment of creating and independent state under white supremacy' should succeed. Highlighting the ongoing dilemma for minority settler colonial states of how to increase their white populations, the same document also argued for the importance both of maintaining the 'existing composition of the European population and its way of life'.[59] The immigration policies of both Smuts and Malan were influenced by the specific political and economic circumstances that they faced. Above all they were driven by the existential dilemma of the minority settler colonial state: how to increase the settler population while maintaining its privileged position. Despite a different demographic balance and history, this dilemma also shaped immigration policy in South Africa's neighbour, Southern Rhodesia.

'Immigration Indigestion': Immigration restriction and quotas in Southern Rhodesia

Southern Rhodesia also experienced a large influx of immigrants in the years after the war. Despite a political climate more supportive of British immigration, however, the Southern Rhodesian government soon implemented a more restrictive immigration policy than that of South Africa. Officials worried that too many immigrants arriving too quickly might, without adequate provision, disturb the racial labour hierarchy. Despite the rhetorical and ideological differences between the South African and Rhodesian governments, both states implemented policies that aimed to maintain the status of their minority settler colonial population. These policies reflect the existential tension inherent to the minority settler colonial state between increasing the white population to safeguard minority rule and the imperative to retain the racial privilege and associated lifestyle of the ruling minority population.

In May 1946, the population classified as 'European' by the Southern Rhodesian government stood at 82,386 including 7,000 wartime internees who were repatriated the following year.[60] As shipping became available, large numbers of immigrants entered the colony: 8,924 in 1946, 12,958 in 1947, and 14,593 in 1948.[61] As discussed in Chapter 2, many in favour of increasing European immigration sought to take advantage of the circumstances of the war to achieve their aims. Yet, despite a general agreement among Rhodesian parliamentarians and other policymakers on the desirability of increasing the European population through immigration, especially from Britain, there was also tension between this goal and concern that the interests of those settlers already resident in Rhodesia should be protected first.[62] This was similar to the situation described above in South Africa, though without the added complication of Afrikaner nationalism.

Because there was no influential competing settler colonial nationalism in Southern Rhodesia, official policy and rhetoric was more supportive of encouraging British immigration and included plans to subsidise immigrant passages. By 1946, the Rhodesian and British governments planned to provide free passages for British ex-service men and women 'approved by the Colonial authorities as suitable for life in the Colony'. A formal agreement between the two governments was signed in October 1946 and was to be implemented when the shipping position and housing situation in Southern Rhodesia had improved. The British government would pay for the sea passage and the Southern Rhodesian government would pay for rail transportation from the port of arrival to the immigrant's destination as well as accommodation. The same scheme would also pay the passages of the families of British service men who had elected to take demobilisation in Southern Rhodesia.[63]

This scheme proved unnecessary, however, as large numbers of immigrants came on their own initiative and at their own expense and it was cancelled before it began. As the above-cited migration numbers imply, there was a large interest in the United Kingdom in moving to Southern Rhodesia, even without government incentives. Returning from a trip to England, the Minister of Internal Affairs, Sir E. Lucas Guest reported in January 1946 that Rhodesia House had a waiting list of 800 approved for passages and a further 1,350 people had applied, with more applications coming in daily.[64] At this point, when shipping difficulties meant that few immigrants had arrived in Southern Rhodesia, most MPs were very supportive of government immigration schemes. One suggested that the government could charter a boat to bring immigrants to Southern Rhodesia and another advocated the recruitment of the skilled workers needed to continue the expansion of the iron and steel industries in Southern Rhodesia.[65]

However, after immigrants began to arrive in large numbers, some politicians became concerned and complained that they could not accommodate the influx. In February 1947, Albert Stumbles, the MP for Avondale, introduced a motion in the Legislative Assembly to curtail immigration because of drought, a shortage of maize and other foodstuffs, and the housing shortage. The motion was ultimately overruled but the debate highlights several brewing tensions. All who spoke in response to the motion argued that they were in support of immigration. Even Stumbles aimed to reduce rather than to end immigration. Those opposed to any restriction on European immigration dismissed concerns about the drought and food shortage and argued that the housing shortage could easily be overcome, suggesting the building of basic 'pole and dagga' houses or that those with large enough houses might be induced to take in lodgers. Their major concern was to take advantage of the opportunity for recruiting European immigrants in the immediate post-war period. As before, many argued that Southern Rhodesia's economy would benefit from an influx of immigrants, particularly skilled artisans who could contribute to development in the building trade and other industries.[66]

Those who were in favour of more restriction framed this in terms of concern that unsatisfied immigrants might return to Britain and spread negative publicity about Southern Rhodesia which might deter others from coming. Stumbles, for example, cited that thirty or forty people, 'some six families' had arrived and then left because they were unable to find accommodation. According to government figures, though there was little emigration from 1946 to 1949, 24,500 Europeans left Southern Rhodesia between 1950 and 1953, the equivalent of 46 per cent of those who had arrived in the same period.[67] While clearly not all those leaving were recent immigrants, many were. As indicated above, housing was a pressing concern and Rhodesia House routinely issued warnings to prospective immigrants that there was a 'temporary' housing shortage. Supporters of restriction also consistently argued that Southern Rhodesia would have no trouble recruiting immigrants later when conditions had improved.[68]

This debate reflected an underlying concern about the preservation of racial prestige and the ever-looming spectre of the 'poor white'.[69] The arrival of European migrants who were unable to take up the lifestyle thought to be appropriate to whites threatened the Rhodesian racial hierarchy, which underpinned the basis of minority settler colonial rule. Though reports such as those in the *Bulawayo Chronicle* that newly arrived European immigrants were sleeping in the park were dismissed as scaremongering by some, to others they posed a threat to white prestige so strong that preventing such problems was more important than increasing the white population in Southern Rhodesia.[70]

In many ways, this discussion paralleled the debate in South Africa over the assimilation of new arrivals into the white community and their contribution to economic development. One notable difference is that in Southern Rhodesia some pro-immigration MPs made the argument that British migration to Southern Rhodesia would benefit the broader Commonwealth and the United Kingdom. Guest, the Minister of Internal Affairs, arguing against curtailing immigration proclaimed, 'We are all part of the same Commonwealth' and asserted that because 90 per cent of immigrants to Southern Rhodesia came from the British Empire, largely from the United Kingdom and South Africa, immigration was helpful in alleviating food shortages elsewhere in the Commonwealth.[71]

This kind of rhetoric found no counterpart in South African debates. Though, particularly in debates about taking in war orphans, some in the South African House of Assembly might make an appeal to taking in immigrants to help rebuild war-torn Europe, a specific appeal to aiding the Empire or Commonwealth was politically untenable. As Saul Dubow has argued, 'after 1905 Anglo-Saxon race patriotism or "British race sentiment" was no longer politically viable: the necessity of reconciling Boer and Brits could proceed only within the ethnically inclusive parameters of white South Africanism'.[72] While there is concern in the Rhodesian debates about protecting the interests of white Rhodesians, for example, ensuring that any new housing built was not automatically offered to immigrants, the general assumption was that British migrants would be easily assimilated into Southern Rhodesia.

Yet despite this rhetoric, the policy pursued was pragmatic and focused on the preservation of settler colonial rule. Though increasing the European population of Southern Rhodesia had long been government policy, the unprecedented post-war increase had strained social services and intensified the housing shortage. In response, the Rhodesian parliament began restricting the immigration of non-British subjects with the Aliens Act of 1946. Such restrictions were expanded to British subjects by 1948 with the Immigrants Regulation and Immigrant Regulation Amendment Acts.[73] Under the terms of the former, prospective immigrants were required to have either the promise of at least six months employment, capital in the amount of £1,500 or £500 in annual income, exclusive of what they might earn once they arrived in Southern Rhodesia. They were required to lodge a deposit of £100 on arrival if coming from Northern Rhodesia, South Africa or Nyasaland or £200 from all other countries. This would be used for 'repatriation' to their country of origin if they or their dependants become a charge on the state in the first three years of their residence in Southern Rhodesia. The only people exempted from these rules were 'skilled artisans of European descent' who worked in the building industry and the elderly parents or relatives of current Rhodesian residents. The 1948 Immigration Regulation Amendment Act provided the Governor with the ability to restrict immigration in the case of a housing or food shortage or 'a shortage of any article, commodity or thing, which in his opinion, is essential to the life of the community'.[74] The naming of housing and food (or the vague 'any other essential commodity') reflects the concern of Rhodesian lawmakers that Europeans might not be able to enjoy the 'appropriate' standard of living.

After the implementation of these laws, immigration numbers fell to 12,422 in 1949 but by 1950, even despite restrictions, 14,516 immigrants classed as European entered Southern Rhodesia and 15,733 entered in 1951.[75] The overall increase of the European population was 11 per cent annually in the period 1946–52. Immigration was responsible for most of the increase, 7.5 per cent, with approximately 1.5 per cent of growth due to natural increase, and another 1.5 per cent to members of the RAF, which continued to a operate a training scheme until 1954.[76]

Most new immigrants, just over 80 per cent, moved to urban areas, drawn by rapid growth in trade and industry, amplifying the strain on housing, transport, and social services causing what one official termed

'Southern Rhodesia's immigration indigestion'.[77] In May of 1952, the Southern Rhodesian government implemented a quota system, which limited immigration to 10,800 annually or 7 per cent of the European population. Within this overall quota were further restrictions by country of origin: 4,560 immigrants classified as European were allowed in from the United Kingdom, the same number from the Union of South Africa, 600 were permitted from other British territories in Africa, 360 from other parts of the British Empire and 720 from 'alien' territories beyond the British Empire and Commonwealth. These limits were increased in 1953 to 6,000 each for the United Kingdom and South Africa, 800 for the rest of British Africa, and 800 for non-British countries.

As well as to slow rates of immigration overall, this policy was also designed to limit the numbers of migrants from South Africa and increase the proportion from the United Kingdom. From 1949 to 1951 there was a steady increase in migration from South Africa and in 1950 the number of migrants from South Africa (10,422) had far exceeded migrants from the United Kingdom (2,752).[78] Reflecting on the impact of these quotas in 1954, a Rhodesian official concluded that they had been effective, as the numbers coming from South Africa and the United Kingdom were almost equal as well as improving, in his view, the 'standard' of immigrants and at least partially easing the housing and services shortage.[79] Even after the implementation of quotas, those for South Africa were consistently filled, while those from Britain were undersubscribed from March 1953.[80] Rhodesian policymakers were concerned that the arrival of too many white South African migrants, especially Afrikaners, might 'dilute' the British character of Rhodesia.[81] In addition, migrants from South Africa, due to the relative ease of return, might prove more transient.

As this suggests, Southern Rhodesia differed from South Africa in its clear preference for British immigrants, however, its immigration policy as a whole was more restrictive.[82] Like the South African government, the Rhodesian government also pursued child migration in the years after the war, although on a much smaller scale than they had initially envisioned. The Fairbridge Memorial College, planned in the 1930s and delayed by the war, opened in 1946.[83] Located on a disused air base outside of Bulawayo, this school for British children admitted 276 boarders and operated till 1961. Though it later took Rhodesian-born children, it was intended to be exclusively for child migrants from Britain, in contrast to the planned South African scheme which aimed for a balance of British and other European children. This reflects the differing national priorities of the Southern Rhodesian government, though planners had similar concerns about assimilation and racial fitness. Seeking to recruit children who would grow up to be members of the ruling settler elite, prospective students were interviewed and had to take an IQ test. It was increasingly difficult to attract large numbers of children to the scheme, however, and it closed in 1962, demonstrating, along with other failed migration schemes, the often-limited impact of government recruitment initiatives.[84]

Conclusion

While certainly an important factor in restricting entry, immigration policy had a limited impact on attracting immigrants. The immigration policy of a potential destination country was only one of many personal, economic, political and cultural factors that shaped the thousands of individual decisions that made up broader immigration patterns. Such personal decisions are often difficult to access for the historian, when compared to the wealth of official sources, making it easy to place too great an emphasis on the importance of state policy. Official sources, often framed by partisan rhetoric, seem at first glance to fit to the familiar narrative of a pro-imperial Smut administration, a Nationalist government hostile to British immigration and a pro-British Southern Rhodesian government. However, a closer examination of the substance of these policies and attention to how they were implemented highlights the similarities between South Rhodesian and South African immigration policies and those implemented across the Smuts and Malan administrations.

In both South Africa and Southern Rhodesia, immigration policy was driven by the competing imperatives inherent to the maintenance of a minority settler colonial regime. Despite differences in stated ideals both were driven by underlying concerns about what type of white migrants should became part of their polities, how these migrants should live, and the role of the state in guaranteeing that lifestyle. Policymakers could limit admission and try, through quotas and other means, to engineer immigration, but ultimately, as their persistent concerns about the amount and quality of immigrants reveal, their role was primarily reactive.

Immigration policy was essentially consistent under the United Party and the National Party in South Africa and in Southern Rhodesia in the years following the war, regardless of partisan rhetoric or national differences. It formed in response to changing political and economic circumstances and was primarily shaped by the tension implicit in minority settler colonial regimes between increasing the population of the ruling minority and maintaining its privilege and character. Despite the differences in the political cultures of South Africa and Southern Rhodesia, it was this tension that fundamentally shaped post-war immigration policy in both cases. Ideologically, the Southern Rhodesian government in this period adhered to the idea of British imperial or Commonwealth unity and was more sympathetic to the promotion of European and especially British migration than the Malan government. However, the practicalities of maintaining settler colonial rule meant that Southern Rhodesia quickly adopted a more restrictive immigration policy.

Notes

1 The Senate of South Africa, *Debates (Official Report) 1946–47* (Cape Town: Nasionale Pers Beperk, 1947), Cols 4154–6.
2 As well as newspaper coverage, this included film reels and television coverage. See, for example, 'Royal Tour of South Africa, 1947', BBC Television Service, First Broadcast 2 June 1947, www.bbc.co.uk/archive/princesselizabeth/6604.shtml (accessed 1 August 2013); 'South Africa's Royal Visit Reel 1', Pathé Pictures, 1947, www.britishpathe.com/video/south-africas-royal-visit-reel-1-1 (accessed 1 August 2013); 'South Africa's Royal Visit Reel 2', Pathé Pictures, 1947, www.britishpathe.com/video/south-africas-royal-visit-reel-2-1/query/South+Africas+Royal+Visit+Reel+2 (accessed 1 August 2013).
3 These figures are approximate as British emigration records measure those who left the United Kingdom, but immigration records in Southern Rhodesia classified migrants by place of birth rather than previous residence. From 1946 to 1949, 466,362 emigrants left the United Kingdom; 64,094 immigrants to South Africa listed their previous country of residence as the United Kingdom; 24,129 immigrants to Southern Rhodesia listed their place of birth as the United Kingdom. Another complicating factor is the movement of British-born migrants between South Africa and Southern Rhodesia. British emigration and Southern Rhodesian immigration figures from Commonwealth Relations Office, *Oversea Migration Statistics 1955* (London, HMSO, 1956), pp. 5, 13, 14. South African immigration figures for 1946 to 1948, Union of South Africa, *Statistics of Migration 1948* (Pretoria: The Government Printer, 1950), p. 43. Figure for 1949 calculated based on specific data for the years 1945 to 1948 as above and a figure for the period 1945–49 in Republic of South Africa Bureau of Statistics, *Report No. 286: Statistics of Immigrants and Emigrants 1924–1964* (Pretoria: The Government Printer, 1964), 3.
4 British migration to southern Africa in this period formed part of a larger migration from the United Kingdom to the so-called 'white' Dominions. Though focused on Australia, Alastair Thomson and A. James Hammerton's nuanced discussion of the motives of post-war British emigrants, especially their analysis of 'push factors' such as the housing shortage, holds true for those who moved to South Africa and Southern Rhodesia. Hammerton and Thomson, *Ten Pound Poms*, pp. 48–96.
5 For more on the tour and particularly the African response to the royal family see Hilary Sapire, 'African Loyalism and its Discontents: The Royal Tour of South Africa, 1947', *The Historical Journal* 54:1 (2011), 215–40.

6 This of course, was not an inevitable path and surprised many at the time. See Saul Dubow, 'Introduction: South Africa's 1940s', in *South Africa's 1940s: Worlds of Possibilities*, eds Saul Dubow and Alan Jeeves (Cape Town: Double Storey, 2005), p. 2.
7 Peberdy, *Selecting Immigrants*; Brownell, *British Immigration to South Africa*; Gwendolen M. Carter, *The Politics of Inequality: South Africa since 1948* (London: Thames and Hudson, 1958), p. 58.
8 William Beinart and Saul Dubow provide an excellent summary of the historiography of apartheid and segregation, arguing that while there are clear continuities, 'apartheid purported to be a rigorous and totalizing ideology in a way that segregation never had been'. William Beinart and Saul Dubow, 'Introduction: The Historiography of Segregation and Apartheid', in *Segregation and Apartheid in Twentieth Century South Africa*, eds William Beinart and Saul Dubow (London: Routledge, 2002), p. 12. Scholars have shown the precursors of apartheid in the practice of segregation in the British imperial context in the late nineteenth and early twentieth century, in the Cape and Natal colonies. Vivian Bickford-Smith, *Ethnic Pride and Racial Prejudice in Victorian Cape Town: Group Identity and Social Practice, 1875–1902* (Cambridge: Cambridge University Press, 1995); Maynard W. Swanson, 'The Sanitation Syndrome: Bubonic Plague and Urban Native Policy in the Cape Colony, 1900–09', in *Segregation and Apartheid in Twentieth Century South Africa*, eds William Beinart and Saul Dubow (London: Routledge); Martin Legassick, 'British Hegemony and the Origins of Segregation in South Africa, 1901–14', in *Segregation and Apartheid in Twentieth Century South Africa*, eds William Beinart and Saul Dubow (London: Routledge, 2002); Shula Marks, 'Natal, the Zulu Royal Family and the Ideology of Segregation', in *Segregation and Apartheid in Twentieth Century South Africa*, eds William Beinart and Saul Dubow (London: Routledge, 2002). Saul Dubow's earlier work outlined the elaboration and entrenchment of segregationist ideology in the interwar period. Saul Dubow, *Racial Segregation and the Origins of Apartheid in South Africa, 1919–36* (Basingstoke: Macmillan, 1989). Another example of continuity is that the clearance of District Six in Cape Town was proposed in the early 1940s under the United Party, though only carried out in the 1960s. Bickford-Smith, Van Heyningen and Worden, *Cape Town in the Twentieth Century: An Illustrated Social History*, pp. 152–4.
9 Minority settler colonies had long faced this dilemma. See, for example, Dane Kennedy's comparative study of the development of settler culture in Kenya and Southern Rhodesia. Dane Kennedy, *Islands of White: Settler Society and Culture in Kenya and Southern Rhodesia, 1890–1939* (Durham: Duke University Press, 1987), pp. 4–6, 187–9.
10 On the implicit racial connation of the phrase 'natural-born British subject' see Bashford, 'Immigration restriction', p. 45.
11 Kennedy, *Islands of White*, p. 168; Smith, 'From Promising Settler'; Bashford, 'Immigration restriction'.
12 Bishi, 'Immigration and Settlement', pp. 59–77.

13 The population stood at 68,954 in 1941, increasing to 136,017 by 1951. Mlambo, *White Immigration*, p. 4.
14 See Table 3.1.
15 Union of South Africa, *Statistics of Migration 1948*, pp. 43, 45, 52. Republic of South Africa, *Report No. 286: Statistics of Immigrants and Emigrants 1924–1964*, 3–4, 8–9, 13. The percentages are my own calculations.
16 NASA, A326, Box 3, Item 7, Immigration Council to the Secretary for the Interior, 7 May 1947, 'Handling of Immigrants on Ships and on Landing'.
17 NASA, TES 6373, Ref. 48/45/3, 'Report for the year ending 31 March 1948', 21 April 1948.
18 NASA, TES 6373, Ref. 48/45/3, Secretary for the Interior to Secretary to the Treasury, 7 August 1947.
19 NASA, MBN 1, Ref. MIN 2/1, Chairman of the Immigration Council, Memorandum, 9 June 1948. They also hoped to send immigration attachés to Paris, Stockholm and Brussels, though it seems this was never implemented. NASA, A326, Box 3, Item 7, Memorandum 'Immigration' sent to the South Africa Legation in Paris, 14 February 1947.
20 NASA, MBN 1, Ref. MIN 2/1, Chairman of the Immigration Council, Memorandum, 9 June 1948, pp. 3, 5–6.
21 NASA, MBN 1, Ref. MIN 2/1, Vernon Thompson to Senator C.F. Clarkson, 4 February 1948. See also Caird Library, National Maritime Museum, London (hereafter Caird Library), UCM/1/7, Union-Castle Mail Steamship Company, Directors Meetings Minute Book, No. 7, April 1942–September 1947, Minute Nos 7764, 7873, 8316, 8334, 8368; UCM/1/8 Minute Book No. 8, October 1947–October 1951, Minutes 8466, 8485, 8521, 8537, 8565, 8613, 8629, 8651, 8692.
22 Dubow, 'How British', p. 14.
23 For more on this organization and its changing relationship with the state see Chapter 4 and Chapter 5.
24 Peberdy, *Selecting Immigrants*, p. 90.
25 NASA, A326, Box 3, Item 7, Memorandum on 'Immigration' by the Commissioner of Immigration and Asiatic Affairs, enclosed in a letter from the Secretary for External Affairs to the High Commissioner of the Union of South Africa in London and to all Overseas Representatives of the Department of External Affairs, 27 October 1947.
26 Emphasis in original. NASA, A326, Box 3, Item 7, Secretary for External Affairs to the High Commissioner of the Union of South Africa in London and to all Overseas Representatives of the Department of External Affairs, 27 October 1947.
27 NASA, MBN 1, Ref. MIN 2/1, Memorandum, Chairman of the Immigration Council, 9 June, 1948, p. 7; Minutes of meeting between officials of the Union-Castle and the Immigration Council, 16 March 1948.
28 NASA, MBN 1, Ref. MIN 2/1 Memorandum, Chairman of the Immigration Council, 9 June 1948, p. 5. See also B.P. Hofstede, *Thwarted Exodus: Postwar Overseas Emigration from the Netherlands* (The Hague: M. Nijhoff, 1964), p. 41.

29 Ibid., pp. 5, 25, 73, 96–7.
30 Union of South Africa, *Debates of the House of Assembly* (Cape Town: Unie Volkspers, 1944), Cols 2157–203, 4734–45, 4811–13; Union of South Africa, *Debates of the House of Assembly* (Cape Town: Unie Volkspers,1945), Cols 5983–9, 6032–6, 6070; The Senate of South Africa, *Debates (Official Report)* (Cape Town: Nasionale Pers Beperk, 1944), Cols 332–5, Cols 518–19, 694–5; The Senate of South Africa, *Debates (Official Report)* (Cape Town: Nasionale Pers Beperk, 1945), Cols 143–52, 166–8; The Senate of South Africa, *Debates (Official Report)* (Cape Town: Nasionale Pers Beperk, 1946–47), Cols 1364–8, 1377, 1385–438; The Senate of South Africa, *Debates (Official Report)* (Cape Town: Nasionale Pers Beperk, 1947), Cols 2001–12, 2022–38, 2167–70, 2183, 2219–42.
31 For more on child migration schemes proposed during the war see Chapter 2.
32 This interest in the adoption of war orphans supports Tara Zahra's argument about the 'special grip on the post-war imagination' held by children. Tara Zahra, 'Lost Children: Displacement, Family, and Nation in Postwar Europe', *The Journal of Modern History* 81:1 (March 2009), 45.
33 A similar idea was reflected in contemporary policy in New Zealand and Canada, which gave migrants from the 'origin' countries of these settler nations priority. Smith, 'Persistence and Privilege', pp. 381, 386.
34 NASA, VWN Vol. 1117, Ref. SW483/1, Vol. 1, 'Child Immigration Scheme', 12 November 1945; Minutes, 7 November 1945.
35 NASA, VWN Vol. 1117, Ref. SW483/1, Vol. 1, 'Child Immigration Scheme', 12 November 1945; 'Child Immigration Scheme', 20 November 1945.
36 NASA, VWN Vol. 1117, Ref. SW483/1, Vol. II, Child Immigration Scheme, 1946; BTS Ref. 59/6C, Vol. 1, Child Immigration Scheme, 1946–51; BTS Ref. 59/6C, Vol. 1, Child Immigration Scheme, 1946–51.
37 NASA, VWN Vol. 1117, Ref. SW483/1, Vol. II, G.M. Bowler to the Secretary of External Affairs, 23 September 1946. There was opposition to this plan in Greece, 'Aid for Children of Greece S.A's offer to take Oprhans Meet Opposition', *Pretoria News*, 2 October 1946.
38 NASA, VWN Vol. 1117, Ref. SW483/1, Vol. II, W.Q. Head to Office of the High Commissioner for South Africa, 2 November 1946.
39 NASA, VWN Vol. 1117, Ref. SW483/1, Vol. II, C.G.B. Bain, 'Note for Record Purposes', 17 August 1946.
40 NASA, VWN Vol. 1117 Ref. SW483/1–2, Union Immigration Scheme, Child Immigration Scheme, Applications for Adoption of Children 1945–48.
41 NASA, VWN Vol. 1117, Ref. SW483/1, Vol. II, 'British War Orphans', 13 July 1946. The Sons of England were a benevolent organization founded in the late-nineteenth century to assist needy English Protestants and promote loyalty to the monarchy. There were branches throughout the empire.
42 NASA, VWN Vol. 1117 Ref. SW483/1–2, Union Immigration Scheme, Child Immigration Scheme, Applications for Adoption of Children 1945–48.
43 Jewish organisations in Europe were given a great deal of autonomy over placement of orphans, which may be why this scheme was successful when other

attempts to bring orphans to South Africa were not. Zahra, 'Lost Children: Displacement, Family, and Nation in Postwar Europe', pp. 74–5.
44 NASA, VWN Vol. 1118, Ref. SW483/1–4, Dietse Kinderfonds application war fund status, 7 September 1946.
45 NASA, VWN Vol. 1118, Ref. SW483/1–4, G.A.C. Kuschke, 'Die Dietse Kinderfonds: Child Immigration Scheme', 15 April 1946.
46 NASA, VWN Vol. 1118, Ref. SW483/1–4, H.G. Lawrence to C.F. Clarkson, 25 April 1946.
47 NASA, VWN Vol. 1118, Ref. SW483/1–4, Secretary of the Treasury to the Secretary for Social Welfare, 22 August 1947; G.A.C. Kuschke, 'Die Dietse Kinderfonds: Child Immigration Scheme', 15 April 1946.
48 Brownell, *British Immigration to South Africa*.
49 Peberdy, *Selecting Immigrants*, p. 99.
50 NASA, MBN 1, Ref. MIN 2/1, Cable, Interior to London, 17 April 1948.
51 NASA, MBN 1, Ref. MIN 2/1, Minutes of meeting between officials of the Union-Castle and the Immigration Council, 16 March 1948.
52 NASA, MBN 1, Ref. MIN 2/1, Draft Press Statement: Procedure in Connection with Immigration, undated.
53 For more on the Immigrants Regulation Act of 1913 see Cd 7111, Union of South Africa, *Correspondence relating to the Immigrants Regulation Act and other matters affecting Asiatics in South Africa* (London: HMSO, 1913).
54 Union of South Africa, Aliens Control Act (No. 1 of 1937).
55 Peberdy, *Selecting Immigrants*, pp. 100–1.
56 NASA, MBN 1, Ref. MIN 2/1, Minutes of the Immigration Council, 16 March 1948.
57 Here I refer to total European immigration. The annual average rate was 6,468 for 1924–29, 4,175 for 1930–34, 7,801 for 1935–39 as compared to 15,838 for 1950–54 and 14,593 for 1955–59. Rates of immigration from the United Kingdom were also higher in the 1950s than in the 1920s, though they made up a smaller proportion of the total. The average annual rate of immigrants whose country of previous residence was the United Kingdom was 3,272 for 1925–29, 1,694 for 1930–34, 3,285 for 1935–39, 5,597 for 1950–54 and 4,375 for 1955–59. Republic of South Africa, *Report No. 286 Statistics of Immigrants and Emigrants, 1924–1964*, 1, 3. These are the earliest reliable immigration statistics generated by the South African government. Earlier statistics were kept by the Board of Trade in the United Kingdom, but they did not differentiate between those arriving in South African ports who intended to settle and those who stayed for a shorter duration. See, for example, Cmd 2738, Board of Trade, *Statistical Abstract for the Several British Oversea Dominions and Protectorates in each from 1909 to 1923*, Fifty-Seventh Number (London: HMSO, 1923).
58 Figures for 1950 to 1953, Republic of South Africa, *Report No. 19–01–01, Migration Statistics: Immigrants and Emigrants, 1966 to 1969*, p. 4.
59 NASA, A326, Box 3, Item 7, Summary of *Immigration on a Selective Basis*, 17 August 1948.

60 Ian Smith Papers, 1/78/002, Memorandum on Immigration, 23 July 1954.
61 Commonwealth Relations Office, *Oversea Migration Statistics 1955*, 14. In addition a large number of members of the RAF and their dependants arrived as well, as wartime training schemes continued up to 1953: 637 in 1947, 2,444 in 1948. Official Southern Rhodesian statistics usually included members of the RAF and their dependants in their accounting of arriving immigrants, perhaps because many did remain in Southern Rhodesia. See Ian Smith Papers, 1/78/002, Memorandum on Immigration, 23 July 1954.
62 Using the case of Polish refugees sent to Southern Rhodesia during the Second World War, Baxter Tavuyanago, Tasara Muguti and James Hlongwana argue that post-war British immigration policy discriminated against non-British Europeans. Baxter Tavuyanago, Tasara Muguti, and James Hlongwana, 'Victims of the Rhodesian Immigration Policy: Polish Refugees from the Second World War', *Journal of South African Studies* 38:4 (2012), 951–65. Alois Mlambo reaches a similar conclusion. Mlambo, *White Immigration*, pp. 49–67.
63 TNA, DO 35/1135, M.822/268 'Government Free Passage Scheme for Ex-Servicemen Men and Women', 23 October 1946.
64 Southern Rhodesia, *Debates of the Legislative Assembly*, Vol. 25, Part 2 (Salisbury: Parliamentary Printers, 1946), Cols 3063–4.
65 Southern Rhodesia, *Debates of the Legislative Assembly*, Vol. 25, Part 2, Col. 3064.
66 Southern Rhodesia, *Debates of the Legislative Assembly*, Vol. 26, Part 2 (Salisbury: Parliamentary Printers, 1947), Cols 2884, 2900, 2903.
67 Ian Smith Papers, 1/78/002, Memorandum on Immigration, 23 July 1954.
68 Southern Rhodesia, *Debates of the Legislative Assembly*, Vol. 26, Part 2, Cols 2890, 2917.
69 This was a long-running preoccupation in Southern Rhodesia as elsewhere. See Kennedy, *Islands of White*, pp. 153–5, 167–86. On the problem of 'poor whites' in the colonial context more generally see Ann Laura Stoler, *Carnal Knowledge and Imperial Power: Race and the Intimate in Colonial Rule* (Berkeley: University of California Press, 2002), pp. 25–6, 34–8.
70 Southern Rhodesia, *Debates of the Legislative Assembly*, Vol. 26, Part 2, Col. 2886.
71 Southern Rhodesia, *Debates of the Legislative Assembly*, Vol. 26, Part 2, Col. 2915.
72 Dubow, 'How British', p. 14.
73 *The Statute Law of Southern Rhodesia 1946* (Salisbury: The Government Printer, 1947), pp. 109–25.
74 *The Statute Law of Southern Rhodesia 1948* (Salisbury: The Government Printer, 1949), pp. 208–10.
75 Commonwealth Relations Office, *Oversea Migration Statistics 1955*, 14.
76 Ian Smith Papers, 1/78/002, Memorandum on Immigration, 23 July 1954. On the RAF training scheme see Golley, *Aircrew Unlimited*, p. 48.

77 Ian Smith Papers, 1/78/002, Memorandum on Immigration, 23 July 1954. See also NAZ, S482/132/49, HD (49) Imm/2, 'Memorandum: The Impact of Immigration on the Southern Rhodesian Economy', 1949.
78 See Table 3.1 for British figures. For South African figures see Commonwealth Relations Office, *Oversea Migration Statistics 1955*, 14.
79 Ian Smith Papers, 1/78/002, Effects of Reigning Immigration Policy, 23 July 1954.
80 Ian Smith Papers, 1/78/002, Memorandum on Immigration, 23 July 1954.
81 The threat of Afrikaner migration to both Northern and Southern Rhodesia and the potential for this to form the basis of growing South African influence leading even to incorporation into the Union was also used by Roy Welensky, Godfrey Huggins and other proponents of Federation to put pressure on British politicians. Philip Murphy, '"Government by Blackmail": The Origins of the Central African Federation Reconsidered', in *The British Empire in the 1950s: Retreat or Revival?*, ed. Martin Lynn (Basingstoke: Palgrave Macmillan, 2006).
82 Ian Smith Papers, 1/78/002, Memorandum on Immigration, 23 July 1954.
83 Boucher, *Empire's Children*; Katja Uusihakala, 'Rescuing children, reforming the Empire: British child migration to colonial Southern Rhodesia', *Identities* 22:3 (2015), 273–87; Sherington and Jeffery, *Fairbridge*. There is also a collection of memoirs written by those who attended the Fairbridge Memorial College. Dean Calcott, ed., *Windows: Rhodesia Fairbridge Memorial College Autobiographies* (Christchurch, New Zealand: Fairbridge Marketing Company Limited, 2001).
84 Boucher, *Empire's Children*, pp. 194, 205–7; Ellen Boucher, 'The Limits of Potential: Race, Welfare, and the Interwar Extension of Child Emigration to Southern Rhodesia', *Journal of British Studies* 48:4 (2009), 914–34; Sherington and Jeffery, *Fairbridge*.

4

From Britons to 'New Rhodesians' and 'New South Africans': The consolidation of racial nationalism in the 1950s

While the South African and Southern Rhodesian governments continued to be selective in their admission of white immigrants throughout the 1950s, they began to recruit white migrants more actively by the middle of the decade. In both cases, this was framed as the remedy to a shortage of skilled labour. Under the racial logic of these settler colonial nations, this was best addressed by importing white workers rather than employing or training local Black workers. In the United Kingdom, while support for emigration as a way to strengthen relationships with the former Dominions continued in some quarters, it diminished over the course of the 1950s. The 1950s also saw increasing concerns about the number of Commonwealth migrants of colour arriving in the United Kingdom. The imperative to maintain British influence in an increasingly independent Commonwealth, however, meant that attempts to limit this migration were informal until the 1962 Commonwealth Immigrants Act. As discussed in previous chapters, the pursuit of the perceived national rather than imperial interest had long defined the migration policies of South Africa and Southern Rhodesia and continued to do so in the 1950s. In the United Kingdom too, national concerns increasingly predominated, as the importance of the Empire (increasingly rebranded as the Commonwealth) diminished.

While increasing the white population was a long-running goal of the South African government, as discussed in Chapters 2 and 3, this was always balanced by the concern of Afrikaner nationalists that the arrival of too many new migrants, especially British migrants, would both dilute Afrikaner culture and thwart their aim of complete independence from the United Kingdom. As the National Party solidified their rule, winning a clear majority in the 1953 election, this became less of a concern and the South African government began to implement initiatives to encourage white, including white British migration. Given the racial labour hierarchy and that the focus of these initiatives was the recruitment of skilled workers who would contribute to the growing industrial economy, immigration policies remained selective on health and financial grounds.

The Federation of Rhodesia and Nyasaland, formed in 1953, through the amalgamation of the colonies of Southern Rhodesia, Northern Rhodesia and Nyasaland (present-day Zimbabwe, Zambia and Malawi) also more actively recruited white migrants from the mid 1950s, although this fluctuated based on the economic situation. As in South Africa, the Federation retained a selective immigration policy. Would-be immigrants were required to prove that they were of good health and character, free of a criminal record and able to support themselves. Unlike in South Africa, the Federal government had a clear preference for British migrants, and concerns continued over white migration from South Africa, specifically that the arrival of too many Afrikaners might dilute white Rhodesia's British character. The Federal government abandoned the quotas discussed in Chapter 3 in 1955 and began a publicity campaign to attract new white migrants as well as a small-scale programme that provided loans to cover the passages of selected skilled migrants. Quotas were reinstated in 1958, however, as the Federation faced an economic downturn due to a drop in copper prices and an even more selective policy was implemented. Though this was loosened again in 1959 when economic prospects improved, concerns over the looming break-up of Federation meant that the government continued to take a cautious and selective approach to immigration.[1]

These policies of selective immigration, and particularly the recruitment of skilled and professional British workers, were at odds with the British government's emigration policy in the 1950s. Though reluctant to abandon its support of emigration to the Commonwealth entirely, ongoing labour shortages in the United Kingdom led British officials to advocate for the migration of what they termed a 'cross-section' of the British population, including people of all ages and of all skill levels and qualifications. There was also widespread official and increasing popular concern about the rising number of Commonwealth immigrants of colour arriving in the 1950s. In both cases, formal policy changes that would end British support for emigration to the Commonwealth and restrict immigration from the Commonwealth were considered. These were ultimately rejected due to concerns for their potential impact on Commonwealth relations, which were, especially in the early to mid 1950s under the Churchill and Eden governments, still considered to be important.[2] Vocal advocates for British emigration to the Commonwealth, including members of the House of Lords and MPs, remained active, but were increasingly marginal figures. The British approach to both emigration and immigration signalled the growing importance of national rather than imperial concerns in the 1950s.

Rates of British migration to South Africa were steady through the 1950s, ranging from around 4,500 to 6,500 annually from 1950 until 1958. They began to decline in 1959 due to political uncertainty leading up to the

The consolidation of racial nationalism in the 1950s   101

South African declaration of republic and exit from the Commonwealth in 1961, reaching a post-war low in 1960 of 2,292 before the recovery and then dramatic increase in the 1960s and 1970s described in Chapter 5. Throughout the 1950s, it was easier for white migrants of British nationality to enter South Africa than all other migrants, provided they met health, financial and 'character' requirements. The rates of British migration to South Africa in the 1950s, were also, though a substantial reduction from the surge of the immediate post-war years, higher than rates in the 1920s and 1930s.[3] The implementation of subsidised migration schemes to other Commonwealth countries, most notably the 'Ten Pound Pom' scheme to Australia, may well have attracted those who would otherwise have considered South Africa, which offered no such subsidies until the 1960s. Potential British migrants may also have been deterred by the increasing strength of Afrikaner nationalism and looked to Southern Rhodesia or indeed Australia, New Zealand or Canada. Some white English speakers left South Africa in this period, many going to Southern Rhodesia.[4]

The figures available for Southern Rhodesia are less precise, as separate records for each colony were not consistently kept during the period of Federation. They do indicate, however, that between 4,000 and 6,000 British-born migrants arrived in Southern Rhodesia annually from 1950 to 1955. The Federation as a whole saw higher rates of British migration (between 7,000 and 11,000 annually) from 1955 to 1958, dropping to 4,558 in 1959 and 3,897 in 1960. British migrants also generally made up a larger proportion of the total in Southern Rhodesia than in South Africa. This was in part due to Rhodesian government policy, which gave priority to migrants coming from Britain under a quota system, as discussed in Chapter 3. The migration figures overall also reflect changing Rhodesian immigration policy, showing an increase in 1956 and 1957 when the quotas were removed, followed by a decrease after they were reinstated in 1958. As well as removing the quotas in 1955, the Federal government also embarked on a publicity campaign to recruit skilled migrants and implemented a small-scale, short-lived loan programme for selected migrants. The economic downturn that prompted the reimposition of quotas may also have made the Federation less attractive to would-be migrants.

Migration policy in the United Kingdom

While supportive in rhetoric of both emigration from Britain to the Commonwealth and of the free entry of Commonwealth citizens to the United Kingdom, British governments in the 1950s provided limited practical support to emigration and worked to limit the entry of Commonwealth

Table 4.1 British migration to South Africa and Southern Rhodesia, 1951–60

Year	Migration from the United Kingdom to South Africa[i]	Percentage of total migration to South Africa from the United Kingdom	British-born migrants to Southern Rhodesia[ii]	Percentage of total migration to Southern Rhodesia born in Britain	Migration from the United Kingdom to the Federation[iii]	Percentage of total migration to the Federation from the United Kingdom
1951	5,903	38.73	6,130	38.96		
1952	6,491	35.14	6,808	54.37		
1953	5,416	33.31	5,290	51.33		
1954	4,629	28.20	4,089	41.82		
1955	4,444	27.43			7,736	38.65
1956	4,476	30.01			11,270	43.01
1957	4,723	32.32			10,347[iv]	42.73
1958	4,450	30.33			7,313	43.14
1959	3,782	30.10			4,588	36.66
1960	2,292	23.41			3,897	32.15

[i] Figures for 1950–1954, Republic of South Africa Department of Statistics, *Report No. 19–01–01, Migration Statistics: Immigrants and Emigrants, 1966 to 1969* (Pretoria: Government Printer, 1969), 4.
[ii] Commonwealth Relations Office, *Oversea Migration Statistics 1955* (London, HMSO, 1956), 14.
[iii] After the formation of the Federation, statistics broken down by nationality or country of last permanent residence were no longer routinely compiled for Southern Rhodesia. Ian Smith Papers, 1/78/004, Southern Rhodesian Cabinet Minutes, Ninth Meeting, 23 February 1955. It seems likely that the majority of British migrants went to Southern Rhodesia. For instance, figures for Southern Rhodesia are available for 1958, 5,238 British migrants came to Southern Rhodesia out of a total of 7,313 who arrived in the Federation or 71.6 per cent. NASA, BNS 1/1/365, Ref. 117/74, Vol. 5, Central African Statistical Office, 'Review of Immigration into the Federation during the Month of December 1958 and the Year Ended 31 December 1958'. Figures for 1955 and 1956, Cmnd 336, Commonwealth Relations Office, *Third Report of the Oversea Migration Board December 1957* (London: HMSO, 1957), 30. Figures for 1957 and 1958, Cmnd 975, Commonwealth Relations Office, *Fifth Report of the Oversea Migration Board March 1960* (London, HMSO, 1960), 38. Figures for 1959 and 1960, Cmnd 1586, Commonwealth Relations Office, *Seventh Report of the Oversea Migration Board December 1961* (London: HMSO, 1961), 26. These figures are taken from the Central African Statistical Office.
[iv] The figure for 1957 includes migrants from the Republic of Ireland. It is unclear why this year's statistics were collected in this way, as all the other years under consideration list Ireland separately. However, according to the Oversea Migration Board, only 'a hundred or two' of the migrants listed came from the Republic of Ireland. Cmnd 619, Commonwealth Relations Office, *Fourth Report of the Oversea Migration Board December 1958* (London: HMSO, 1958), 22.

citizens of colour. Concern both about emigration, especially of skilled workers, and the increasing number of migrants of colour from the Commonwealth led British officials to consider formal policies to restrict both. In the end restrictions were not implemented because of the potential damage to Commonwealth relations. Instead, these concerns were addressed through informal means.

In terms of immigration, though the 1948 British Nationality Act confirmed the abstract equality of all British subjects throughout the Empire and Commonwealth and their right to live and work in the United Kingdom, the official response to the arrival of West Indian migrants and other migrants of colour in the years after the war demonstrate that this was not the Act's intended purpose. Rather, the legislation aimed to formalise existing nationality and citizenship arrangements in light of increasing moves by the Dominions to create their own separate citizenship, beginning with Canada in 1946.[5] British subjects of colour who came to Britain after the Second World War, even as their right to live and work in the United Kingdom was legally affirmed, were cast as unfairly taking advantage of their status as British subjects in contemporary official and popular discussions.[6] Such migrants were implicitly challenging the imperial system and its hierarchies and ideologies of race by moving to the imperial centre on their own initiative and for their own reasons, rather than as wartime workers or at the behest of the Colonial Office.

Despite the labour shortage that led to the recruitment of Irish and other European workers in this period, the Atlee government began to seek ways to limit the migration of British subjects of colour after the arrival of the HMS *Ormonde* in 1947, a year before the arrival of the *Windrush* and the passage of the British Nationality Act in 1948.[7] Officials sought to accomplish this while avoiding charges of racial discrimination that might jeopardise colonial relations. They implemented informal measures intended both to discourage migrants from coming and to make it more difficult for them to do so. One tactic was to prevent passengers from travelling on the troop deck on troopships returning from the Caribbean as they had done on the *Windrush*, and the *Ormonde* and *Almanzora*, its less famous predecessors, thereby cutting down on the availability of affordable passages. Another was to instruct shipping companies only to issue passages to those with a definite offer of employment.[8] There was also a return to the pre-1942 protocol for immigration officers at British ports, which gave more discretion to officials and required more documentation of arriving passengers. Alongside these measures were attempts to make it more difficult for passengers to stowaway and a stricter approach to the prosecution of stowaways. In 1950, the holder's nationality was removed from the British Travel Certificate make it more difficult for some migrants to prove that they were British subjects. As Lydia Lindsey has argued, these measures contributed to the reduction in the number of migrants arriving in the United Kingdom from the Caribbean until the introduction of cheaper and more available travel via the United States beginning in 1950.[9]

The British government also placed pressure on colonial and newly independent Commonwealth governments not to issue passports to those who could not prove that they had the means of paying for their passage and maintenance once in the United Kingdom.[10] The Pakistani government increased the application fee, required a deposit against the potential cost of repatriation as well as proof of literacy and competence in English. The Indian government required proof of literacy as well as financial status and required special permission in addition to a passport for those travelling by sea.[11] The main passport office moved to Delhi in 1950 and bureaucratic delays meant that it could take up to two years for passports to be issued. In addition, applications could be refused if the reasons given for travel were not thought to be valid. As well as discouraging would-be migrants, this also led to a flourishing black market in forged travel documents.[12] Although it was not as difficult to get a passport in the Caribbean colonies as in India and Pakistan, there were restrictions. In Jamaica for instance, passports were not granted to those with criminal convictions, people over the age of fifty and pregnant women.[13]

Another method used to discourage would-be migrants was the circulation of propaganda warning of the potentially difficult conditions awaiting them in Britain. In India and Pakistan, the UK High Commissioner arranged for the publication in local newspapers of stories emphasising the difficulties migrants to Britain might encounter. The Colonial Office arranged for similar materials to be circulated by the High Commissions in the Caribbean including posters made by the Ministry of Labour warning of unemployment, cold weather, difficulty finding housing, unexpected expenses and even the duty on importing rum and cigarettes.[14]

By the mid 1950s, more overt restriction on immigration were debated by the Churchill government. This was partly precipitated by the increase in migrants from the West Indies to Britain in the early 1950s as more affordable passages became available and the 1952 McCarran-Walter Act made it more difficult to move to the United States.[15] Proposals included requiring all arriving migrants to prove that they would not become dependent on public funds, or those possessing British passports issued outside of the United Kingdom to prove they had accommodation or employment lined up. By leaving this to the discretion of British immigration officers, it would be possible to exclude arriving British subjects of colour, while admitting white British subjects from the Dominions without a formal colour bar.[16] Such an approach would make it easier to exclude other 'undesirable' migrants from the Commonwealth regardless of race and was similar to methods long employed by South Africa, Rhodesia and the other settler colonies of the British Empire.[17]

Ultimately the Churchill government did not go ahead with these proposals because they feared the political consequences if it was perceived that the true motivation was racial. Churchill's private secretary, Sir David Hunt, described their dilemma: 'The minute we said we've got to keep these black chaps out, the whole Commonwealth lark would have blown up.'[18] How to keep out British subjects of colour, while maintaining the rights of white Commonwealth subjects to live in Britain without the appearance of racism, continued to be a dilemma, although less so as time went on and Commonwealth unity became less important to British policymakers.

Preserving Commonwealth unity and influence in former Dominions was also the reason for the continuing, if limited, practical support provided by the government to British emigration to the Commonwealth in the 1950s, despite growing concerns about its desirability. Opponents of emigration pointed to the labour shortage and the lost investment in terms of education and social welfare spending especially of young working-age migrants. These arguments, as explored further in Chapter 5, were increasingly linked to concerns about rising migration to the United Kingdom from the Commonwealth, based on the often racist assumption that the United Kingdom was losing skilled and productive migrants and gaining those with less education and ability. Vocalising concerns about emigration to other destinations, such as the United States, became one way around this dilemma. Another was to continue public support for migration schemes, while reducing practical and financial support for them.

While debates over British emigration to the Commonwealth in the 1950s drew on many of the long-running arguments for what had previously been termed 'empire settlement' these were adjusted to the geopolitical context of the time. Supporters argued that as well as reinforcing Commonwealth unity and bolstering Britain's faltering international position, it would also contribute to the development of Commonwealth countries, especially, but not only, in Africa. In the context of the Cold War, some argued that the distribution of British population and industrial capacity across the wide area of the Commonwealth would be desirable in the case of a nuclear attack or the outbreak of a third world war.

Proponents of British migration to South Africa and Southern Rhodesia argued that it would help to safeguard British interests in southern Africa, especially after the electoral victory of the National Party in South Africa in 1948.[19] More broadly, advocates of migration to the Commonwealth argued that it would lead to economic development while reviving Britain's diminished post-war position.[20] Such development in the Commonwealth, some argued, would also stem the flow of immigrants coming from the Commonwealth to Britain.[21] By this logic, as the colonies and former colonies developed, with the aid of British migrants, the opportunities available at home would make a move to the United Kingdom less enticing. Migration schemes were cast, then, not only as a way to revive Britain's post-war economic and geopolitical position but also to reduce another post-war development, the mass migration of Commonwealth subjects of colour to the United Kingdom. This underscores the ways in which the promotion of emigration was an attempt to return to a previous world order, and the racial logic by which white migration was considered desirable and assumed to contribute to the receiving countries economy while the migration of people of colour was not.

Such positions were also advocated by the Migration Council an independent, voluntary organisation set up to promote Commonwealth migration in 1950, whose board included such supporters of empire migration as Leo Amery and Lord Beaverbrook.[22] The Council was particularly concerned, in the context of the early Cold War to promote migration as a safety measure and complement to rearmament in the context of a potential nuclear attack and food shortages in the event of third world war. The Council also advocated migration as a solution to the housing shortage after the war, drawing on long-running tropes of the crowded United Kingdom and the 'empty' lands of Canada, Australia, New Zealand, South Africa and Southern Rhodesia. Its 1951 publication *Operation British Commonwealth* is illustrated with photographs of 'over-congested London' contrasted with 'Spacious Canada'. As well as promoting the well-worn trope of 'empty lands' that ignored the very existence of indigenous communities, this line of argument also ignored the ongoing housing shortages in all the settler colonies of the Commonwealth. The pamphlet drew on the nineteenth-century language of settlement, describing post-war migrants as '20th century pioneers to develop the idle resources of the British Commonwealth'.[23] Notwithstanding its prominent supporters, the Council was never very successful in influencing policy and officials in the Commonwealth Relations Office frequently expressed their irritation at the Council's efforts, deferring or refusing requests for meetings and dismissing their efforts as fanatical and lacking realism.[24]

Although the Empire Settlement Act was renewed in 1952 and then again as the Commonwealth Settlement Act in 1957, funding for emigration was significantly cut in the 1950s. At the inception in 1946 of the 'Ten Pound Pom' scheme, the British government had shared the cost equally with the Australian government. By 1951, the British annual contribution stood at £885,000. It was reduced to a maximum of £500,000 in 1952 and then reduced to £150,000 in 1953 (which funded about 1,000 migrants).[25]

At same time funding for other migration schemes under the Empire Settlement Act was also cut, for instance, those organised by the Church of England.[26] Overall, the total amount spent under the Empire Settlement Act dropped dramatically after 1952, so that significant financial support by the government was only provided for four years with expenditures of £1,421,142 in 1948/49, £2,028,882 in 1949/50, £1,306,389 in 1950/51 and £751,599 in 1951/52. Thereafter up until 1961 the amount spent ranged from £164,267 (1960/61) to £269,989 (1954/55).[27]

As well as cutting funding for emigration schemes, the government's policy was to encourage the migration of a 'cross-section' of the population in terms of age and profession. By adopting this approach, British officials hoped to avoid mass migration of those of prime working and reproductive age and in particular skilled workers. Such migrants were the very people, however, most sought by the recruiting countries. While there were some small-scale schemes for the elderly relatives of those who had already migrated, all the subsidised schemes had age limits or required applicants to have skills and qualifications in demand or both. Migrants were also required to have no criminal record and meet health requirements.[28] South Africa and the Central African Federation were even more selective in their immigration policies than the other recruiting countries (Australia, Canada and New Zealand) requiring proof, either in terms of skills and qualifications or financial assets, that migrants would be able to support themselves.

This put South Africa and Southern Rhodesia (and later the Federation) particularly at odds with the British government over migration policy, as they were explicitly only seeking exactly the kind of migrants that Britain hoped to retain. Increasing criticism of racial discrimination in South Africa and the Federation further widened this division. The arrival of more white migrants to the settler colonies of southern Africa, critics argued, would contribute to the ongoing oppression of their Black African populations, through the increasing appropriation of land and by strengthening the white minority regimes both in economic and demographic terms. This made the official encouragement of British migration to southern Africa increasingly difficult in political terms.

Despite the efforts of the Migration Council and other supporters of British emigration to the settler colonies of the Commonwealth, official support remained limited in the United Kingdom. High rates of migration from the United Kingdom to the Commonwealth in the 1950s, were largely due to the assisted passage programmes offered by Australia, Canada and New Zealand in this period.[29] While official support for British migration to the Commonwealth was waning in the United Kingdom, it was gradually growing in both the Federation and South Africa, although this very much depended on political and economic considerations.

'Unskilled persons should not apply': Southern Rhodesia in the Central African Federation

After the formation of the Central African Federation in 1953, and despite its multi-racial rhetoric and such gestures as the provision of limited African representation in the Federal and territorial parliaments, the recruitment of white immigrants became a renewed priority. The quota system was abandoned for British subjects in 1955, signalling a renewed enthusiasm by both the Federal and Southern Rhodesian governments for promoting European immigration, although they continued to operate a selective scheme.[30] Enthusiasm for the recruitment of European migrants also, as ever, depended on economic circumstances. To secure a loan with the World Bank for the Kariba Dam, the Federal government was required to scale back their financial investment in recruiting European immigrants from 1957 and a downturn in 1958 resulting in a reimposition of quotas, albeit at a higher level than previously.[31]

In the Federation, in line with some of the arguments made in the United Kingdom as described above, the promotion of white migration was largely framed by the rhetoric of development, asserting that the arrival of skilled white migrants would hasten economic development and therefore ultimately benefit the African population.[32] This was part of the Federation's broader attempt to position itself as a more progressive alternative to the increasingly hard-line apartheid regime in South Africa.[33] As African nationalist opposition to Federation at the time and the subsequent history of Rhodesia would suggest, this rhetoric of multi-racialism and partnership did little to alter the balance of power, which was still very much held by the minority white population. Whatever its benefits to the Black majority might be, economic development would certainly benefit the resident white settler population of the Federation, and, it was hoped, serve to attract more white migrants.[34]

This is reflected in the Federation's migration policy, which was premised on the recruitment of skilled white labour, with a preference for British migrants. Migrants not classified as white were subject to much greater restriction, and new restrictions for those classified as 'Indians' by the state were introduced post-Federation in 1954.[35] As well as ending immigration quotas for British subjects in 1955, the Federal government joined the Intergovernmental Committee on European Migration (ICEM), an international organisation dating from the post-war refugee crisis that sought to coordinate migration from Europe. The Federation recruited 100 building workers from Western Europe through ICEM and signed a migration agreement with the Dutch government. The same year, the Federation posted an Immigration Attaché to Rhodesia House in London to undertake a promotional tour of the British Isles and operate a clearing house for job opportunities. They made grants to both the Society for the Oversea Settlement of British Women and to the 1820 Memorial Settlers' Association, which helped with publicity, recruitment, arranging passages, reception on arrival, housing, employment and social integration.[36] The Federal government also established a separate immigration branch, setting aside £12,000 for publicity, made a promotional film and sent new brochures and photographs to 800 travel agents around the United Kingdom. The film, *Two Generations*, highlighted the achievements accomplished in industry, mining and agriculture since the arrival of European settlers and showcased the Federation's natural beauty. Other short 'Rhodesian spotlight' films were also produced by the Central African film unit and aired on the BBC.[37]

In addition to promoting migration, the Federal government also began a system of providing loans to immigrants from the United Kingdom 'qualified in an essential occupation in which there is demand for skilled workers'. These loans, ranging from £30 to £120, were to be used to pay for the passage out and were interest-free for three years. As of June 1955, sixty-five immigrants had received loans averaging £75.16, and £47,000 had been set aside for the loan programme.[38] In 1957 the scheme provided loans to 524 migrants and the Federal government had made loans totalling £168,835 by the end of that year.[39]

There was a particular emphasis on the recruitment of skilled workers in the building trade. An advertisement in the *Wiltshire Times* in 1955 noted opportunities for 'building artisans (all trades), motor mechanics, engineer-mechanics for earth moving equipment, pharmacists, surveyors and shorthand-typists'.[40] This list describes the workers needed to continue the 'development' of the Federation, to survey the land, operate the machines that would clear it and then build factories, homes, schools, offices and hospitals. The Federation's promotional literature presented the story of the rapid, but crucially ongoing 'civilisation' of central Africa following European colonisation. A 1955 brochure, 'Achievement: Modern Living in Rhodesia and Nyasaland' highlights '60 years of Progress' with photographs illustrating the transformation 'from Bush-track to City Street'.[41] The brochure also includes numerous photographs of grand government buildings and 'modern' city streets, as well as industrial images showing mines and power plants.

In this telling, the development brought by European settlement had also benefited the indigenous African population, contrasting this 'new civilisation' with the previous 'slave despotism and the slave trader'.[42] This drew on long-running tropes of the 'civilising mission' which cast British conquest and colonisation of central and East Africa in the nineteenth century as an anti-slavery crusade, featuring such well-known figures as David

Livingstone.⁴³ While most of the brochure is focused on the opportunities for work and the adventurous outdoor lifestyle available to the European immigrant, there is also a section entitled 'Africans are learning many trades under European supervision' illustrated with images of Black workers in industrial settings and picking cotton, in line with often paternalistic 'partnership' rhetoric of the Federation as a whole.⁴⁴ It was clearly intended to counter criticism from African nationalists and anti-colonial activists that Black people were losing jobs and land to European immigrants. In response to such a critique from Moses Shankanga, an African National Congress official based in Lusaka in what was then Northern Rhodesia, Benjamin Goldberg, Federal Secretary for Home Affairs argued that the selective immigration policy brought only skilled immigrants who would contribute to the development of the Federation and thereby benefit the Black population.⁴⁵

Implicit in this argument is an assumption that although Black workers might slowly advance to the level of the 'semi-skilled', the racial labour hierarchy would remain intact. While the recruitment of white immigrants was seen as crucial for the continued development of the Federation, only skilled migrants were sought to take their place at the top of hierarchy. As the advertisement in the *Wiltshire Times* cited above makes clear, 'Unskilled persons should not apply.' Even after ending migration quotas, the Rhodesian government still operated a selective immigration policy.⁴⁶ This is reflected in much of the promotional literature. For instance, a 1955 publication states: 'There is no place for the white man who is classed in the United Kingdom as a labourer.'⁴⁷ Even the most favoured category of migrants, 'British subjects of European descent' were required to provide proof of their training and qualifications as well as character testimonials, details of their finances and evidence of their health. They were also required to follow the profession listed on their application for the first two years after their arrival, although it is not clear whether and how this rule was enforced.⁴⁸

As this suggests the Federal government sought immigrants of the 'right type', reflecting ideas about racial fitness. As well as being physically and mentally healthy, of 'good character' and possessing the skills or finances to ensure that they would not risk becoming 'poor whites', the ideal migrants described also possessed a resilient and adventurous outlook. While the promotional literature portrayed Southern Rhodesia and the wider Federation as modern and developed, with numerous photographs of buildings including grand hotels, churches and factories, they also stressed that this development was an ongoing process, warning that in newer areas, immigrants should not expect 'a pub on every corner … a cinema on the High Street' or indeed that all roads would be paved.⁴⁹

The ideal immigrant was one who would not complain about the lack of such amenities but would throw themselves into the task of developing the Federation. As the information pack sent to British travel agents from the Rhodesian High Commission put it, 'escapists and complainers are not welcomed' and would-be migrants should expect 'growing pains'.[50] This is also reflected in the application form for a residence permit, which includes the question, 'Are you and your wife prepared to put up with a variety of minor inconveniences during the initial period of settling down and making a home for yourselves in a new country?'[51] Even as these brochures sold the settler lifestyle, they also made clear that not all Britons were suitable settlers.[52]

One difficulty for new migrants to overcome was the housing shortage. Even as the brochures included photographs of detached bungalows on large plots and modern blocks of flats in city centres, they repeatedly warned about the potential problems of finding housing, suggesting that men go out ahead of their families and only send for them when they had secured appropriate accommodation. One brochure included in bold capital letters: 'ONCE AGAIN IT SHOULD BE EMPHASISED THAT IN MOST CENTRES OF EUROPEAN POPULATION THE HOUSING SITUATION IS DIFFICULT.'[53] In part to address the housing shortage, the Federation implemented a Nomination Scheme in 1955. Local residents who knew of someone 'likely to obtain satisfactory employment and be an asset to the Federation' were invited to send their details to the Ministry of Home Affairs, where they would be given 'priority consideration' and might be granted a loan toward their passage if they fell into an occupational category in which there was a skills shortage. The advantage of such a programme, like Australia's 'Bring Out a Briton' scheme, was that it was expected that accommodation for the new immigrants would be provided by the nominator when they first arrived.[54]

The nomination scheme was also intended to help with the assimilation of migrants. To encourage integration, the 1955 official 'Immigration Bulletin' explained that European immigrants should be referred to as 'New Rhodesians' because 'the terms "immigrants" and "settlers" do not convey that degree of warmth which we should offer to our new friends, nor do they imply our acceptance of them into the life of the Federation'. European immigrants also received 'Welcome Cards', attached to their Permanent Residence Permit, consisting of 'a short address of welcome to the Federation as well as the names of over 100 branches of 33 Patriotic and Social Societies throughout the three territories whose members have volunteered to assist New Rhodesians to settle contentedly into the Federation'.[55] This illustrates the importance placed on the successful integration of white arrivals into white Rhodesian society, tied to the same concerns behind selective immigration policies.

However, even with these measures not all migrants settled 'contentedly' into the Federation, particularly after an economic downturn in the late 1950s. This is reflected in high rates of emigration.[56] A notable example of dissatisfied migrants were three Scottish bricklayers who mounted a hunger strike and demonstration in 1958 complaining that they been misled into coming to Southern Rhodesia by promises of well-paid employment that never materialised. They had initially arrived as part of 'Operation Brickie', five plane-loads of Scottish and English bricklayers, plasterers and carpenters given loans towards their passages in December 1957. By March 1958, they had been laid off several times and led a protest march of forty unemployed British migrants to the statue of Cecil Rhodes in central Salisbury (now Harare) where they began a hunger strike. One man ended his strike after being offered employment, but the other two continued for three days, receiving coverage in *The Scotsman* and the *Liverpool Post* as well as Rhodesian newspapers.[57] In another case, two carpenters and a motor mechanic who had moved to the Federation from the United Kingdom in 1957 applied to be repatriated just a week after arrival, claiming that they had been unable to find work in either Ndola (in Northern Rhodesia) or Salisbury and that they had been misled by officials at Rhodesia House. In bringing up their case, Albert Stumbles, the Minister of Justice and Internal Affairs, claimed that they had refused offers of work and noted that public money had been spent on providing them with accommodation.[58] Such problems provide an indication of why the Rhodesian government was so concerned with the selection of immigrants deemed to be appropriate and why their immigration regime was so sensitive to the vicissitudes of the economy and demand for labour.

Despite this, the underlying existential requirement to fortify the minority white nation through immigration remained and would become more acute after the collapse of the Federation and the Unilateral Declaration of Independence, which led to increasing rates of white emigration. After the Rhodesian Front came to power in 1964 and especially after UDI in 1965 the Rhodesian government recruited white immigrants, while attempting to prevent large-scale white emigration, even as concerns about maintaining white prestige and the privileged lifestyle of the white minority continued. Though scholars have largely focused on the recruitment drives of the 1960s, as this chapter and the previous one has demonstrated, this was a policy pursued in the immediate post-war years and again in the mid-1950s heyday of the Federation, though shaped, as ever, by political and especially economic constraints.[59]

Migration policy in South Africa

By the mid 1950s, the South African government also began to pursue a more active immigration policy, foreshadowing the more comprehensive immigration programme undertaken in the 1960s after republic. Given that the immediate post-war problems – the housing shortage and the demobilisation of the armed forces – were less pressing, white migrants were less likely to seen as competition to returning South African veterans for jobs and state resources. Rather, due to the selective immigration policy and racial labour hierarchy, white migrants were largely seen as providing the skilled labour crucial to the continuing development of the growing South African economy.[60] The more active government initiatives on immigration were also in part a reaction to increasing rates of white emigration, including to Southern Rhodesia.[61] As well as these pragmatic concerns, the increasing push for white immigration, including from the United Kingdom, reflects a broader, if gradual, shift towards the official promotion of white racial solidarity, albeit still under Afrikaner leadership. This is also illustrated by changes in public holidays in this period, towards a celebration of the history of white, including British, settlement of South Africa.

This more open official approach to white (including British) immigration was also related to political considerations. The 1949 South African Citizenship Act changed the procedure for gaining citizenship and the franchise from an automatic right granted to British subjects after two years' residence in South Africa to one that was granted only on application after five years.[62] This, along with the National Party's electoral victory in 1953, which consolidated their political position, meant that British immigrants, who might be more likely to support the United Party or continuing ties with the British Empire, were less of a threat to Afrikaner nationalism or republicanism.

While the main rationale behind the recruitment of white migrants was the recruitment of skilled labour, the late 1950s also saw developing concerns about maintaining the relative size of the white population. Official commissions in both 1955 and 1958 predicted the collapse of what they termed 'white civilisation' without increased European immigration. In 1955 the Tomlinson Commission raised fears about the relative size of the Black and white populations in South Africa and their projected growth, given the much lower white birth rate.[63] In order to continue current rates of economic growth, the Viljoen Commission in 1958 called for at least 25,000 white immigrants annually.[64]

The South African government increasingly saw the arrival of white migrants as crucial given the lower growth rate of the white population compared to other racial groups. In 1955, the South Africa sent an observer to ICEM and joined the following year.[65] That same year saw the establishment of a new Directorate of Immigration and more sympathetic statements on immigration by National Party MPs in Parliament.[66] In 1956, the government provided £10,000 to ICEM to facilitate the immigration of refugees from Hungary and by 1959, 1,309 refugees had moved to South Africa.[67] In 1957, they agreed to contribute to an ICEM scheme providing subsidised passages for migrants from the Netherlands.[68] The government also offered to accept as migrants 1,000 'displaced Hollanders' from Indonesia in the run-up to the Indonesian expulsion of Dutch nationals in October 1957, provided they and their wives were white.[69] Given the National Party's long-running preference for migrants from the Netherlands and anti-communist stance, it follows that they would focus their efforts on recruiting Dutch immigrants and would assist Hungarian refugees.

As their welcome of Dutch migrants from Indonesia suggests, there was also particular sympathy for white settlers displaced by the end of colonial rule. By 1960, measures were announced that made it easier to move to South Africa for the white residents of African countries where the end of colonial rule loomed. Such migrants would be able to bring in vehicles and household goods and in urgent cases temporary visas could be issued and permanent residency could be sought after arrival. Generally, such migrants were admitted even if they did not meet the usual health and financial criteria and were thought to be more easily assimilated given their experience of living in colonial Africa. Contemporary commentators correctly predicted that these measures were likely forerunners of a subsidised migration scheme.[70]

The South African government also began to provide more support to migration organisations. In November 1960, it began providing financial support to the South African Immigration Organisation (Samorgan), founded in 1958 by John Foggit, a South African businessman, which recruited skilled men in the United Kingdom and provided loans for their passages to South Africa and to Transa, a similar organisation that operated in West Germany, Austria and Switzerland. These organisations received a subsidy for each approved immigrant that they recruited.[71] At the same time state funding was provided for the 'after care' and integration activities of the Maatskappy vir Europese Immigrasie (Organisation for European Immigration), an organisation founded in 1954 by Afrikaner church and cultural organisations that focused its efforts on migrants from continental Europe. By 1961, this financial support had also been extended to the 1820 Memorial Settlers' Association, whose focus was on British migrants and is discussed in further detail below.[72]

As these measures indicate, there was a gradual move towards greater state support for immigration, which presaged the implementation of the subsidised scheme described in further detail in Chapter 5. This shift was the result of several developments: the consolidation of political power by the National Party, the increasing international isolation of South Africa, and the shortage of skilled labour. Related to this was the greater state promotion of white racial solidarity. This was reflected in the changing celebration of public holidays in South Africa across the 1950s. In 1952, the South African government instituted Settlers' Day, a public holiday celebrating the 1820 Settlers, early English colonists. A similar holiday had long existed in Southern Rhodesia, Pioneer Day (originally Occupation Day) which commemorated the Pioneer Columns of the 1890s.

As Eric Hobsbawm has argued, the institution of public holidays and their celebrations, are one way that states 'broadcast' particular understandings of the nation.[73] Such celebration often focus on heroes, symbolism, and on myths surrounding the foundation of a particular nation, such as Independence Day in the United States or Bastille Day in France. In the context of South Africa, T. Dunbar Moodie has shown how, the 'Afrikaner civil religion' was promulgated in the early twentieth century. This included events such as re-enactment of the so-called 'Great Trek', the movement into the interior, undertaken by those Dutch settlers who did not wish to live under British rule, especially after the abolition of slavery in 1834. It also included celebrations of the Day of the Vow, commemorating the unlikely victory of a group of outnumbered Voortrekkers over the Zulu leader Dingane.[74]

South Africans of British descent had their own mythology, commemorations and heroes. As John Lambert has shown, the First World War Battle of Delville Wood, the 'Springboks on the Somme', became a focus for Anglo-South African identity and patriotism in a similar way to Gallipoli for Australians and New Zealanders.[75] So did the 1820 Settlers, the first large group of British migrants who came to South Africa. These settlers were sent to the Eastern Cape in a scheme sponsored by the British government, which had recently taken control of the Cape Colony. Over time the 1820 Settlers became an important symbolic reference point to British-descended South Africans, like the Voortrekkers for Afrikaners. To this day, if you mention an interest in British migration to South Africa, South Africans will assume that you mean the 1820 Settlers, even though far larger waves of British migration followed around the discovery of diamonds and gold later in the nineteenth century, after the Boer War in the early twentieth century and after the Second World War.[76] Though numerically a small proportion of the British settlers to South Africa, the 1820 Settlers loom large in the popular imagination of British settlement.

In part this was due to the activities of the 1820 Memorial Settlers' Association. Founded around the centenary of the arrival of the 1820

Settlers, the Association 'proposed to commemorate the work of the Settlers of 1820 by introducing more like them'.[77] The 1820 Memorial Settlers' Association did much to promote the mythology surrounding the 1820 Settlers, including historical articles and excerpts from Settler diaries, memoirs and letters in their magazine, *The 1820*, and organising celebrations such as festivals and re-enactments, as well as memorials in Port Elizabeth and Grahamstown in the Eastern Cape.

But while Dingane's Day, which would later be renamed the Day of the Vow, became a public holiday when the Union of South Africa became a Dominion in 1910, there would be no similar holiday commemorating the early British settlers of South Africa until 1952, when Settlers' Day was instituted by the Public Holidays Act of 1952. The Act also renamed Dingane's Day, the Day of the Vow, instituted a holiday celebrating Jan Van Riebeeck, the leader of the first European settlement established at the Cape under the Dutch East India Company in 1652 and a holiday celebrating Paul Kruger, the Afrikaner hero and president of the South African Republic defeated by the British in the South African War. And while the Act continued the celebration of the King's Birthday (soon to be the Queen's Birthday), it abolished Empire Day as a public holiday.

While the abolition of Empire Day and the institution of holidays in honour of Afrikaner heroes by an Afrikaner nationalist government comes as no surprise, the institution of Settlers' Day, a holiday celebrating British settlement in South Africa was less predictable. Yet it makes more sense when viewed as an attempt to unify white South Africa. Significantly, Settlers' Day emphasised the long presence in South Africans of settlers of British descent. In this way, the South African government emphasised a celebration of British settlement as part of the larger project of European colonisation of the region over a celebration of South Africa as part of the wider British Empire. As mentioned above, the same bill also instituted Van Riebeeck's Day, later called Founder's Day, which similarly emphasised the long history of European settlement in South Africa, since 1652. This emphasis on a shared history of white settlement became stronger through the 1950s and especially after the declaration of the South African republic in 1961. At this time, public holidays changed again, with Union Day becoming Republic Day and the abolition of the Queen's Birthday as a holiday.[78]

That is not to say that such efforts to promote white solidarity were successful and clearly individual ethnic, regional and other identities persisted among the white South African population, at times alongside and at times in opposition to a broader sense of themselves as white South Africans. In Natal for instance, often described as the most 'British' of the colonies that had joined together to become the Union of South Africa, there was a long-running tradition of separatism and an active campaign against republic. In the referendum on the question of republic conducted among white voters in 1960, Natalians overwhelmingly voted 'No'. Fifty-two per cent of the white electorate nationally voted in favour of republic, however, and the British government made it clear that even if Natal seceded from the Union, already a fairly remote possibility, it could only return to Crown control on the basis of universal suffrage. Despite their affinity to the monarchy and the British Empire, Natal separatists could not countenance the prospect of ending white minority rule and though a distinct Anglo-Natalian culture persisted, reinforced by the arrival of white migrants to the province from Rhodesia, this marked the end of separatism in political terms.[79]

Decolonisation and South Africa's increasing isolation shaped the options available to Natal separatists and the same forces influenced the National Party's increasing promotion of white racial solidarity. This was reflected in the pro-republic slogan, 'To Unite and Keep South Africa White' and had some impact, given the increased electoral support for the National Party from white English speakers in the 1961 election. This shift towards a broader white nationalism, did not mean the abandonment of Afrikaner nationalism, but rather its expansion as signalled by the inclusion of two conservative English speakers in the cabinet after the 1961 election. It was also reflected in the increasing recruitment of white migrants.[80] As well as celebrating the history of European settlement in Africa, state policy also aimed to continue that process in the immigration drives of the 1960s, which increasingly focused on the perceived race rather than nationality or class of potential immigrants.

Conclusion

In all three nations, governments aimed to shape their populations by recruiting certain migrants and discouraging others while also trying to retain existing residents whom they saw as desirable. In part this was undertaken to meet the perceived needs of each national economy. This is clear from the focus on skilled labour in the official discussion about migration in South Africa, Southern Rhodesia and the United Kingdom alike. Yet, the perceptions of who was skilled or unskilled or who would contribute to economic development was never immune from political and indeed ideological considerations. Imperial affiliation became less important, but imperial ideologies of race persisted.

The primary concern in the minority settler colonial nations of South Africa and Rhodesia was the recruitment of white migrants that met their health, financial and moral criteria, while the main concern in Britain was to discourage the mass immigration of migrants of colour from the Commonwealth. In all three nations there was also concern over the emigration of their existing white citizens. This approach to what James Hampshire has called 'demographic governance' reflects broader changes in the shift from empire to nation.[81] In South Africa, as well as the political movement towards republic, the 1950s saw moves towards the official promotion of white South African solidarity. In Southern Rhodesia, while an affiliation to Britishness, particularly in its white imperial form remained strong, there was also an increasing sense of white Rhodesian nationalism. While white nationalism in the United Kingdom was more covert, it is evident in growing concern over both the migration of people of colour and the emigration of white Britons. In all three cases, migration policies focused on the reinforcement of nations understood in racial terms as white would intensify in the 1960s.

Notes

1 Cmnd 975, *Fifth Report of the Oversea Migration Board* (London: HMSO, 1960), p. 23; Brownell, *Collapse of Rhodesia*, 117.
2 Martin Lynn, 'Introduction', in *The British Empire in the 1950s: Retreat or Revival?*, ed. Martin Lynn (Basingstoke: Palgrave Macmillan, 2006), pp. 1–7.
3 Peberdy, *Selecting Immigrants*, pp. 260–72.
4 Brownell, *British Immigration to South Africa*, pp. 38–9.
5 Karatani, *Defining British Citizenship*, pp. 116–26; Paul, *Whitewashing Britain*, pp. 9–24; Hansen, *Citizenship and Immigration*, pp. 35–56.
6 Paul, *Whitewashing Britain*, p. 118.
7 Lindsey, 'Halting the Tide', p. 63.
8 This echoed the approach taken in Australia, South Africa and colonial British West Africa of effectively outsourcing the imposition of migration restrictions to shipping companies. Smith, 'From Promising Settler', pp. 506, 508–9, 515; Matthew M. Heaton, 'Elder Dempster and the transport of lunatics in British West Africa', in *Beyond the State*, ed. Anna Greenwood (Cambridge: Cambridge University Press, 2016), p. 119.
9 Lindsey, 'Halting the Tide', pp. 77–86. Bob Carter, Clive Harris, and Shirley Joshi, 'The 1951–55 Conservative Government and the Racialization of Black Immigration', in *Inside Babylon: The Caribbean Diaspora in Britain*, eds Winston James and Clive Harris (London: Verso, 1993), pp. 57–8.
10 Hampshire, *Citizenship and Belonging*, p. 21. Hansen, *Citizenship and Immigration*, p. 59; Dummett and Nicol, *Subjects, Citizens*, p. 178; Karatani, *Defining British Citizenship*, p. 128; Lindsey, 'Halting the Tide', pp. 80–2.
11 Paul, *Whitewashing Britain*, pp. 151–3.
12 Wills, *Lovers and Strangers*, p. 57.
13 Paul, *Whitewashing Britain*, p. 152.

14 Ibid., pp. 152–3, 160; Hampshire, *Citizenship and Belonging*, p. 21; Karatani, *Defining British Citizenship*, p. 128.
15 Lindsey, 'Halting the Tide', pp. 88–9.
16 Paul, *Whitewashing Britain*, p. 143.
17 Smith, 'From Promising Settler', pp. 505–7.
18 Quoted in Paul, *Whitewashing Britain*, p. 142.
19 See, for instance, the debate over the renewal of the Empire Settlement Act in 1952. *Parliamentary Debates, Commons*, 5th Ser., Vol. 499, 21 April 1952, Cols 72, 89–90, 98, 115–16, 120.
20 *Parliamentary Debates, Commons*, 5th Ser., Vol. 497, 5 March 1952, Col. 616. *Parliamentary Debates, Commons*, 5th Ser., Vol. 499, 21 April 1952, Col. 101. *Parliamentary Debates, Commons*, 5th Ser., Vol. 500, 7 May 1952, Cols 495–6.
21 *Parliamentary Debates, Commons*, 5th Ser., Vol. 500, 7 May 1952, Col. 492. See also *Parliamentary Debates, Commons*, 5th Ser., Vol. 499, 21 April 1952, Col. 132.
22 TNA, DO 35/10220, 'Migration Council Activities Statement', 6 July 1953.
23 See, for instance, the 1951 publication *Operation British Commonwealth*, NASA, A326, Box 7.
24 See, for instance, covering correspondence, TNA, DO 35/10220.
25 TNA, LAB 8/2736, 'British Emigration Policy: Report by Interdepartmental Committee of Officials', 1961, p. 8. See also Hammerton and Thomson, *Ten Pound Poms*, p. 30; Paul, *Whitewashing Britain*, pp. 53–5.
26 Sarah Stockwell, 'Greater Britain and its Decline: The View from Lambeth', in *The Break-up of Greater Britain*, eds Christian Damm Pederson and Stuart Ward (Manchester: Manchester University Press, 2021), p. 202.
27 Cmnd 1586, Commonwealth Relations Office, *Seventh Report of the Oversea Migration Board December 1961*, London: HMSO, 1961, 27.
28 Smith, 'Persistence and Privilege'.
29 Ibid.
30 At the creation of the Federation, the Federal government took control of immigration, although the territorial governments were able to influence policy. Mlambo, *White Immigration*, p. 15.
31 Julia Tischler, *Light and Power for a Multiracial Nation: The Kariba Dam Scheme in the Central African Federation* (Basingstoke: Palgrave Macmillan, 2013), pp. 24, 45.
32 This was also evident in the largest and most visible development project in the Federation, the Kariba Dam, which was framed as a benefit even to the African communities that it displaced. Ibid., p. 65.
33 Ibid., p. 2; Alison K. Shutt, *Manners Make a Nation: Racial Etiquette in Southern Rhodesia: 1910–1963* (Rochester: University of Rochester Press, 2015), pp. 103, 106.
34 Tischler, *Light and Power*, pp. 33, 65, 225.
35 Mlambo, *White Immigration*, p. 15.
36 For more on the Society for the Overseas Settlement of British Women see Smith, 'The Women's Branch'.

37 'Rhodesia Ends Restriction on Britons' *Daily Telegraph*, 10 August 1955; Ian Smith Papers, 1/78/004, 'Immigration Bulletin No.1' August 1955, pp. 2–5; TNA: DO 35/10184, 'Brief on Migration to the Federation of Rhodesia and Nyasaland'.
38 Ian Smith Papers, 1/78/004, Immigration Policy, 24 October 1955, pp. 3–5; 'Immigration Bulletin No.1', August 1955, pp. 2–5.
39 TNA, CO 1015/1248, Annex A, The Federation of Rhodesia and Nyasaland Assisted Passage Scheme for Immigrants from the United Kingdom, 18 January 1958.
40 TNA, LAB 13/985, *Wiltshire Times*, 8 March 1955.
41 TNA, LAB 13/985, 'Achievement: Modern Living in Rhodesia and Nyasaland', p. 8.
42 Ibid., p. 3.
43 For an interrogation of this anti-slavery mythology particularly in regard to Livingstone see Landeg White, *Magomero: Portrait of an African Village* (Cambridge: Cambridge University Press, 1987), p. 18.
44 TNA, LAB 13/985, 'Achievement: Modern Living in Rhodesia and Nyasaland', p. 41.
45 TNA, CO 1015/1248, Press Communique No. 864, B.D. Goldberg's Statement, 29 October 1957. The issue of land was particularly sensitive and there were also objections to increased European settlement by African politicians in Nyasaland. As a result, officials in Colonial Office and Commonwealth Relations Office were hesitant to provide too much public support to immigration schemes proposed by the Federal and Southern Rhodesian government. TNA, CO 1015/1248, Submission agreed with Commonwealth Relations Office on Mr Mustoe's Letter to the Secretary of State About Migration to the Central African Territories, undated.
46 TNA, LAB 13/985, *Wiltshire Times*, 8 March 1955.
47 TNA, LAB 13/985, 'A New Life in the Federation of Rhodesia and Nyasaland: Facts and Figures for the Immigrant', p. 2.
48 TNA, LAB 13/985, IMM. 20, Form No. 1 (S), 'Application by a British Subject to Enter the Federation of Rhodesia and Nyasaland as an Immigrant'.
49 TNA, LAB 13/985, 'Achievement: Modern Living in Rhodesia and Nyasaland' pp. 6–7. See also NAZ, FG-P/HIG, 'There's a Welcome for you in Rhodesia and Nyasaland', 1955.
50 TNA, LAB 13/985, W.H. Hammond, Immigration Advisor to the High Commissioner, undated circular letter.
51 TNA, LAB 13/985, Form 2, Immigration Questionnaire.
52 This is in line with long-running concerns about racial fitness in Britain itself. Stephen Howe, 'When (if ever) did Empire End? "Internal Decolonisation" in British Culture since the 1950s', in *The British Empire in the 1950s: Retreat or Revival?*, ed. Martin Lynn (Basingstoke: Palgrave Macmillan, 2006), p. 219.
53 TNA, LAB 13/985, 'A New Life in the Federation of Rhodesia and Nyasaland: Facts and Figures for the Immigrant', p. 1.
54 Ian Smith Papers, 1/78/004, Immigration Policy, 24 October 1955, p. 5.

55 Ian Smith Papers, 1/78/004, Immigration Policy, 24 October 1955, pp. 1–2, 5. See also the card itself, NAZ, S3609142, Local Advisory Immigration Committees, 'Welcome to Rhodesia and Nyasaland'. For more on the role of these associations in forming a unified white Rhodesian identity, see Chapter 7.
56 Josiah Brownell, 'The Hole in Rhodesia's Bucket: White Emigration and the End of Settler Rule', *Journal of South African Studies* 34:3 (2008), 595–6.
57 TNA, LAB 13/985, 'Bricklayers for Rhodesia: Emigration by Air' *Manchester Guardian*, 31 December 1957; 'Immigrants end hunger strike', *Liverpool Post*, 24 March 1958: 'Protest March by Immigrants: 2 Scots in Rhodesia end Hunger strike', *Scotsman*, 24 March 1958.
58 Ian Smith Papers, 1/78/006, S.R.C. (57) 114, 'Deportations and Repatriations', 12 June 1957.
59 Though efforts to increase the white population intensified in the 1960s, Brownell downplays similar immigration drives in the 1940s and 1950s. Brownell, *Collapse of Rhodesia*, pp. 17, 14. Alois Mlambo's work is concerned with the period up until the establishment of the Federation. Mlambo, *White Immigration*.
60 Brownell, *British Immigration to South Africa*, p. 43.
61 Such concerns had long been expressed in the English-speaking press, given the increase in white emigration to Southern Rhodesia and elsewhere from 1949. See, for instance, NASA, A2, File 158, Press clippings, *The Star*, 8 November 1950. Rates of emigration remained high through the 1950s. Peberdy, *Selecting Immigrants*, pp. 257–8. Rates of white migration from South Africa to the Rhodesias showed a steady increase after the war, reaching a peak of 12,916 in 1951 before the imposition of quotas described above. From 1952 to 1957, they averaged between 7,000 and 9,000 before dropping to approximately 5,000 annually from 1958 to 1961 and then approximately 2,500 up until 1970. The 1960s onwards saw higher rates of white migration from the Rhodesias to South Africa. Brownell, *British Immigration to South Africa*, p. 178.
62 Gwendolyn Carter points out that the 1949 Act had only a limited effect on the 1953 election given that most of the recent immigrants who were denied citizenship lived in urban United Party strongholds rather than marginal electoral areas. Carter, *Politics of Inequality*, pp. 48–60. This Act like similar, contemporary legislation in other Commonwealth countries including the United Kingdom aimed to clarify citizenship status in the emerging Commonwealth. The South African Act was distinctive in that it did not include the term 'British subject' or 'Commonwealth citizen' indicative of a common status.
63 Peberdy, *Selecting Immigrants*. The Tomlinson Commission concerned the economic development of the so-called 'Bantustans' or African 'homelands' came to form a pillar of the apartheid ideology of 'separate development'. See Saul Dubow, *Apartheid: 1948–1994* (Oxford: Oxford University Press 2014), pp. 61, 66–7, 108.
64 Brownell, *British Immigration to South Africa*, p. 47.

65 NASA, MBN 2, Ref. MIN 2/14, Vol. 1, Text of a speech made by Mr W.C. Naude, Representative of the Union of South Africa at the 38th Meeting of the Intergovernmental Committee for European Migration, 1 October 1956.
66 Brownell, *British Immigration to South Africa*, p. 43.
67 NASA, MBN 2, Ref. MIN 2/14, Vol. 1, T.E. Donges (Minister of the Interior) to Harold Tittman (Director of ICEM), 14 December 1956; NASA, BTS Vol. 44, Ref. 59/5, V.G. Stock (Secretary for External Affairs) to Consul-General of the Unions of South Africa, New York, 7 August 1959.
68 NASA, MBN 2, Ref. MIN 2/14, Vol. 2, 'More hope for immigration', *The Star*, 7 October 1957.
69 NASA, BTS Ref. 59/3, Vol. 1, 'S. Africa to offer homes to Indonesian refugees', *The Star*, 10 December 1957, p. 27. For more on this expulsion see Elizabeth Buettner, *Europe After Empire: Decolonization, Society, and Culture* (Cambridge: Cambridge University Press, 2016), pp. 218–22.
70 NASA, BTS Ref. 59/3, Vol. 1, 'South Africa Opens Doors to Settlers', *The Christian Science Monitor*, 17 June 1960. On official sympathy for white migrants from other parts of Africa see H.F. Verwoerd to A.T. Culwick, 13 August 1960, Annexure L, in Brownell, *British Immigration to South Africa*, p. 177.
71 Ibid., pp. 47–8, 128–9.
72 The MEI received a grant of £5,000 in 1960 and both organisations received an annual grant of R12,000 for 'aftercare' beginning in 1961, this grant gradually increased reaching R72,000 by 1969. Ibid., pp. 135–6. For more on the MEI see Roland Slater, 'Die Maatskappy vir Europese Immigrasie: A Study of the Cultural Assimilation and Naturalisation of European Immigrants to South Africa 1949–1994' (Thesis, University of Stellenbosch, 2007).
73 According to Hobsbawm, such 'broadcasting' was only one part of this equation, it must resonate with the public to be successful. Eric Hobsbawm, 'Mass Producing Traditions: Europe, 1870–1914', in *The Invention of Tradition*, eds Eric Hobsbawm and Terence Ranger (Cambridge: Cambridge University Press, 1983), pp. 263–4.
74 T. Dunbar Moodie, *The Rise of Afrikanerdom: Power, Apartheid, and the Afrikaner Civil Religion* (Berkeley: University of California Press, 1975).
75 John Lambert, 'South African British? Or Dominion South Africans? The Evolution of an Identity in the 1910s and 1920s', *South African Historical Journal* 43:1 (November 2000), 213–14; Bill Nasson, *Springboks on the Somme: South Africa in the Great War, 1914–1918* (Johannesburg and New York: Penguin, 2007).
76 This happened without fail when I mentioned that I was studying British migration in South Africa.
77 1820 Memorial Settlers' Association, *The 1820 Memorial Settlers' Association, its aims, objects, constitution, organisation, etc.*, 1920, p. 2.
78 Public holidays changed again at the end of apartheid with the institution of Human Rights Day in March, commemorating the Sharpeville massacre, Freedom Day, which commemorates the first democratic election held in

South Africa on 27 April 1994, Youth Day, which commemorates the Soweto Uprising, and National Women's Day which commemorates the role of women in a protest against pass-laws in 1956. The Day of the Vow was renamed the Day of Reconciliation.
79 Thompson, *Natalians First*, pp. 151–74; Lambert, 'The Last Outpost', pp. 165–75.
80 Dubow, *Apartheid*, p. 85.
81 Hampshire, *Citizenship and Belonging*, pp. 2–3.

5

The demographic defence of the white nation, 1960–75

A 1963 article in the *Financial Times* highlighted rising rates of emigration from the United Kingdom, detailing the assistance would-be migrants could receive from the governments of Australia, New Zealand, Canada, South Africa and the Federation of Rhodesia and Nyasaland. While Australia received the largest number of British migrants, the article reported that migration to South Africa was rapidly increasing. Intending emigrants cited the weather and employment opportunities as motivations, as well their perceptions that the United Kingdom was in decline:

> Comments like ... 'we are not able to dictate terms on anything anymore', and 'Britain has had it' are frequent ... The semi-skilled tool-store man, with his wife, two children, and grandmother, aged 69 ... wants to give his children more scope. 'We don't really have a reason, have got all we want, anyway: a house, a car, but in Brentford the coloured people have taken over and they are not nice to work with.'[1]

The connection between the idea of 'more scope', of greater opportunities available elsewhere, especially for the next generation, was often related to a perception of British decline, which was frequently, as in this quotation, linked to the increasing presence of people of colour in Britain.[2]

Solutions to the perceived problem of national decline were often articulated in terms of migration both at the level of the individual and of the state. Many British emigrants, like the 'semi-skilled tool-store man' framed their decision to move as a way of attaining a better future than was available in the United Kingdom while policymakers looked to migration and its restriction as a solution to racial and demographic trends they saw as threatening to national stability and cohesion. In the United Kingdom this largely took the form of increased restrictions on migrants of colour from the Commonwealth, though it also appeared in concerns about mass emigration from Britain. In South Africa and Rhodesia it took the form of the recruitment of white immigrants to shore up their minority settler populations.

The demographic defence of the white nation, 1960–75   125

This chapter examines policies surrounding migration in the United Kingdom, Rhodesia and South Africa in the 1960s and early 1970s alongside the experiences of migrants. It argues that in all three cases, the end of formal imperial ties led to state efforts to strengthen and preserve nations imagined in racial terms as white. The challenge that decolonisation brought to the previously held racialised order of things contributed to a backlash in the 1960s and 1970s, which can be seen in both the intensification of segregation and racial oppression in South Africa and Rhodesia, and the racism and opposition to immigration in Britain signified by the popularity of Enoch Powell and the rise of groups from the National Front to the Monday Club.[3] This backlash was also evident in migration policy. It is well known that the migration policies of Rhodesia and South Africa in this period were centred on race. This chapter places this history in broader context and highlights the related processes and ideologies underway in the United Kingdom.

Ongoing connections including migration flows have been obscured by the political separation between the United Kingdom and both South Africa and Rhodesia that occurred in the 1960s. South Africa's declaration of republic in 1961 and Rhodesia's Unilateral Declaration of Independence in 1965 broke formal ties with Britain and the Commonwealth to continue explicitly racially based settler colonial rule. Both had come under increasing pressure to end minority rule, especially from newly independent countries in the Commonwealth and the United Nations. In the case of Rhodesia, the refusal of Britain to grant independence without majority rule prompted the Smith regime to cut ties unilaterally. This commitment to minority rule was also reflected in both countries' immigration policies. As prior chapters have shown, these had long discriminated on the basis of race, but in the 1960s and 1970s both nations recruited immigrants they defined as white more actively than ever before as they sought to mount a demographic defence of minority rule on a rapidly decolonising continent. Much of the recruitment effort focused on the United Kingdom, which was the largest source of immigrants to both countries throughout the period.

As South Africa and Rhodesia embarked on immigration drives, formal restrictions on migration from the Commonwealth to the United Kingdom were enacted with the Commonwealth Immigrants Acts of 1962 and 1968. Though these laws ostensibly regulated the entry of all Commonwealth citizens, as Kathleen Paul and others have shown, they were intended to restrict Commonwealth migrants of colour even as they allowed for continuing migration from the white Dominions.[4] Amid concerns over the loss of skilled labour, the British government also moved away from its previous support of British emigration to the Commonwealth, decreasing financial subsidies and ending them completely in 1972.

This chapter begins with a discussion of the dramatic increase in British emigration in this period – especially to South Africa – and how conditions in the United Kingdom including the increasing numbers of migrants of colour from the Commonwealth contributed to the decisions of many Britons to move. It then examines the South African and Rhodesian immigration drives of the 1960s and 1970s and concludes with a discussion of how British migration policy also aimed towards a demographic defence of the white nation through restriction and retention rather than recruitment.

'I've no wish for coloured grandchildren': Race and the decision to move to southern Africa

From 1963, there was a large increase in emigration from the United Kingdom overall, which reached a peak of 309,000 in 1967 and largely continued at these higher rates throughout the 1970s and 1980s, and into the 1990s, with a small slowdown from 1982 to 1984.[5] There was also a dramatic increase in British migration to South Africa in the 1960s, which continued, with periodic short downturns until the mid 1980s. Rates of migration to Rhodesia, although much lower than those to South Africa, increased from the mid 1960s and began to decline from the mid 1970s.

Though South African recruitment efforts were also aimed at continental European countries, especially the Netherlands, they were most successful in the United Kingdom. British immigrants had long been the largest group arriving in South Africa, and remained so until the late 1970s, when they were overtaken temporarily by those leaving Rhodesia in the run-up to the end of minority rule in 1979, many of whom had, as described in earlier chapters, originally moved to Rhodesia from Britain.[6] The 1960s increase in immigration to South Africa was more gradual than in the immediate post-1945 years, but also longer lived. Aside from short-term dips in British migration to South Africa in 1973 and again from 1977 to 1979, rates remained high in this period.[7] Despite the increasing intensity of the anti-apartheid struggle, rates of immigration from Britain only began to decrease permanently in 1983, and only dropped below the average rates of the 1950s from 1986, as the South African government wound down its subsidised migration scheme.

In Southern Rhodesia the early 1960s saw a decline in immigration likely caused by uncertainty over the looming break-up of the Central African Federation. The same period also saw an increase in emigration with a negative net migration of Europeans from 1961 to 1964. This was followed by a recovery in the late 1960s and early 1970s as post-UDI Rhodesia implemented incentives and subsidies to attract white migrants. By the

Table 5.1 White migration to Southern Rhodesia/Rhodesia and South Africa, 1960–79

Year	'European' immigration to Southern Rhodesia/Rhodesia[i]	'White' immigration to South Africa[ii]	Immigration to South Africa from the United Kingdom[iii]	Percentage of immigrants to South Africa from the United Kingdom
1960	7,430	9,789	2,292	23.41
1961	6,627	16,309	2,323	14.24
1962	6,062	20,916	4,970	23.76
1963	5,093	37,960	10,138	26.71
1964	7,000	40,865	12,807	31.34
1965	11,128	38,326	12,012	31.34
1966	6,418	48,048	13,130	27.33
1967	9,618	38,937	12,993	33.37
1968	11,864	40,548	16,044	39.57
1969	10,929	41,466	16,954	40.89
1970	12,227	41,523	21,323	51.35
1971	14,743	35,845	17,347	48.39
1972	13,966	32,776	15,828	48.29
1973	9,433	24,016	11,057	46.04
1974	9,649	35,910	17,380	48.40
1975	12,425	50,464	24,805	49.15
1976	7,782	46,239	20,347	44.06
1977	5,730	24,822	7,304	29.43
1978	4,360	18,669	4,550	24.37
1979	3,288	18,680	4,260	22.81

[i] Immigration statistics were not collected systematically for country of previous residence, citizenship or birth for Southern Rhodesia/Rhodesia. Figures for 1960 to 1970, *Monthly Migration and Tourist Statistics for March 1970* (Salisbury: Central Statistical Office, 1970). Figures for the Federation period (up to 1963) do not include migration from Northern Rhodesia and Nyasaland. Figures from 1971 to 1979, Brownell, *The Collapse of Rhodesia*, p. 125.
[ii] All data from South Africa as follows: figures for 1960 to 1964, Republic of South Africa Bureau of Statistics, *Report No. 286: Statistics of Immigrants and Emigrants 1924–1964*, (Pretoria: The Government Printer, 1964), p. 4; figures for 1965 to 1979, Peberdy, *Selecting Immigrants*, pp. 276–85, from 1960–69.
[iii] Figures based on country of previous residence.

1970s, the intensification of the Second Chimurenga, the war between the Rhodesian state and anti-colonial forces, meant that white immigration fell and white emigration (often to South Africa) soared in the run-up to the end of minority rule in 1979 and thereafter. The last peak of immigration to Rhodesia in the mid 1970s was largely due to white Portuguese migrants arriving from Mozambique and Angola as these nations became independent.[8]

The incentives offered by the South African and Rhodesian governments, discussed in the next section, played an important role in the increase in British migration in the 1960s. So too did the situation in the United Kingdom. The lingering humiliation of Suez, the so-called permissive society and the shifting demographics of the United Kingdom, meant that many people believed that Britain was in decline, despite relative prosperity, rising living standards and low unemployment.[9] A sociological study of 200 migrants arriving in Durban from the United Kingdom in 1967 found that they 'often expressed a general disgust with the United Kingdom'. This was often connected to racism: 'One said that a Pakistani family had come to live next door to them ... Some ... disliked the race policies of the United Kingdom ... They said that social security was given to people who did not want to work, such as Pakistanis and West Indians and also White layabouts.'[10] As James Hammerton and Alistair Thomson have shown, many migrants to Australia in this period expressed negative assessments about Britain's future and complained about high taxes and low wages. Hammerton and Thomson also found that for many, the arrival of people of colour 'contributed to white pessimism about the future'.[11] For those who felt threatened by the increasing number of Commonwealth migrants of colour, Australia, whose 'white Australia' policy would only be dismantled in 1973, and South Africa and Rhodesia, with their racially based systems of discrimination and explicit white privilege, were appealing. In this context, somewhat counter-intuitively, white flight could mean a move to Africa rather than a retreat to the suburbs. Regardless of whether they understood this in racial terms, migrants were attracted by the opportunities and lifestyle available to them because of the discriminatory and exploitative policies enacted by the South African and Rhodesian states.

Understanding migrant motivations can be difficult, especially since the decision to move was often based on a combination of things including economic opportunity, the perception of the possibility for an improved lifestyle, pre-existing relationships with people abroad, prior travel to a destination country, or government incentives.[12] Indeed, as Conway and Leonard have argued, migrants to South Africa often moved because of 'serendipity and contingency' rather than as a result of 'exhaustive planning or careful deliberation'.[13] The way that migrants retrospectively make sense of their decision may also be, as Karen O'Reilly puts it, a *post hoc* justification, constructed from the perspective of the new context within which they have found themselves'.[14] This is especially true if migrants are asked about their decisions years later. The role that the changing racial demographics of the United Kingdom or the institutionalised racial segregation of southern Africa played in migration decisions is particularly difficult to ascertain. Migrants interviewed decades later may have been influenced by changed attitudes to race and apartheid and different ideas of what is socially acceptable to say. In oral history interviews conducted by the author from 2009 to 2012 many migrants, for example, said that they were not really aware of apartheid in South Africa or the reality of segregation and racism in Rhodesia when they made the decision to move.[15] It is entirely possible that some migrants had only vague ideas about the racial politics of South Africa and Rhodesia, especially earlier in the 1960s. It is also possible that they took for granted or did not really question the racial hierarchies of these nations and their own resulting racial privilege. They were, after all, hierarchies grounded in centuries of British imperial practice and cultural representations, albeit ones that were always evolving and contextually specific. But the possibility also remains that for some, stating ignorance or even coming to believe retrospectively that they had not known, or avoiding the topic, is a way to evade complicity with apartheid or racism and to smooth out potential contradictions in the narratives they have constructed about their lives.[16]

Some migrants interviewed by the author did acknowledge their reservations about the racial policies of Rhodesia and South Africa. Carolyn Hastings went to South Africa on the government-sponsored subsidised migration scheme in 1970 with a friend.[17] Rather than a permanent migration, she saw this as a chance to travel with her nursing qualification, 'a kind of a passport to go anywhere'. She had originally intended to go first to Canada but because it was more complicated to have her nursing training recognised, Hastings and her friend decided to go straight to South Africa. She had always wanted to spend time in Africa as her parents had lived in Kenya, the Sudan and Swaziland, where she was born and lived until her family returned to the United Kingdom when she was four years old. Her father worked for the British Empire Leprosy Relief Association and her mother was a teacher. Hastings mentioned that her brother, who had taken a position in independent Zambia as a teacher, gave her a hard time about going to South Africa because of the apartheid regime. She reflected:

> I actually knew very little about it. I knew apartheid existed insofar as I knew that the whites were privileged, but practically I shouldn't think I knew more than that there were separate lines in post office queues and things. Umm. [pause] So I was a bit silly in that sense. I mean I could have investigated far more before I went. But we were offered a job ...[18]

Here the opportunity for travel, work and a cheap fare along with her long-running desire to see Africa combined to persuade her to go.

This kind of ambivalence continued once she was in South Africa. Hastings worked first at a hospital for white and 'Coloured' patients in

Pietermaritzburg.[19] Reflecting on this she mentioned her regret that she never pushed harder to spend some time working at the hospital for Black patients further out of town and that she particularly enjoyed her time working at Victoria Hospital in Wynberg near Cape Town where she was able to work on the 'Coloured' wards which 'felt more normal'. She also mentioned having 'furious arguments' with her South African boyfriend about apartheid. Nevertheless, the overall sense in her account of her time in South Africa and later Rhodesia was positive. She travelled extensively and described the warm welcome she received along with the beauty of the landscape and wildlife.

This kind of ambivalence or concern about apartheid was not uniformly the case, some migrants admitted that it was part of what made South Africa appealing. Another interviewee, Ian Jones, who had moved to South Africa in 1968, mentioned as one of the attractions the idea that 'Africa looked very glamorous then with ... lots of black people standing around to do the work'. He mentioned reading pamphlets produced by the South African government and the appeal of having servants:

> They all said that every South African has their own servant. They would have a picture of a black nanny in some nice pink or yellow overalls doing the ironing. So that was always pushed as a great thing ... Your wife could do things apart from slave and do the housework and you had a gardener as well.[20]

This vision of a lifestyle where Black servants rather than your wife would do all the domestic labour, particularly the seemingly unthinking use of the term slave, reflect the acceptance of a racial (and gender) hierarchy, and speak to the appeal of class elevation, the promise that even working-class immigrants to South Africa, like Jones, an air-conditioning mechanic, could, because of their whiteness, enjoy a lifestyle that was unattainable to all but the extremely wealthy elite in Britain.[21]

Some of those interviewed shortly after their migration were similarly candid about their desire to move away from increasingly diverse areas of the United Kingdom. An immigrant from Lancashire profiled in the *Rhodesia Herald* in 1968, stated this decision to move was in part because of the 'flood' of immigrants of colour to the United Kingdom.[22] John Stone's 1973 study of British immigration to South Africa cites a number of migrants who mentioned the arrival of immigrants of colour in their neighbourhoods in explaining their decision to move.[23] Stone argues that political agreement with the racial ideology of the apartheid state was not the primary reason that most migrants moved to South Africa. Yet, the racial motivations of many are apparent. One man stated, for example, that '[i]t was particularly the rising number of Coloureds ... I'm not prejudiced but I've no wish for Coloured grandchildren'.[24] Here, his claim of not being 'prejudiced' is undercut by this concern about the possibility of his children starting a family with a person of colour.[25] Others interviewed by Stone also repeated the inaccurate, although common, perception that immigrants came to take advantage of the welfare state and were given priority over the British-born as part of the rationale for moving.[26] One man, discussing how the housing shortage in Britain contributed to his decision to move, stated, 'We couldn't get anywhere to live … we had waited three years for a flat while three hundred Coloureds moved to new flats in Paddington.'[27] He concluded that the arrival of immigrants of colour was to blame for his difficulties and perhaps a more generalised decline. One migrant was even aware of the apparent contradiction involved in going to Africa to avoid Black people in Britain, 'Some parts of Britain *are* black … I was concerned [pause] … and yet I've come out here.'[28] Yet, this is not quite so contradictory a move as he implied. Living as part of a privileged racial minority in South Africa, supported by the government in his employment and housing search was quite different to living in a country or neighbourhood, whose increasing racial diversity he viewed in negative terms.

Another respondent included what he called 'racial mixing in Britain' as one of a long list of reasons to move, including the election of a Labour government, his fear of renewed austerity, the weather, high taxes, his previous experience of South Africa in the merchant navy and dislike of his mother-in-law.[29] This demonstrates the complexity of such decisions, but racial motivations should not be disregarded simply because they are one among many reasons to move. One respondent illustrates how these various factors could merge into a single explanation. He stated that he had moved to South Africa because he came to believe that the 'British reaction' to the 1960 Sharpeville massacre was 'biased' after hearing 'glowing reports about the work and the weather' from friends in South Africa.[30] Here the perceived advantages of moving for a better climate and economic opportunity become grounds to dismiss one of the most infamous, well-documented and publicised atrocities committed by the apartheid regime, of which the respondent is clearly well informed, specifically mentioning the Anglican Bishop of Johannesburg, Ambrose Reeves, who was deported from South Africa because of his criticisms of the government over Sharpeville. This idea of bias against South Africa was also reflected by British migrants to South Africa interviewed for the *Daily Sketch* in 1968. Philip Jones, for instance, a 'newspaperman' who had moved from Cardiff to the coastal city of Port Elizabeth with his family 'gave an emphatic, "No."' when asked whether South African politics bothered him, adding that he was 'more bothered' by 'those who knock South Africa without knowing the background'.[31] Jones and the other migrants and prospective migrants interviewed highlighted the low rate of taxation, the climate and the lifestyle available to them in South Africa, including domestic help and larger houses as part of South Africa's appeal.

Setting aside the question of whether British immigrants would have admitted the ideological attraction of apartheid, at the time or retrospectively, many were plainly attracted to the lifestyle and opportunities offered by the racial privilege made possible by the apartheid regime, mentioning high wages or an increase in status.[32] Many came to agree with apartheid after arrival. In Stone's sample of British migrants in the late 1960s and early 1970s, 76 per cent stated that they were either 'favourable' or 'very favourable' to apartheid after they had lived in South Africa.[33] Whether or not British immigrants agreed with the racial policies of those states, they certainly benefited from them and were attracted by the resulting social mobility.

The politics of recruitment: Selling South Africa and Rhodesia

The higher standards of living available in South Africa and Rhodesia were featured in the recruitment campaigns of both nations. In the 1960s South Africa and Rhodesia more actively recruited white immigrants, offering new incentives including subsidised passages. They also embarked on publicity campaigns highlighting the climate and way of life available in southern Africa, drawing on tropes that had long been used to promote European settlement. Like earlier guides and pamphlets, this literature portrayed South Africa and Rhodesia as modern places of opportunity and highlighted the social mobility and outdoor lifestyle available to white immigrants, a lifestyle implicitly underpinned by racial privilege.

Two years after the Unilateral Declaration of Independence in 1967, the Rhodesian government launched a new drive for white migrants, including assisted passages comprising of a £60 grant towards the fare, the reimbursement of expenses to the port of embarkation in their home country, transit expenses to their final destination in Rhodesia and in some cases board and lodging on arrival. This assistance was granted on the condition that migrants remained in Rhodesia for three years. Those who left Rhodesia earlier would be required to repay the costs *pro rata* based on how long they had stayed.[34]

In South Africa, incentives for white migrants included subsidised passages, onward travel and temporary housing as well as help with finding permanent housing and employment. Approved immigrants were offered the cost of a passage up to R120, roughly the same as the £60 offered by the Rhodesian state, and comparable to the £10 subsidised passage to Australia.[35] The South African scheme was more generous than these other schemes given the additional assistance provided and that it did not require a period of minimum residency.[36] New arrivals could arrange to be met by officials of the Department of Immigration who would offer advice and assistance. Second-class train fares to their final destination were provided by the state along with temporary accommodation if required.[37] Ian Jones, mentioned above, who arrived in 1968, even described receiving beer money on the weekends from immigration officials who came to the transit accommodation where he was staying.[38] These recruitment efforts also extended to white South Africans who had moved abroad. Those who returned to South Africa after an absence of more than three years were eligible for loans, travel grants, temporary accommodation and assistance with finding employment.[39]

To encourage white immigration, the South African government created a substantial administrative structure. The new Department of Immigration, established in 1961, employed 258 staff in South Africa and expanded overseas adding new immigration offices in Brussels, Athens, Lisbon, Paris, Milan, Vienna and Munich to the already existing ones in Berne, The Hague, Hamburg, Cologne, London and Rome. The largest of these remained the office in London which had twelve assistant attachés for immigration followed by The Hague, which had four and Cologne, which had three.[40] To provide a sense of the assistance provided, in 1966, department officials met 37,041 immigrants, more than 77 per cent of those arriving, provided accommodation at government expense to 8,695 and placed 6,249 in employment.[41]

Recruitment efforts included the distribution of illustrated pamphlets in seven European languages, the screening of a film highlighting conditions in South Africa, a slide show, and advertisements in newspapers across Europe (in Britain, the Netherlands, Belgium, France, West Germany and Austria).[42] The Department of Immigration also invited foreign officials to come to South Africa to observe the 'prospects offered by South Africa as an immigration country' and see how well their own nationals had settled. By 1968 South Africa had hosted four officials from the Netherlands, two from West Germany, one from Belgium and one from Switzerland. In addition, successful immigrants were sent on recruitment tours of their countries of origin. As this suggests, the preference was for immigrants from northern Europe, especially the Netherlands, though, all who would be classified by the apartheid state as white and met the health and financial criteria were eligible for these subsidies. Out of solidarity with other minority-ruled and colonial regimes in the region, the South African government did not provide incentives to white migrants from these countries but did provide them the same customs concessions (in terms of importing personal property), access to social services and assistance with finding employment on arrival enjoyed by other immigrants.[43] In addition to these initiatives, though long-running health and financial or skills-based restrictions remained in place, the South African government streamlined the process for potential immigrants, allowing overseas staff to grant permanent residence in most cases, with only difficult cases referred to the Immigrants Selection Board in South Africa.[44] Taken together, these policies reflect a dramatic shift towards the active recruitment of white immigrants.

As discussed in Chapter 4, the South African government also provided subsidies to private organisations including Samorgan, which recruited migrants in the United Kingdom, and Transa, which recruited migrants in West Germany, Switzerland and Austria.[45] State funding for organisations focused on the care of migrants after arrival and their integration in white South African society also continued. As well the 1820 Memorial Settlers' Association, which focused on British migrants, the Maatskaapy vir Europese Immigrasie (the Society for European Immigration), which focused on Dutch migrants, from 1963, the South African government also provided support to the Southern Africa League, founded in Kenya, which aided those coming from newly independent African countries in the wake of decolonisation.[46]

Promotional materials emphasised the assistance available to new immigrants. A series of pamphlets provided extremely detailed information about every step of the immigration process. *Assisted Immigration to the Republic of South Africa* outlined the assisted immigration programme and how to apply for it. *The Immigrant's Journey to South Africa* laid out in detail the steps of the journey by air or sea, what to pack, and even what kind of clothing would be suitable on arrival. *The Immigrant's Arrival in the Republic of South Africa* explained the warm welcome that immigrants would receive and that flights would be met by officials wearing distinctive rosettes in the orange, white and blue of the South African flag who could provide assistance.[47]

These pamphlets emphasised the attractions of the climate and depicted an idealised outdoor lifestyle available in South Africa.[48] The cover of *Land of Sunshine* (Figure 5.1) shows a young blond girl on the beach hugging a giant ball, with a modern resort in the background. The pamphlet includes pages of data about the climate, average temperatures and rainfall and numerous scenes of the outdoors including several beach scenes, an attractive young woman surfing in a bikini, fishing, hiking, horse racing, and sailing.[49] These brochures sought to draw on the appeal of South Africa's climate to would-be British emigrants. After the freezing winter of 1962–63, Stanley Uys wrote in *The Scotsman* of immigrants to South Africa: 'They wanted to escape from Britain's climate. They wanted an outdoor life and

The demographic defence of the white nation, 1960–75 135

Figure 5.1 Department of Immigration, *Land of Sunshine*, 1970.

better prospects for their children.'[50] As this statement and the frequent depiction of children in the promotional materials suggest, the idea of social mobility for the next generation was a powerful draw.

This is also reflected in *The Immigrant Housewife in South Africa*, which emphasises family life and promises a luxurious lifestyle. It is illustrated with numerous photographs of holiday destinations from the beach to the mountains. Assuming married women will stay at home, the pamphlet emphasises the welcome that new immigrants will receive and the opportunities for social contact. The guidance on the hiring and management of domestic servants also signals the potential for social mobility, which as noted above, was appealing to many. Though a paragraph at the end does include a brief mention of women's role in public life and the professional world, the pamphlet primarily emphasises women's domestic role, in line with the patriarchal and pro-natalist policies of the South African state.[51]

The promotional materials also highlight the opportunities for home ownership available in South Africa, another indication of the potential for social mobility. *Housing Facilities in the Republic of South Africa* includes images of suburban homes and gardens as well as modern blocks of flats.[52] In later editions produced in 1972 and 1975/6, the illustrations primarily feature suburban detached houses, with only a few depictions of flats, perhaps in response to the greater appeal of a house and large garden.[53] Though acknowledging a housing shortage, these publications highlighted an ambitious government building plan and asserted that remaining shortages are the result of rapid industrial development. They promised that 'owning a house is within the reach of every family man' and describe a range of loan programmes available including employer-sponsored plans at below-market interest rates. The size of the houses available is also emphasised, complete with garage, servants' quarters and large gardens, underlined by the assertion that 'semi-detached houses are practically non-existent'.[54] Many of the images, such as Figure 5.2 below, depict children playing outside in large and lush gardens under the supervision of their fashionably dressed mothers, highlighting the opportunity for an outdoor family lifestyle.

The connection between appropriate housing for growing white families and the health of the nation is made explicit in the pamphlet, which opens with 'Suitable housing is the corner-stone of a happy family life and plays

Figure 5.2 'Playtime in the Garden', Department of Immigration, *Housing Facilities in the Republic of South Africa*, 1972.

an important role in the development of a nation'.⁵⁵ This, like the implicit assumption that white women will primarily be housewives and mothers, reflects the perceived importance to the South African state not only of recruiting white migrants but also of creating conditions for higher white fertility. Long-running official concerns about comparatively low rates of white fertility took on increasing urgency in the 1960s and 1970s.⁵⁶

Taken together, these pamphlets present South Africa as a modern country with a desirable lifestyle for white immigrants. They address many of the concerns cited by migrants regarding the United Kingdom including the weather, the housing shortage, high taxes and low wages. Black South Africans do not appear at all, not even as servants or service workers. Beach scenes, street scenes, depictions of schoolchildren and a housewife in a supermarket all exclude Black South Africans. Instead, the pamphlets feature the climate, the landscape and young, attractive white men and women engaged in a variety of leisure activities.

Though Rhodesia was less successful than South Africa in recruiting immigrants from Britain or elsewhere, the Smith regime employed similar tactics, emphasising the Rhodesian climate and the lifestyle available to a privileged racial minority. The 1965 publication *Rhodesia: Assisted Passages to Land of Sunshine: Golden Opportunity* depicted an outdoor way of life in a sunny climate. In landlocked Rhodesia, pool scenes replaced South African beach scenes as in the cover shown in Figure 5.3. Four attractive young white women in swimsuits are attended by two white men, who are more formally dressed in suits. The setting is luxurious, a building with Mediterranean-style arches in the background.⁵⁷

Inside, the pamphlet promises 'Opportunity, Sunshine and Dynamic Development' and describes Rhodesia as the 'modern Eldorado with unequalled riches in agriculture, mining and manufacturing for massive industrial immigration'. Like the South African publications, it promised 'pleasure at work and leisure', showing outdoor recreation in the bush and in swimming pools as well as modern workplaces where young, white men are shown with test tubes or banks of electrical equipment. The buildings shown are also modern, including 'Salisbury shopping centre' and 'Modern hospital, Bulawayo' emphasising, like the work scenes, the sophistication and development of Rhodesia, as well as the climate and opportunity for leisure. Like the South African promotional material, Black people do not appear, except in the background of one street scene, echoing nineteenth-century depictions of Africa as empty and in need of, to quote the pamphlet, a 'large intake of European population'.⁵⁸

Although the Rhodesian immigration drives were far less successful than their South African counterparts, both shared similar motivations. To survive as minority-ruled settler colonial regimes on a rapidly decolonising

138   Settlers at the end of empire

Figure 5.3 Department of Immigration and Tourism, *Rhodesia: Assisted Passages to the Land of Sunshine: Golden Opportunity*, 1965.

continent, officials in both countries believed it was crucial to increase their white populations. And, for reasons of history and language, the United Kingdom was the largest, though by no means the only, recruiting ground for new immigrants.

The politics of restriction and retention: British migration policy

Although the United Kingdom did not have the same kind of explicitly racist immigration regulations as South Africa and Rhodesia, successive British governments, Conservative and Labour alike, sought to control the entry of Commonwealth immigrants of colour. As discussed in Chapter 4, this was largely through informal means in the 1940s and 1950s, such as the deployment of propaganda to discourage would-be immigrants and measures to make it more difficult for them to gain passports and other identity documents in their countries of origin.⁵⁹ Beginning in 1962, however, the British state began to implement legal controls on immigration from the Commonwealth. At the same time, amid increasing concerns about the emigration of skilled workers – the so-called 'brain drain' – there was a move away from official support, including financial support, for British emigration to the Commonwealth.

These policies were implemented in a political landscape where many explicitly linked British decline to the immigration of Commonwealth immigrants of colour. This was increasingly articulated in the aftermath of the Nottingham and Notting Hill riots of 1958 and the racially charged Smethwick by-election of 1964. Probably the most notorious exponent of anti-immigrant sentiment, Enoch Powell, made a direct reference to emigration in his infamous 1968 'Rivers of Blood' speech. Powell, at that time Shadow Defence Secretary, referred to a 'quite ordinary working man' who had told him that he would emigrate if he had the money because, in what became one of the most infamous lines of an infamous speech, 'in 15 or 20 years' time the black man will have the whip hand over the white man'.⁶⁰ Here emigration is posed as a solution to what Powell and the 'ordinary working man' posit as the threat of increasing racial conflict in Britain and a future in which white domination was not only ended but reversed. Powell's public avowal of what were for many privately held views led to his dismissal from the shadow cabinet but also an outpouring of public support. Polling after the speech reveals a high level of agreement with Powell; Gallup recorded 74 per cent, Opinion Research Corporation 82 per cent and National Opinion Poll 67 per cent.⁶¹

Opposition to the immigration of people of colour from the Commonwealth played a large part in the passage of the 1962 Commonwealth Immigrants Act (CIA), which the Macmillan government hoped, as Home Secretary Rab Butler put it, would seem 'non-discriminatory' even though 'its restrictive effect is intended to, and would in fact, operate on coloured people almost exclusively'.⁶² Only those born in the United Kingdom or who held passports issued by the United Kingdom and their dependants would have an automatic right of abode. All other Commonwealth citizens were allowed admission to Britain under a system of employment permits based on whether they were sponsored by an employer or fulfilled categories based on education or skill. The Act made it easier for migrants from the white Dominions than other Commonwealth migrants in several ways including the classification of shorthand typists (many of whom were women from the Dominions) as professionals and eligible for visas under the Type B voucher, the recognition of any degree from Australia or New Zealand while only recognising a first-class honours degree from India or Pakistan and the blind eye shown to working-holidaymakers.⁶³

The 1968 CIA further tightened these restrictions. Passed in just five days, the legislation was prompted by concerns that the Africanisation policies of the Kenyan government would lead to the mass migration to Britain of Kenyan residents of South Asian descent. After independence up to 150,000 Kenyan residents of South Asian descent opted to retain their status as Citizens of the United Kingdom and Colonies (CUKC) and held passports issued under the authority of the British High Commissioner in Kenya. As a result they had the legal right of abode in the United Kingdom and many chose to exercise this right as they faced increasing difficulties under Kenyatta's government.[64] The 1968 Act revised the 1962 Act so that exemption from immigration controls would only be granted to those holders of CUKC passports who were themselves or had one parent who had been born, naturalised or adopted in the United Kingdom, thereby excluding the majority of Kenyan residents of Asian descent who had opted for CUKC passports. Highlighting the intent of the Act to exclude on racial grounds, Parliament had previously passed the British Nationality Act of 1964, which reaffirmed the right of white Kenyan residents to British citizenship and the right of abode in the United Kingdom.[65]

The 1971 Immigration Act made concrete this distinction based on descent. 'Patrials', largely from the former colonies of settlement, who could claim a parent or grandparent born in Britain, were unrestricted in their ability to live and work in the United Kingdom. Non-patrials were henceforth treated the same as 'aliens' from beyond the Commonwealth. Ostensibly passed to restrict the flow of immigrants, its true purpose was to restrict the flow of immigrants of colour, as through the implementation of patriality the Act actually expanded the pool of migrants with the automatic right of abode in the United Kingdom.[66] The 1981 British Nationality Act went even further, abolishing birthright citizenship and granting British nationality and the right of abode only to those with a parent born, adopted or naturalised in the United Kingdom.[67]

At the same time as this shift towards a more restrictive and racialised immigration policy, there was also increasing official concern about the growing volume of British emigration. These were often expressed in conjunction with concern over the arrival of people of colour in the United Kingdom, highlighting the implicit racism often underlying these discussions. During Prime Minister's Questions in January 1957, Cyril Osborne, MP for Louth, made an explicit link between the two asking for the government's policy, 'regarding the increase in emigration of young British men and women with high scientific qualifications, and the corresponding increase in immigration into this country of coloured people without tests of either health, technical skills or criminal record'.[68] Osborne was a long-time opponent of the immigration of people of colour and later a member of the Monday Club.⁶⁹ In his response Macmillan defended the health and conduct of Commonwealth immigrants and stated that there was no firm evidence about the emigration of scientists.

Even so, this link between emigration and immigration continued to appear in official discussions. A memorandum produced by the Oversea Migration Board in 1960, for example, wondered whether exchanging 'a good portion of our best citizens' with 100,000 migrants from the Caribbean was 'making a good bargain'.⁷⁰ Again, the implicit assumption is that immigrants of colour were unskilled or otherwise undesirable. Race played a significant role in this, 'coloured', Caribbean or 'new Commonwealth' immigrants are those most often invoked in this comparison rather than immigrants from Europe or the largest immigrant group, the Irish.⁷¹

Though there had been long-running tensions between concerns about the supply of labour in Britain, especially skilled labour, and the encouragement of British migration to the Dominions, these had always been overruled in the interest of maintaining Commonwealth links through the export of 'British stock'.⁷² Gradually, however, the balance began to shift. In 1956, the Advisory Council on Scientific Policy undertook an official investigation of how many chemistry and physics graduates and academics had emigrated, sending out surveys to universities across the United Kingdom.⁷³ This was part of a wider initiative to increase skilled manpower in the sciences and engineering, which also led to reforms of technical education.⁷⁴ There was a particular concern regarding emigration to the United States, as this loss of skilled labour would not even have the potential compensation of reinforcing Commonwealth ties. Though this survey did not reveal a significant exodus, concerns that such emigration *could* escalate led to a series of measures to keep scientists and engineers in Britain or to lure them back. The Civil Service Commission and Atomic Energy Authority began to offer grants to returning scientists in 1958. In 1963, the Treasury began to pay the fares for British scientists returning from North America to take up appointments in the United Kingdom and sent representatives to recruit British scientists in North America for public sector positions.⁷⁵ In 1967, there was a further state-funded initiative to recruit British scientists and those in technical fields in the United States for private industry.⁷⁶

As well as these initiatives to retain skilled workers, support for British emigration to the former Dominions continued to wane. The Oversea Migration Board, which had come in existence in 1953 as a revived version of the interwar Overseas Settlement Board, was wound down in 1964. Located within the Commonwealth Relations Office, the Board, as discussed in previous chapters, had primary responsibility for coordinating and measuring emigration from Britain to the Dominions. It had taken a less active role since 1962, no longer producing 'annual narrative reports' although it continued to publish migration statistics until 1964.[77] The final annual report of the Board, published in December 1961, recommended the renewal of the Commonwealth Settlement Act (the successor to the Empire Settlement Act) in 1962 for a further five years, but also that 'the attention of the four main receiving countries of the Commonwealth should be drawn to the present limited manpower resources of [the United Kingdom] in certain skilled and professional categories' with the implication that those countries should not aggressively recruit workers in these fields.[78] Along these lines were requests made by the British government that Commonwealth countries should 'not direct their publicity solely to the recruitment of skilled people in certain occupations and professions'.[79] Though the Commonwealth Settlement Act was renewed in 1962 for five years, it was not renewed thereafter.

Reduced support for emigration was also reflected in government expenditure. Treasury funding was withdrawn from the Women's Migration and Overseas Appointments Society (previously the Society for the Overseas Settlement of British Women) in 1964. This led to the closure of an organisation that had been promoting and assisting the migration of women largely to British settler colonies since the nineteenth century.[80] Funding was also reduced for other emigration initiatives. As described in Chapter 4, British funding for the 'Ten Pound Pom' migration scheme with Australia had been reduced in 1952 and then again in 1953 to just £150,000. Australia had long covered the bulk of the costs of the scheme, contributing for example, £4 million in 1964.[81] British funding was withdrawn altogether in 1972.[82] Taken together with the policies of restriction described above, these policies of retention, of moving away from the support of emigration, worked towards a demographic defence of the white British nation.

Conclusion

The politics of migration in the United Kingdom, South Africa and Rhodesia in the 1960s all aimed at the social engineering of nations imagined in racial terms. The increasing incentives offered to white migrants by the South African and Rhodesian states aimed to increase their white populations just as the United Kingdom began to implement policies designed to slow down British emigration and limit the entry of Commonwealth migrants of colour. While not all of these initiatives were successful, they illustrate the intentions of those who implemented them. When racism in Britain and its relationship to migration policy in this period is discussed, this is rarely in the context of similar issues in South Africa and Rhodesia even though links were seen by contemporaries, from activists who campaigned against racism in both Britain and southern Africa to right-wing groups such as the National Front and the Monday Club which supported white minority rule in South Africa and Rhodesia as well as immigration restriction and repatriation in Britain.

The declaration of South African republic in 1961 and UDI in 1965, though ruptures in formal political relations, were not sharp breaks with the United Kingdom in terms of racial ideology or ongoing connections through migration.[83] Rather, the attempted retreat to the racialised nation that Republic and UDI signified was underway in the United Kingdom at the same time and for many of the same reasons. Though they took different forms, in the 1960s and 1970s the politics of migration in the United Kingdom, South Africa and Rhodesia all centred on the defence of the white nation. This is not simply because the shifting racial demographics of the United Kingdom led Britons to move to South Africa or Rhodesia. The processes unfolding in both locations were far more entangled and mutually constitutive. Racial ideologies, policies or practices were never identical in each location. They were always inflected by local political struggles and economic circumstances. Yet, they were all responding to challenges to a racial ideology and a racialised ordering of things that was foundational to the nations of South Africa, Rhodesia and the United Kingdom alike. All were products of an imperial system, which both produced and was based on white supremacy. This emerged more urgently when it was challenged in the post-war era by decolonisation, the decline in Britain's global position and the mass migration of people of colour to the United Kingdom.

Notes

1 'The Rising Flood of Emigrants' *Financial Times*, 16 August 1963.
2 On this point see Conway and Leonard, *Migration, Space*, pp. 154, 171–4.
3 On this backlash see Schwarz, *White Man's World*, pp. 18–26; Gilroy, *After Empire*.
4 Paul, *Whitewashing Britain*, pp. 111–90; Hampshire, *Citizenship and Belonging*, pp. 1–78; Karatani, *Defining British Citizenship*, pp. 128–33, 151–4; Nadine El-Enany *(B)ordering Britain: Law, Race and Empire* (Manchester: Manchester University Press, 2020), pp. 4–5, 73–132.
5 Series MN, Office of Population, Censuses and Statistics, *International Migration: Migrants Entering or Leaving the United Kingdom*, 1964–2000.
6 The data from Rhodesia is not broken down by nationality. Due in part to sanctions from 1968, discussed in Chapter 6, and the increase in migration from Europeans leaving newly independent African nations such as Kenya and Mozambique, it seems likely that the rate of migration directly from Britain

dropped in this period. Brownell, *Collapse of Rhodesia*, pp. 126–7. In South Africa data is available for approved immigrants based on citizenship, birthplace and previous country of residence throughout the 1960s and 1970s. British citizens and those born in Britain were the largest group of immigrants in those categories throughout the 1960s and 1970s, those listing the United Kingdom as their previous country of residence were also the largest group for every year up to 2002, with the exception of 1977–80 and 1983–85 when immigrants listing Rhodesia/Zimbabwe as their previous country of residence were the largest group, and 1999 when immigrants listing Mozambique were the largest group. For a useful collation of this data see Peberdy, *Selecting Immigrants*, pp. 272–83.
7 This latter dip was likely related to the 1976 Soweto Uprising.
8 Brownell, *Collapse of Rhodesia*, pp. 125–6.
9 Jim Tomlinson, 'Inventing "Decline": The Falling Behind of the British Economy in the Postwar Years', *Economic History Review* XLIX:4 (1996), 731–57; Jim Tomlinson, 'Thrice Denied: "Declinism" as a Recurrent Theme in British History in the Long Twentieth Century', *Twentieth Century British History* 20:2 (2009), 235, 238, 245.
10 P.H.W. Johnston, *British Emigration to Durban, South Africa* (Durban: Institute for Social Research: University of Natal, 1970), pp. 27–8.
11 Hammerton and Thomson, *Ten Pound Poms*, p. 72. See also Hammerton, *Migrants of the British Diaspora*, pp. 57–8.
12 Dick Hoerder provides a compelling discussion of these myriad motivations for migration, comprising what he refers to as the 'holistic material-emotional approach'. Hoerder, *Cultures in Contact*, p. 20. See also, a similar discussion in relation to British migration to Australia in the decades after the Second World War, Hammerton and Thomson, *Ten Pound Poms*, pp. 28–78.
13 Conway and Leonard, *Migration, Space*, p. 62.
14 Karen O'Reilly, *The British on the Costa del Sol: Transnational Identities and Local Communities* (New York: Routledge, 2000), p. 28. See also Conway and Leonard, *Migration, Space*, p. 49.
15 Conway and Leonard found that many British migrants described themselves as 'not political' as a way of evade their complicity with apartheid. Conway and Leonard, *Migration, Space*, p. 139.
16 On this aspect of self-narration see Portelli, 'What Makes Oral History Different', p. 38. On the specific case of British migrants to South Africa see Conway and Leonard, *Migration, Space*, p. 155.
17 Interview with Carolyn Hastings, Cambridge, United Kingdom, 2 September 2011. Other migrants recounted a similar experience of ending up moving to South Africa after initially hoping to move elsewhere. Stone, *Colonist or Uitlander*, pp. 168–9.
18 Interview with Carolyn Hastings, Cambridge, United Kingdom, 2 September 2011. James Hammerton describes a similar attitude in the case of Rod Blackburn, who moved to South Africa in 1972 to take up a job at Shell. Blackburn describes himself as 'politically naive' and notes that he 'had not

given it much thought other than vaguely understanding that apartheid was not a good thing'. Quoted in Hammerton, *Migrants of the British Diaspora*, p. 175.
19 In this context 'Coloured' refers to a specific racial group in South Africa, those of multi-ethnic or Malay descent, rather than to people of colour more generally.
20 Interview with Ian Jones, Grahamstown, South Africa, 16 April 2011. At the interviewee's request I have used a pseudonym.
21 See also Conway and Leonard, *Migration, Space*, p. 182.
22 This was part of a general understanding of British decline including 'socialism gone mad'. Quoted in Josiah Brownell, '"One last retreat": Racial Nostalgia and Population Panic in Smith's Rhodesia and Powell's Britain', in *Global White Nationalism: From Apartheid to Trump*, eds Daniel Geary, Camilla Schofield and Jennifer Sutton (Manchester: Manchester University Press, 2020), p. 178.
23 Stone's study was based on 500 interviews of British migrants to South Africa conducted in the late 1960s and early 1970s. Stone, *Colonist or Uitlander*, p. 166.
24 Quoted in ibid.
25 On this fear more generally see Hampshire, *Citizenship and Belonging*, pp. 111–49.
26 Ibid., pp. 79–110.
27 Quoted in Stone, *Colonist or Uitlander*, p. 166.
28 Quoted in ibid.
29 Quoted in ibid., p. 164.
30 Quoted in ibid., p. 169. On the perception among British migrants of British media bias see also Conway and Leonard, *Migration, Space*, pp. 157–9.
31 'It's a sweet sunshine life … in South Africa', *Daily Sketch*, 26 October 1968, p. 8.
32 Stone, *Colonist or Uitlander*, pp. 165–6, 168; Conway and Leonard, *Migration, Space*, pp. 120–7.
33 Stone, *Colonist or Uitlander*, p. 224; Conway and Leonard, *Migration, Space*, p. 155.
34 Ian Smith Papers, 1/78/019, Enclosure, R.C. (S)(65) 173, *Rhodesia: Assisted Passages to the Land of Sunshine Golden Opportunity*, 2 July 1965. For more on these schemes see Brownell, *Collapse of Rhodesia*, pp. 97–131.
35 Stanley Uys writing in *The Scotsman* cites South Africa as providing a £60 subsidy towards the passage, leaving migrants to pay 'roughly £10' towards their passages. Stanley Uys, 'More British go to South Africa', *The Scotsman*, 4 July 1963.
36 That there was no obligation to stay for any fixed period was appealing to intending immigrants interviewed in the *Daily Sketch*, who felt they could easily return if things didn't work out. 'It's a sweet sunshine life … in South Africa', *Daily Sketch*, 26 October 1968, p. 8. See also Conway and Leonard, *Migration, Space*, p. 40; Johnston, *British Emigration to Durban*, p. 39.
37 NASA, A326, Box 7, *Assisted Immigration to the Republic of South Africa*, 1972, pp. 1–5.

38 Interview with Ian Jones, Grahamstown, South Africa, 16 April 2011.
39 NASA, A326, Box 7, *Come Home South Africans*, 1961.
40 All the other offices had either only one assistant attaché or vice-consul for immigration or the attaché or consul for immigration worked alone. R.P. 31/1969, *Report of the Department of Immigration for the period 1 April 1961 to 30 June 1968* (Pretoria: The Government Printer, 1968), pp. 12, 4.
41 R.P. 31/1969, *Report of the Department of Immigration, 1961–1968*, p. 10.
42 For an example in *The Sun* in 1973 see Conway and Leonard, *Migration, Space*, p. 45.
43 R.P. 31/1969, *Report of the Department of Immigration, 1961–1968*, pp. 5–7. See also Peberdy, *Selecting Immigrants*, pp. 123–4.
44 R.P. 31/1969, *Report of the Department of Immigration, 1961–1968*, p. 7.
45 Brownell, *British Immigration to South Africa*, pp. 47–8.
46 The Southern Africa League operated until 1969. R.P. 31/1969, *Report of the Department of Immigration, 1961–1968*, p. 11; R.P. 21/1971, *Report of the Department of Immigration for the period 1 July 1968 to 30 June 1970* (Pretoria: The Government Printer, 1971), p. 11.
47 NASA, A326, Box 7, *The Immigrant's Arrival in the Republic of South Africa*, 1972.
48 On the appeal of an adventurous, outdoor life for British emigrants see Hammerton, *Migrants of the British Diaspora*, pp. 54–6.
49 NASA, A326, Box 7, *Land of Sunshine*, undated.
50 Stanley Uys, 'More British go to South Africa', *The Scotsman*.
51 NASA, A326, Box 7, *The Immigrant Housewife in the Republic of South Africa*, 1972, pp. 2, 4, 8; see also Peberdy, *Selecting Immigrants*, p. 133; Susanne M. Klausen, *Abortion Under Apartheid: Nationalism, Sexuality, and Women's Reproductive Rights in South Africa* (Oxford: Oxford University Press, 2015), pp. 12, 66–8.
52 NASA, A326, Box 7, *Housing Facilities in the Republic of South Africa*, 1970.
53 NASA, A326, Box 7, *Housing Facilities in the Republic of South Africa*, 1972; *Housing Facilities in the Republic of South Africa*, 1975/76.
54 NASA, A326, Box 7, *Housing Facilities in the Republic of South Africa*, 1970, pp. 2, 7, 10.
55 NASA, A326, Box 7, *Housing Facilities in the Republic of South Africa*, 1970, p. 2.
56 Susanne M. Klausen, '"Reclaiming the White Daughter's Purity": Afrikaner Nationalism, Racialized Sexuality, and the 1975 Abortion and Sterilization Act in Apartheid South Africa', *Journal of Women's History* 22:3 (2010), 41–2, 53, 56.
57 Ian Smith Papers, 1/78/019, Enclosure, R.C. (S)(65) 173, *Rhodesia: Assisted Passages to the Land of Sunshine Golden Opportunity*, 2 July 1965.
58 Ibid.
59 El-Enany, *Bordering Britain*, pp. 86–7; Hampshire, *Citizenship and Belonging*, p. 21; Dummett and Nicol, *Subjects, Citizens*, pp. 177–8.

The demographic defence of the white nation, 1960–75 147

60 As quoted in Tom Nairn, *The Break-up of Britain: Crisis and Neonationalism* (London: Verso, 1981), p. 256.
61 Cited in Schwarz, *White Man's World*, p. 48.
62 Quoted in Paul, *Whitewashing Britain*, pp. 111–90.
63 El-Enany, *Bordering Britain*, pp. 95–102; Paul, *Whitewashing Britain*, pp. 172–3.
64 Hampshire, *Citizenship and Belonging*, p. 35.
65 El-Enany, *Bordering Britain*, pp. 103–16; Dummett and Nicol, *Subjects, Citizens*, pp. 197–205; Paul, *Whitewashing Britain*, p. 179.
66 El-Enany, *Bordering Britain*, pp. 116–21; Paul, *Whitewashing Britain*, p. 181.
67 El-Enany, *Bordering Britain*, pp. 125–32; Hampshire, *Citizenship and Belonging*, p. 43.
68 *Parliamentary Debates*, Commons, 5th Ser., Vol. 563, No. 37, 24 January 1957, Col. 296.
69 Founded on 'Black Monday' in 1961, the day Macmillan gave his famous 'winds of change' speech heralding the decolonisation of Africa, the Club consistently argued against sanctions on Rhodesia, against the ban on the sale of arms to South Africa, for a reduction in immigration and the repatriation of immigrants and their descendants from Britain. Though considered by many, especially retrospectively, to be a fringe right-wing group, in the 1960s and 1970s, the Monday Club was influential, claiming, by 1969, 30 local branches, 55 groups at universities and further education colleges, and 5,000 members including 35 sitting members of parliament. Lisa Mason, 'The Development of the Monday Club and its Contribution to the Conservative Party and the Modern British Right, 1961–1990' (PhD dissertation, University of Wolverhampton, 2004), 52. This membership number is disputed, with Patrick Seyd claiming between 1,600 and 2,500 based on annual subscription figures. Patrick Seyd, 'Factionalism within the Conservative Party: The Monday Club', *Government and Opposition* 7:4 (1972), 470.
70 Quoted in Paul, *Whitewashing Britain*, p. 57.
71 Wills, *Lovers and Strangers*, p. xii; Dummett and Nicol, *Subjects, Citizens*, p. 179.
72 Paul, *Whitewashing Britain*, pp. 25–63.
73 TNA, CAB 124/2731, 'Emigration of Scientists', 13 February 1957.
74 Tomlinson, 'Inventing "Decline"', p. 747.
75 TNA, T 334/13, G.R. Ashford to T.A. Oxley, 19 November 1963; Supplementary Notes, Parliamentary Question, 12 May 1966. See also Paul, *Whitewashing Britain*, p. 57.
76 TNA, T 334/13, Anthony Benn, 'The Brain Drain', 25 April 1967.
77 TNA, LAB 8/2736, D.G. Storer to Morgan, 12 July 1963.
78 Cmnd 1586, Commonwealth Relations Office, *Seventh Report of the Oversea Migration Board* (London: HMSO, 1961). The four countries referred to are Australia, Canada, New Zealand and the Federation of Rhodesia and Nyasaland. Although South Africa received more British migrants than the Federation, by this time it had left the Commonwealth.

79 TNA, LAB 8/2736, LA Paper No. 56, 'Ministry of Labour: United Kingdom Migration Policy', March 1963.
80 Smith, 'The Women's Branch ', pp. 520–35.
81 TNA, LAB 8/2736, PMM (U.K.) (64)B11, 'Meeting of Commonwealth Prime Ministers 1964, Emigration Policy, Brief Prepared by Commonwealth Relations Office, Talking Points', June 1964.
82 Hammerton and Thomson, *Ten Pound Poms*, p. 30. TNA, LAB 8/2736, 'British Emigration Policy: Report by Interdepartmental Committee of Officials', 1961, p. 8.
83 There is a growing literature on the legacies of empire after decolonisation. Bailkin, *Afterlife of Empire*; Howe, 'Internal Decolonization?', pp. 286–304; Hopkins, 'Rethinking Decolonization', pp. 211–47. For more on the continuing economic, military and political relationship between South Africa and the United Kingdom in particular see Hyam and Henshaw, *The Lion and the Springbok*.

6

'The last bastion of the British Empire': The politics of migration in the final days of Rhodesia and apartheid South Africa, 1970–94

In 1972 the anti-apartheid movement in the United Kingdom produced a poster opposing emigration to South Africa. Showing the South African Prime Minister John Vorster, arms open wide in an apparent gesture of welcome, superimposed on a photograph of police beating Black South African women, it read, 'Prominent South African figure seeks white workers to help maintain racist regime'. Highlighting the exploitation of Black workers, and naming British companies, including Dunlop and British Leyland, involved in this 'semi-slave labour system', the poster's message was: 'Don't support them. Don't emigrate.'[1] While there had long been critiques of white migration to South Africa and Rhodesia in this vein, as campaigns against white minority rule in both nations intensified from the 1960s opposition to white migration became more prominent and widespread.

Despite these campaigns and increasing international condemnation, British migration, especially to South Africa, continued at high rates throughout much of the 1970s and into the early 1980s. Rhodesia had some success in attracting white migrants, especially from within Africa in the early 1970s, but this was not sustained as the war between anti-colonial forces and the Rhodesian government escalated and rates of white emigration increased dramatically. Although the Rhodesian subsidised migration scheme continued until the end of minority rule in 1979, UN sanctions and legal restrictions imposed by the British government made the recruitment of white migrants difficult. Rates of white migration to South Africa in the 1970s, however, increased from the already high rates of the 1960s, reaching a peak in 1975. Rates fell in 1977 in the wake of the 1976 Soweto Uprising, but recovered by 1980 and only began to fall permanently in 1984. Rates of migration from the United Kingdom to South Africa also remained high in the 1970s, increasing by close to 40 per cent from the elevated rates of the 1960s. As well as this continued migration from the United Kingdom, both South Africa and Rhodesia received white migrants from other African countries, notably from Mozambique and Angola

Figure 6.1 Anti-apartheid Movement (London) poster, 1972.

which gained independence from Portugal in 1975, and many moved to South Africa from Rhodesia/Zimbabwe in the run-up to and following Zimbabwean independence in 1980.

High rates of British migration to South Africa continued despite increasing public awareness and condemnation of the apartheid regime and the escalating violence and instability in the Republic. One important factor, as discussed in Chapter 5, was the generous subsidised migration scheme offered by the South African state which continued until 1991 although it was only open to skilled migrants with a job offer from 1982. This became an increasing draw as the subsidised schemes in the other former Dominions wound down. Canada stopped offering interest-free loans in 1967, New Zealand ended its subsidised passage scheme in 1975 and Rhodesia's scheme concluded in 1979.[2] The largest of these schemes, Australia's 'Ten Pound Pom' scheme continued until 1982, however, so a lack of other subsidised options is not the only explanatory factor.[3] The appeal of a privileged life in the sunshine persisted, particularly as the South African economy was strong, bolstered by the rising gold price and state spending on infrastructure projects, especially in the early 1970s.[4] Certainly, the opportunities for class and lifestyle elevation discussed in Chapter 5 remained attractive for white migrants, and were, perhaps, all the more appealing given the difficult economic situation in the United Kingdom in this period.

As in the 1960s, migration decisions were motivated not only by economics but also by a sense of relative opportunity and a perception of British decline. The sense of national decline in the United Kingdom described in Chapter 5 was exacerbated by the economic difficulties of the 1970s and as before was often linked to the presence of people of colour. Given that the 1971 Immigration Act had placed restrictions on the migration of people of colour from the Commonwealth, those who had previously advocated restriction turned their attention to what they termed 'repatriation', the removal of people of colour already resident in the United Kingdom. This took a range of forms, from the 'voluntary repatriation' included in both the 1970 Conservative Party election manifesto and the 1971 Act, to the mandatory expulsion of people of colour advocated by the National Front. There were also continuing calls for an even more restrictive immigration policy, particularly regarding the admission of the dependants of those already resident. These politics of removal and restriction were both intended to defend a nation understood implicitly as white. This is underlined by the term 'repatriation', the return of someone to their own country. By this logic, people of colour, regardless of their citizenship, legal status or historic links to the United Kingdom, belonged somewhere else. The British Nationality Act of 1981, which ended automatic birthright citizenship, also reflected this racialised understanding of the British nation.

Many of those advocating 'repatriation', from the Monday Club to the National Front, also expressed strong support for both Rhodesia and apartheid South Africa, underlying the ongoing connections between the United Kingdom and the settler colonies of southern Africa. This chapter examines the concluding phase of white, and especially British, migration to South Africa and Rhodesia and then turns to the politics of migration in the United Kingdom.

White migration to Rhodesia and South Africa in the 1970s and 1980s

By the 1970s both the Rhodesian and South African minority regimes came under increasing political and economic pressure both internally and internationally. One of the results of this increasing isolation is that both nations redoubled their efforts to recruit white migrants as a demographic defence of minority rule. While these efforts remained to some extent dependent on economic conditions, they became less selective than in previous years, especially in relation to white migrants from within Africa. There was some official concern, especially about the large numbers of largely Roman Catholic Portuguese migrants who came to both Rhodesia and South Africa as Mozambique and Angola gained independence in 1975. Overall, however, white migrants from decolonising Africa were generally treated with sympathy.[5] In part, they were considered more easily assimilated than migrants from Europe, but these increasingly isolated regimes were also more and more concerned with increasing their white populations, especially as rates of white emigration rose dramatically by the late 1970s. Attempts to slow emigration were also implemented, including limits on the assets that emigrants could take with them. These efforts, as well as those to recruit new migrants were, however, increasingly unsuccessful as it became more and more clear that majority rule was inevitable, from the late 1970s in Rhodesia and by the mid 1980s in South Africa.

As outlined by Table 6.1, white migration to Rhodesia continued to rise in the early 1970s and then began a gradual fall from 1973, with a temporary increase in 1975 due to an influx of Portuguese migrants with the independence of Mozambique and Angola. Rates of white migration fell dramatically as the war between the Rhodesian settler state and anti-colonial forces intensified from 1972. Though the Rhodesian state continued its recruitment campaign throughout the 1970s, it was largely unsuccessful. The war and the threat of military conscription were contributing factors to this failure, as were international sanctions including a ban on the advertising and promotion of migration to Rhodesia in the United Kingdom and limits imposed on the assets that prospective migrants could take.[6] Rates of white emigration from Rhodesia also increased after 1974 for many of the same reasons. However, it is worth noting that, in part because of the arrival of Portuguese migrants in 1975, Rhodesian statistics only reveal a net loss of white population on an annual basis from 1976.[7] All things considered, and especially given the legal prohibitions on migration to Rhodesia and its advertisement, it is surprising how many people did move there in this period.

By contrast, white migration to South Africa in the 1970s increased even from the historically high rates of the 1960s, reaching a post-war peak in 1975. Rates of migration from the United Kingdom also increased in this period and only began to decline, along with wider white migration in the mid 1980s as the conflict between the South African state and anti-apartheid movements escalated and economic conditions became more difficult in South Africa. More white migrants came from the United Kingdom than from anywhere else except for 1977 to 1980 and 1983 to 1985, when more came from Rhodesia/Zimbabwe, many of them British-born, in the run-up to and after Zimbabwean independence.[8] As in Rhodesia, there were

Table 6.1 European immigration to and emigration from Rhodesia, 1970–79

Year	'European' immigration to Rhodesia[i]	'European' emigration from Rhodesia	Net 'European' migration to/from Rhodesia
1970	12,227	5,896	+6,331
1971	14,743	5,336	+9,407
1972	13,966	5,141	+8,825
1973	9,433	7,751	+1,682
1974	9,649	9,069	+580
1975	12,425	10,497	+1,928
1976	7,782	14,854	−7,072
1977	5,730	16,638	−10,908
1978	4,360	18,069	−13,709
1979	3,288	14,472	−11,184

[i] Immigration statistics were not collected systematically for country of previous residence, citizenship or birth for Rhodesia in this period. All figures from Brownell, *Collapse of Rhodesia*, p. 125.

also high rates of white migration from Mozambique and Angola as these nations became independent from Portuguese rule in 1975.

The South African government continued the subsidised migration scheme described in the previous chapter, increasing the subsidy to account for the rising cost of travel in 1972, 1973 and 1976.[9] This was broadly successful in the early 1970s as reflected by the figures in Table 6.2. South Africa House in London was so inundated with 'spontaneous interest' in the peak year of 1975, that they stopped advertising in the United Kingdom until all the applications could be processed.[10] Rates of white migration dropped following the 1976 Soweto Uprising, although there was a final peak in the early 1980s as an increase in the global price of gold gave a boost to the South African economy.[11]

There was also increasing official concern about rising rates of emigration from South Africa, especially from the late 1970s onwards, and the South African government, though officially continuing with a selective immigration policy, in practice relaxed restrictions, especially for white migrants from elsewhere in Africa. Such migrants, particularly those leaving newly independent countries were treated with a good deal of sympathy in terms of both admission and assistance after they arrived. They were considered more likely to assimilate and to understand South Africa's racial politics given their previous colonial experience.[12] Stricter measures were imposed on ideological grounds, however. Supporters of communism, atheism and those opposed to the racial ideology of the South African state were excluded.[13]

Table 6.2 White immigration to and emigration from South Africa, 1970–94

Year	'White' immigration to South Africa[i]	'White' emigration from South Africa	Net 'white' migration to/from South Africa	Immigration to South Africa from the United Kingdom[ii]	Percentage of immigrants to South Africa from the United Kingdom
1970	41,523	9,278	+32,245	21,323	51.35
1971	35,845	8,407	+27,438	17,347	48.39
1972	32,776	7,884	+24,892	15,828	48.29
1973	24,016	6,401	+17,615	11,057	46.04
1974	35,910	7,428	+28,482	17,380	48.40
1975	50,464	10,255	+40,209	24,805	49.15
1976	46,239	15,641	+30,598	20,371	44.06
1977	24,822	26,000	−1,178	7,304	29.43
1978	18,669	20,686	−2,017	4,550	24.37
1979	18,680	15,694	−2,986	4,260	22.81
1980	29,365	11,363	+18,002	10,117	34.45
1981	41,542	8,791	+32,751	18,464	44.45
1982	45,784	6,832	+38,952	20,347	44.44
1983	30,483	8,247	+22,236	10,942	35.90
1984	28,973	8,550	+20,243	9,252	31.93
1985	17,284	11,401	+5,883	5,168	29.9
1986	6,994	13,711	−6,717	2,012	28.77
1987	7,953	11,174	−3,221	2,168	27.26
1988	10,400	7,767	+2,633	2,904	27.92
1989	11,270	4,911	+6,359	3,088	27.40
1990	14,499	4,722	+9,777	3,395	23.42
1991	12,379	4,256	+8,123	2,489	20.11
1992	8,686	4,289	+4,397	1,370	15.77
1993	9,824	8,078	+1,746	1,794	18.26
1994	6,398	10,235	−3,837	1,047	16.36

[i] All figures for South Africa from Peberdy, *Selecting Immigrants*, pp. 276–85.
[ii] Figures based on country of previous residence rather than birthplace or citizenship. The figures based on birthplace are broadly similar to country of previous residence, those based on citizenship are higher, including those with British nationality coming from former British colonies largely within Africa.

Active recruitment of migrants continued until 1982, although the Department of Immigration was merged with the Department of the Interior in 1978, following the drop in numbers beginning in 1977. Officially this was attributed to a decline in economic conditions and a concurrent drop in demand for labour, although the Soweto Uprising and increased international condemnation of the apartheid regime likely also played a role. Though the official line was that this merger would not mean the end of the recruitment of the 'best immigrants for the Republic', even prior to the merger, the department had cut down its own staffing levels, eliminating seventy-five posts. This smaller administrative structure as well as lower rates of migration that year is reflected in the much smaller numbers of new immigrants greeted by officials (1,595) and provided with accommodation (207) in 1979 compared to 1966, when 37,041 new migrants were met by officials and 8,695 were provided with accommodation, as discussed in Chapter 5.[14] Samorgan and Transa, the private recruitment agencies funded by the South African state, shut down in 1978 and 1977 respectively.[15]

The upswing in the South African economy from 1979 to 1981 combined with the independence of Zimbabwe in 1980, led to a final peak in white immigration to South Africa including from the United Kingdom. The annual report of the Department of Internal Affairs for 1980, for instance, notes that the London office was unable to manage 'the sudden flood of applications' and asked employers to consult with the department before placing advertisements.[16] The same report, however, also states that 'selective immigration' should be only a short-term solution to the demand for skilled labour and should not come at the expense of the training of 'local population groups', reflecting reforms under P.W. Botha, including changes in the racial labour hierarchy, which saw increased, although limited, opportunities for social mobility for Black South Africans.[17] South Africa left ICEM in 1980 and active recruitment ended in 1982. Although the assisted passage scheme remained open to skilled migrants with offers of employment until December 1991, rates of migration dropped from 1983. In 1991 the Aliens Control Act removed racial discrimination in immigration law.[18]

In Rhodesia, the increasingly embattled minority regime continued to promote immigration schemes in the 1970s, although these were largely unsuccessful. The Settler '74 campaign, launched in January 1974, called on white Rhodesians to personally appeal to their friends and relatives overseas to move to Rhodesia in the hope of gaining 100,000 new immigrants. Advertisements for the scheme to white Rhodesian residents cast white migration as a benefit to both existing and potential Rhodesian residents: 'They will enjoy a much better life out here, and they'll ensure YOUR future. So, do them, and yourself, a favour.'[19] It soon became clear, however, that the initial goal of recruiting 100,000 white migrants was unrealistic and the goal was dropped to 10,000. By May 1974 only 4,200 potential immigrants had been suggested and the campaign was abandoned.

Undeterred by this failure, Rhodesian MPs continued to make proposals to attract white migrants, including the provision of paid holidays for middle-aged professionals and tradesmen, who might then be tempted to stay, and the creation of a Scouting centre in the Matopos, which again might encourage those who visited to stay.[20] Both of these ideas reflect the conviction that if people came and experienced life in Rhodesia, they could be convinced to remain, echoing the migration enthusiasts of the 1940s. Even after 1976, when the Rhodesian Prime Minister Ian Smith acknowledged the inevitability of majority rule, the subsidised migration programme was still funded by the Rhodesian government. From this point, however, more money was allocated to assisted passages than was spent, reflecting a dramatic decrease in migration after the last influx of Portuguese migrants from Mozambique and Angola.[21]

These difficulties in recruiting new immigrants made it increasingly difficult for the Rhodesian government to maintain a selective immigration policy. Given the opposition, especially from Black African MPs but also more broadly in the Rhodesian parliament, to an unselective mass immigration policy, this was never openly admitted, but, as Josiah Brownell has argued, it seems clear that as it became more difficult to recruit white migrants the state became less selective. The international sanctions on migration to Rhodesia also made it practically more difficult for immigration officials to vet prospective migrants. As a result, many of the migrants who arrived in Rhodesia, especially by the late 1970s were 'white kooks, criminals, racists, and misfits' including those attracted by Rhodesia's defiant defence of white supremacy in a changing world.[22] As one prospective migrant to Rhodesia put it: 'I see Rhodesia as the last bastion of the British Empire.'[23]

Increasingly, the Rhodesian state was most concerned by dramatically rising rates of white emigration. A 1970 report raised concern about emigration, particularly of the emigration of young families and argued that the even more proactive recruitment of white migrants was the only way, not only to increase the white population, but also to convince those already resident to stay.[24] Rates of emigration began rising from 1973, increasing dramatically from 1976, when emigration exceeded immigration on an annual basis for the first time since 1964. It was only the increase in migration from Mozambique and Angola in 1974 and 1975 that had prevented this from happening sooner. The extent of this difficulty is perhaps best illustrated by the emigration of a former Immigration Minister, Wickus de Kock in 1977.[25] In an attempt to reduce emigration the Rhodesian government made leaving the country more difficult, limiting the assets that emigrants could take out of the country. The emigration allowance was reduced from RH$5,000 to RH$1,000 in 1976, for instance.[26] Some intending emigrants were rumoured to employ ingenious plans to get around restrictions on the removal of assets, including wealthy couples divorcing prior to leaving as they could take out more money as individuals and 'ex-wives' could draw maintenance abroad from assets frozen in Rhodesia.[27] In the late 1970s precious stones reportedly sold for three or four times their value in Salisbury

The final days of Rhodesia and apartheid South Africa, 1970–94

(present-day Harare), as they were easier to smuggle out of the country.[28] Because of these restrictions, many of those who planned to take what many diehard Rhodesians scornfully called the 'chicken run' or the 'yellow route' did not announce their intentions, or went away on holiday and did not return, arranging their affairs from a distance.[29] Those who disclosed their plans to leave Rhodesia received a personal letter from the Immigration Promotion Department, asking, 'in a tactful way' whether they might be able to provide any help or change the intending immigrant's mind.[30]

Despite such efforts, white emigration from Rhodesia continued in the run-up to Zimbabwean independence and beyond. As discussed above, many emigrants from Rhodesia went to South Africa, but they also moved to the United Kingdom and other Commonwealth destinations.[31] One man, who had moved from Rhodesia to South Africa in 1978 and was planning to move on to Australia, described his decision in the following terms: 'The fight for Rhodesia is over and lost and now the fight for South Africa is about to begin.'[32] As will be discussed in Chapter 7, this kind of serial migration was a common occurrence for white Rhodesians and white South Africans in the run-up to and after the end of the minority rule in both countries.

Despite employing similar recruitment methods, Rhodesia was less successful at attracting European immigrants than South Africa. The escalating war and likelihood that white men would be conscripted made it less attractive as a destination, especially after the period of exemption from military service for new immigrants was decreased from five to two years in 1975.[33] More comprehensive international sanctions and legal prohibitions of migration, discussed in the next section, as well as limits placed on the money migrants could take to Rhodesia also made the move difficult in practical terms. In both Rhodesia and South Africa, white migration decreased as it became increasingly clear that the days of minority rule were numbered. In Rhodesia this was from the early 1970s, whereas in South Africa it came a decade later. But both nations, and South Africa especially, also experienced relatively high rates of migration prior to this due to both the state subsidies offered, and the continued allure of a privileged life in a sunny climate. Opponents of the Rhodesian and apartheid states recognised the important role of white migration both in contributing to and sustaining confidence in the longevity of minority rule.

'Don't support them. Don't emigrate': Opposing emigration to South Africa and Rhodesia

Opposition to white migration to both Rhodesia and South Africa was actively pursued as part of the larger movements opposing white minority rule in both countries. This movement was more successful regarding Rhodesia, although had some success, especially by the 1980s, in regard to South Africa. The greater sanctions imposed both by the United Nations and the United Kingdom on Rhodesia reflected, in part, the way in which it had unilaterally declared independence and was considered an 'illegal' regime. Though, equally illegitimate, especially when viewed from the perspective of the disenfranchised Black majority in South Africa, South Africa's independence first as a Dominion and later as a Republic were achieved through means recognised by international law at the time. This, combined with South Africa's greater economic strength and military and strategic importance, meant that sanctions in general came later and were less severe, including those against white migration. Nevertheless, there was vocal opposition to white migration to South Africa from a wide range of groups both within South Africa and internationally including in the UN General Assembly, religious organisation, trade unions, student groups and the international anti-apartheid movement.

Very soon after the Rhodesian Unilateral Declaration of Independence in 1965, the United Nations imposed sanctions on Rhodesia, first in 1966 and then in 1968. The 1968 mandatory comprehensive sanctions included a section in the Security Council Resolution calling on member states to 'prevent activities ... promoting, assisting, or encouraging emigration to Southern Rhodesia, with a view to stopping such emigration'.[34] This was followed by British legislation prohibiting the promotion of migration to Rhodesia and limits on the assets that British migrants to Rhodesia could take. Several publications were prosecuted for violating this law and subsequently fined, including, in 1974, *The Economist* and *The Spectator*.[35] Though it was possible to evade these restrictions by moving first to South Africa and then on to Rhodesia, this extra difficulty likely deterred many as did the requirement that subsidised migrants had to stay for at least three years or repay the fare.

Despite these disincentives, as well as the escalating war and the threat of conscription, the Rhodesian Front government was successful enough in recruiting white immigrants in the early 1970s that Bishop Abel Muzorewa, the anti-colonial leader (and later Prime Minister of the short-lived interim Zimbabwe Rhodesia) complained in a speech to the United Nations Security Council in 1972:

> Africans in Rhodesia have been extremely surprised to see streams of Europeans continuing to come to Rhodesia displacing Africans from their land and their jobs despite Security Council resolution 253 (1968) explicitly calling on member states not to allow their citizens to emigrate to Rhodesia. I hope that from now on Member States will do their best to stop such immigrants, who continue to prop up the racist regime in Rhodesia.

Muzorewa went on to suggest that the British government use the £50 million it had offered for the development in the proposed settlement between Rhodesia and the United Kingdom to assist those 'white people who do not want to live under majority rule to leave for various parts of the world where there are white governments'.[36]

The settlement failed, but the following year the Foreign and Commonwealth Office (FCO) did consider paying white residents to leave Rhodesia as a way of weakening the Smith regime and hastening its collapse. In the discussion of whether financial incentives could be offered to lure Europeans away from Rhodesia, an FCO memorandum notes:

> For so long as net White immigration into Rhodesia continues, the morale of the Whites stays high. Property prices are sustained. The Whites feel that, however hostile the outside world may be, they are still winning. Nothing would be more likely to induce amongst them a readiness to compromise than a significant White exodus.[37]

It was eventually determined that such a scheme would be too expensive, impractical and might have the unintended result of encouraging more moderate Rhodesians to leave, leaving only the most intransigent behind, which would make ongoing negotiations more difficult.[38]

The idea of facilitating the emigration of whites from Rhodesia was again considered by the FCO in 1974, after the coup in Portugal and the prospective independence of Mozambique and Angola led to more enquiries by Rhodesian residents as to whether the British government might help them return to the United Kingdom. Sanctions and the financial restrictions placed on emigrants by the Rhodesian government made it difficult for Rhodesian residents, British citizens or otherwise, to leave Rhodesia. Though the idea of paying for repatriation was largely abandoned, assisting people to leave Rhodesia or providing British passports to those who were not already entitled to them was considered. Imagined as a reversal of the Rhodesian immigration campaigns, the FCO considered a plan that aimed to target recent immigrants, without deep roots in the country, who were generally in their assessment, 'not too intelligent, not interested in politics, not concerned with political ethics, and in general seeking only a well-paid job in a pleasant country with all the manifold trimmings of racial superiority'. According to a rather fanciful proposal, such immigrants might be identified through passport files and approached through unmarked mailings from around Britain or through a broadcast on Radio Lourenço Marques.[39] In the end this was determined to be too difficult and dropped in favour of a secret press propaganda campaign.[40]

Had this policy been implemented, it would have marked a complete reversal from the position of the British state in the 1940s and 1950s, a shift from encouraging Britons to move to a British colony to encouraging them to return to the United Kingdom from a regime who had broken away from the British Empire to continue majority rule. This speaks to the change both in geopolitics and in the British government's priorities. It is striking, however, how British officials in the 1970s imagined a similar kind of migrant to the one South African and Rhodesian officials hoped to attract: 'The ideal candidate for this scheme would be the young, middle or working class couple with children, who had perhaps recently emigrated and where the husband had a skilled or semi-skilled job.' In a further parallel to the national and racial prejudices of South African and Rhodesian officials, which underlines the similar racial preoccupations of British migration discourse in this period, one comment on the proposal expressed concern that the offer of British passports to Rhodesian residents 'could land us with all sorts of undesirables (e.g. Greeks, Portuguese, Arabians who might simply use Rhodesia as a staging post to get the U.K.)'.[41] In the end, as the war intensified, large numbers of Europeans left Rhodesia without incentives from the British government. As Josiah Brownell has argued, the demographic collapse of white Rhodesia was a substantial factor in its demise, as it became increasingly difficult to man the armed forces.[42]

In reaction to the continued high rates of British migration to South Africa, the 1970s also saw increasing campaigns against white migration to South Africa as part of the international anti-apartheid movement. Although advertising migration to South Africa was not prohibited by law as was the case with Rhodesia, and it is hard to say how successful these campaigns were, they did, along with wider anti-apartheid activism including the boycotting of South African sports teams and products and calls for divestment, contribute to greater public awareness of the realities of apartheid South Africa in the United Kingdom and elsewhere.

Although the promotion of migration to South Africa was not banned by the UN Security Council, a 1968 UN resolution called for member states to 'discourage the flow of immigrants, particularly skilled and technical personnel to South Africa' and similar resolutions continued thereafter.[43] ICEM, the intergovernmental agency which facilitated migration (including the migration of refugees) from Europe was criticised in 1974 for their role in assisting migration to apartheid South Africa by the UN General Assembly Special Committee on Apartheid, although South Africa continued as a member until 1980.[44] By the late 1970s, West Germany, the Netherlands and Switzerland all banned the promotion of migration to South Africa.[45]

Unlike these countries, the United Kingdom did not impose legal restrictions on the promotion of emigration to the South Africa as it had with the promotion of migration to Rhodesia. Under the Race Relations Act of 1968, however, advertisements indicating the intention to discriminate were unlawful including those advertising employment opportunities abroad. In practice, however, it was usually possible for advertisements for jobs in South Africa to be framed in such a way that they did not break the law. For instance, the Race Relations Board brought a case against the Nurses Association and the Associated Newspaper Groups that went to trial in March 1977. The advertisement in question, recruiting nurses for the Florence Nightingale Hospital in Johannesburg, did not specify that only white nurses would be employed, but did mention that as well as enjoying, 'All the year sunshine', free meals and serviced apartments, successful applicants would care for 'All white patients only'. The Race Relations Board argued that this statement along with a basic understanding of the situation in South Africa, would make it clear that only white nurses would be hired, but the judge and a subsequent appeal found that the advertisement did not 'indicate an intention to discriminate'.[46] The South African Department of Immigration worked with employers recruiting in Europe, offering guidance on how they could comply with local laws.[47]

As well as legal challenges, those opposed to migration also employed other tactics. On the same lines as campaigns against companies with investments in South Africa, there were attempts to target companies and organisations that either recruited in the United Kingdom for South African branches or cooperated with South African companies and the South African government to recruit white workers. However, the campaign against emigration faced particular difficulties. For instance, it was hard to identify potential emigrants or to place emigrants under pressure once they had moved abroad.[48]

These same difficulties occurred with union activism against emigration to South Africa. The Trades Union Congress passed resolutions against emigration to South Africa beginning in 1969, but it was difficult for unions to exert influence on members who moved abroad. Unions in the music, film and television industries such as the Musician's Union and the Association of Cinematograph, Television and Allied Technicians had the most success. Given that workers in those industries were frequently on short-term contracts rather than settling in South Africa permanently, such unions were more likely to have leverage in terms of threatening blacklisting or negative publicity to those who did go. The National Union of Students passed resolutions against emigration to South Africa in 1970 and 1973 and organised protests against recruiters on university campuses. These protests and the negative publicity they caused did have some impact, as fewer South African firms undertook such recruiting missions by the later 1970s or turned to less obvious means of recruitment.[49]

Barclays was a particular target of anti-apartheid campaigners because of its extensive operations in the Republic and its role in promoting emigration.

Barclays published a guidebook for emigrants to South Africa in 1971. Very similar in tone and appearance to the official South African publications discussed in the previous chapter, the guide also featured a section on 'the new South Africans', four families who had moved to four South African cities from the United Kingdom. The guide discussed the specifics of these cities: Cape Town, Johannesburg, Durban and Port Elizabeth, and gave examples including photographs of successful migrants and the opportunities South Africa offered to white migrants for career advancement and home ownership.[50] The campaign against Barclays, which included the disruption of the bank's annual general meeting in April 1972 as well as divestment campaigns and protests at branches was widely covered by the British press. Student activism and the National Union of Students also played a crucial role in the campaign against Barclays, which pulled out of its South African operations in 1986.[51]

Critiques of British migration to South Africa also came from religious organisations.[52] As early as 1965, the British Council of Churches called for measures to discourage emigration to South Africa, suggesting that an 'apartheid tax' could be levied on the air and sea passages of those travelling to South Africa to emigrate and that a limit of £10 could be imposed on the assets that could be taken out of the country.[53] In 1973, the Council published the pamphlet 'Emigration to Southern Africa'. The pamphlet is clearly designed to counter the arguments put forward by both the South Africa and Rhodesian governments that the migration of skilled white workers benefited Black workers by contributing to economic development. Outlining these arguments point by point, the pamphlet asserted that the migration of skilled white workers slowed the training and promotion of African workers and that the benefits of any economic development were not shared with the majority Black population of these countries. There was also a lot of soul-searching on the question of whether missionary societies should continue to send European staff to the region and whether this helped the anti-apartheid cause or not, ultimately concluding that this was a matter for further reflection.[54]

Organisations based in South Africa also launched campaigns against white migration. The Christian Institute, which would be banned by the apartheid government in 1977, published a pamphlet in 1974 that made a very passionate case against further white immigration, drawing on Christian theology and the idea of 'corporate guilt and responsibility' that all white South Africans and white migrants benefited from the exploitation of Black South Africans. Firmly opposing the much-cited argument that the arrival of every skilled white worker created jobs for ten Black workers, the pamphlet argued that to the contrary, white immigration bolstered both the racial labour hierarchy and the apartheid state and that a better way to assist Black workers was to train and promote them. The pamphlet called for an 'immediate end to organised white immigration to the Republic', for foreign governments to ban recruitment in their countries and 'dissuade their citizens', for newspapers and journals to refuse to carry advertisements for positions in South Africa, for employers, trades unions, universities and churches to actively oppose such migration and even for white immigrants already in South Africa to consider whether their presence was contributing to the unjust system in South Africa and either leave or 'work vigorously' against apartheid if they chose to stay.[55]

Another example of opposition from within South Africa was a 1983 letter written by the South African Bishop's Commission for Justice and Reconciliation, a Catholic organisation, aimed at refugees, many of them Catholic, from the communist regime in Poland, who had been offered visas by the South African government. Acknowledging and condemning the economic difficulties and political repression such refugees had faced in Poland, the letter, banned in South Africa, but published internationally by the Irish anti-apartheid movement, aimed to convince potential refugees that they would be contributing to similar repression by moving to South Africa.[56]

It is difficult to assess how successful these campaigns were in dissuading emigrants to South Africa. While there was a drop in British migration to South Africa in the late 1970s following the Soweto Uprising, rates of migration increased again from 1980 to 1982, before beginning their final decline. The curtailment of the subsidised migration scheme after 1982 is also likely to have played a role in the decline in British migration, as well as the escalation of the conflict between anti-apartheid forces and the regime and a downturn in the South African economy. Even so, these campaigns, along with broader campaigns against Rhodesia and apartheid South Africa certainly contributed to increasing awareness of the realities of segregation and exploitation in those nations. It became increasingly difficult for emigrants to Rhodesia and South Africa to claim ignorance or a disinterest in politics.

The politics of restriction and removal in the United Kingdom

While British opposition to apartheid and minority rule in Rhodesian was significant, it is also important to recognise that this was not the only form of engagement with the region in this period. Ongoing migration especially to South Africa, formed another important aspect of this interaction, and so did outspoken support for the Rhodesian and South African minority regimes and the racial ideologies upon which they were based, which were often linked with opposition to the immigration of people of colour to the United Kingdom. After the 1971 Immigration Act those advocating restriction increasingly turned their attention to the migration of the dependants of those already resident, which was allowed under the Act, arguing that there were high rates of fraud.[57] Alongside this continuation of the politics of restriction, emerged a new emphasis on the politics of removal, the so-called 'repatriation' of migrants of colour on the far right. A less extreme version of this, the idea of funding 'voluntary repatriation', aiding the return of migrants who wished to return to their countries of origin was a more mainstream position.

There were also continued concerns about emigration from the United Kingdom, which, as in earlier periods, were often entangled with concerns about the migration of people of colour to the United Kingdom. As they had been previously, high rates of emigration were put forward as evidence of the deterioration of the United Kingdom, in economic but also in social and cultural terms. This loss through emigration was frequently linked to the arrival of migrants of colour by advocates of immigration restriction and repatriation. The Conservative MP and member of the Monday Club, John Stokes, for instance, described in a letter to *The Times* in 1976: 'Our best people – those with brains and ambition, with energy and drive – are now increasingly leaving our shores and in replacement we are receiving mainly uneducated coloured people many of whom cannot even speak English.' Stokes cast this as an issue of 'national survival' for a 'once great nation'.[58] Here the racial ideology is clear, as is the emphasis on the nation, the concern that national decline was driving white emigration, which in turn accelerated that decline.

This was also evident in the publications of the Monday Club. A 1974 pamphlet, *Right Reason: A Monday Club Policy Document* asserted, 'The Monday Club insists on the historic claims of Conservatives to be a National Party. We are patriots.' This nation was one understood in firmly racial terms as white, drawing very explicitly on the racial ideologies of the British Empire, whose end, it described as 'calamitous'. As well as calling for support for a continuing military relationship with South Africa and the end of sanctions on Rhodesia, the document also advocated the repeal of the Race Relations Act, subsidies for the voluntary repatriation of immigrants and the deportation of 'illegal immigrants'.[59]

In terms of immigration, the pamphlet called for 'privileges for Australians, New Zealanders and Canadians of all races at least as favourable as those enjoyed by foreigners from the Community and the Irish Republic' and the cessation of all other immigration. Here again is an echo of imperial ideologies of racial kinship with the 'white Dominions', which continues in the promotion of the Anglo-sphere and CANZUK in contemporary and especially post-Brexit politics.[60] Although there is an attempt to avoid accusations of racism through the inclusion of 'of all races', given that the majority of people in Australia, New Zealand and Canada were white, this is fairly meaningless. Despite the support throughout the document for the white minority regimes in South Africa and Rhodesia, there is no suggestion that migrants 'of all races' from these nations should be included.[61]

The voluntary 'repatriation' of immigrants was also supported by the mainstream Conservative Party. The 1970 Conservative Party Manifesto included a provision for funding 'assistance to Commonwealth immigrants who wish to return to their countries of origin' alongside the disclaimer that 'any attempt to harass or compel them to go against their will' would not be tolerated.[62] This offer was specific to Commonwealth immigrants, and a provision for voluntary repatriation was included in the 1971 Immigration Act.[63] Very few took up the offer of voluntary repatriation, much to the disappointment of some of its advocates.[64]

More extreme groups called for the compulsory removal of people of colour resident in the United Kingdom. One example of this was the 'Send Them Back' campaign, which called for the 'compulsory repatriation of immigrants' in their 1971 manifesto.[65] The National Front also called for the removal of people of colour from the United Kingdom, a policy, which was also advocated by its successor, the British National Party until 1997.[66] While this was a minority view, there was significant support for it. Twenty-nine per cent of voters polled in a national survey shortly after the 1979 election were in favour of the removal of migrants of colour from the United Kingdom.[67] In many ways the economic conditions in the United Kingdom in the 1970s that contributed to increased rates of emigration also fuelled the growth of right-wing populist movements in this period.

Although these campaigns for the removal of people of colour from the United Kingdom were not successful, the racial ideology behind them, the definition of the British nation as a white nation, defined by blood, had an impact on the legal definition of British citizenship. The British Nationality Act of 1981 marked an abandonment of the centuries-old tradition of *jus soli* citizenship, by which any person born on British soil, regardless of their ethnic background or descent would be British.[68] The adoption of *jus sanguinis*, an understanding of British citizenship that prioritised descent or blood, in the 1981 Act was the culmination of the migration restrictions discussed in Chapter 5 and has ongoing ramifications today, as shown by the Windrush scandal.

Conclusion

While international sanctions and an escalating war with anti-colonial forces meant that Rhodesian government efforts to recruit white migrants were largely unsuccessful by the mid 1970s, attracting more white migrants and more importantly stemming the tide of white emigration from Rhodesia remained important priorities for the Rhodesian government until the very end of the regime. By contrast, the South African government was extremely successful in recruiting white migrants for much of the 1970s and into the 1980s. While many came from within Africa, rates of migration to South Africa from the United Kingdom were also high in this period, increasing in the 1970s from the already historically high rates of the 1960s. As well as benefiting from the subsidised migration schemes offered by the South African state, British migrants in the 1970s and 1980s were attracted, like those arriving in previous decades, by the climate and the opportunities and lifestyle available to a privileged white minority. As was the case with Rhodesia, when the prospects for the white minority and correspondingly the opportunities for white migrants in South Africa seemed less secure by the early 1980s and especially when, from 1982, subsidies were less widely available, rates of migration declined.

As this indicates, the story of the British relationship with Rhodesia and South Africa in the 1970s and 1980s cannot be reduced to opposition to apartheid and the Rhodesian regime. Indeed, the need for those opposed to minority rule in southern Africa to campaign against emigration indicates the extent of interest in the United Kingdom in moving to the region especially to South Africa. Though different in the case of Rhodesia, another important aspect of the relationship was official support for apartheid South Africa, especially in the context of the Cold War and ongoing economic engagement. As the volume of British migration indicates, the relationship was also constituted through the movement of individuals and the networks that they formed and this traffic continued even after the collapse of Rhodesia in 1980 and the end of apartheid in 1994. The next chapter considers the experience of British migrants in the aftermath of Zimbabwean independence and majority rule in South Africa.

Notes

1 'Prominent South African public figure seeks white workers to help maintain racist regime', Anti-Apartheid Movement Online Archive, www.aamarchives.org/archive/goods/posters/po019-prominent-south-african-public-figure-seeks-white-workers.html (accessed 25 March 2021).
2 Loans were still available but at a 6 per cent interest rate. Smith, 'Persistence and Privilege', pp. 386–7.
3 Ibid.

4 Although the high growth rates of the 1960s had already begun to slow by the 1970s and would be hastened by sanctions and the increasing withdrawal of foreign investment following the Soweto Uprising, this was mitigated by the rising gold prices and high rates of state spending on defence and infrastructure. Stuart Jones and Jon Inggs, 'An overview of the South African economy in the 1970s', *South African Journal of Economic History* 14:1–2 (1999), 2. Similarly, the increase in gold prices in 1979 and 1980 also provided a boost to the South African economy, which lasted into the early 1980s. By the mid 1980s, however, capital flight and the increasing pressure of sanctions led to a sustained economic decline. Dubow, *Apartheid*, pp. 195, 222–3.
5 Kenrick, *Decolonisation, Identity and Nation*, pp. 39–43.
6 Brownell, *Collapse of Rhodesia*, pp. 121–2.
7 Ibid., p. 125.
8 Migrants from the United Kingdom made up the largest group of white migrants to South Africa throughout the apartheid regime and on a yearly basis were only exceeded by migrants from Southern Rhodesia/Rhodesia in the years stated above and in 1961 and 1962, when concerns about Sharpeville and the South African declaration of republic deterred British migrants and many left Southern Rhodesia due to concern about the break-up of the Federation. Peberdy, *Selecting Immigrants*, pp. 260–90.
9 R.P. 41/1975, *Report of the Department of Immigration for the period 1 July 1972 to 30 June 1974* (Pretoria: The Government Printer, 1975), p. 4; R.P. 18/1977, *Report of the Department of Immigration for the period 1 July 1974 to 30 June 1976* (Pretoria: The Government Printer, 1977), p. 4.
10 R.P. 18/1977, *Report of the Department of Immigration, 1974–76*, p. 1.
11 Dubow, *Apartheid*, p. 195.
12 Peberdy, *Selecting Immigrants*, pp. 123–5.
13 Ibid., pp. 125–30.
14 R.P. 21/1980, Department of the Interior, *Annual Report for the Calendar Year 1979* (Pretoria: The Government Printer, 1980), p. 26.
15 R.P. 17/1979, *Report of the Department of Immigration for the period 1 July 1976 to 30 June 1978* (Pretoria: The Government Printer, 1979), pp. 2–3, 17–18.
16 R.P. 46/1981, Department of Internal Affairs, *Annual Report for the Calendar Year 1980* (Pretoria: The Government Printer, 1981), p. 8.
17 Ibid., p. 9. Dubow, *Apartheid*, pp. 196–9.
18 Peberdy, *Selecting Immigrants*, pp. 120–3, 143–4, 268–89; Conway and Leonard, *Migration, Space*, pp. 39–40.
19 Cited in Brownell, *Collapse of Rhodesia*, p. 121.
20 Peter Godwin and Ian Hancock, *'Rhodesians Never Die': The Impact of War and Political Change on White Rhodesia, c. 1970–1980* (Oxford: Oxford University Press, 1993), p. 138. See also Brownell, *Collapse of Rhodesia*, p. 121.
21 Brownell, *Collapse of Rhodesia*, p. 123.
22 Ibid., pp. 127–8; Luise White, 'The Utopia of Working Phones: Rhodesian Independence and the Place of Race in Decolonization', in *Utopia/Dystopia*:

168 Settlers at the end of empire

Conditions of Historical Possibility, eds Michael D. Gordin, Helen Tilley and Gyan Prakash (Princeton: Princeton University Press, 2010), pp. 106–8; Gerald Horne, *From the Barrel of a Gun: The United States and the War Against Zimbabwe, 1965–1980* (Chapel Hill: University of North Carolina Press, 2001), pp. 201–40.
23 Quoted in Brownell, *Collapse of Rhodesia*, p. 123.
24 NAZ, S3285/14/147/3, M.N. Tsourolis, 'Report of the Chairman of the Executive Sub-Committee on Immigration', 1970.
25 De Kock had resigned from the Smith government two year before emigration in 1975. Godwin and Hancock, *Rhodesians Never Die*, pp. 123, 208, 359. See also Brownell, *Collapse of Rhodesia*, p. 123.
26 Brownell, *Collapse of Rhodesia*, pp. 88, 203.
27 Godwin and Hancock, *Rhodesians Never Die*, p. 208.
28 Brownell, *Collapse of Rhodesia*, p. 88.
29 As Alan Savoury, a Rhodesian MP in opposition to the Rhodesian Front put it, a better name would be the 'wise old owl route'. Quoted in Godwin and Hancock, *Rhodesians Never Die*, pp. 163–4. See also Brownell, *Collapse of Rhodesia*, p. 77.
30 Quoted in Brownell, *Collapse of Rhodesia*, pp. 71–2.
31 For South Africa see Godwin and Hancock, *Rhodesians Never Die*, p. 315. For white migration to the United Kingdom after independence see Christopher Roy Zembe, 'Migrating with Colonial and Post-Colonial Memories: Dynamics of Racial Interactions within Zimbabwe's Minority Communities in Britain', *Journal of Migration History* 2 (2016), 41–8.
32 NASA, MSK Vol. 576, Ref. 9/9/16/02, W.D. Alder to C.P. Mulder, 2 September 1978.
33 Brownell, *Collapse of Rhodesia*, p. 123.
34 The country was generally referred to as Southern Rhodesia in international fora such as the UN, as the Unilateral Declaration of Independence and resulting state of Rhodesia was not recognised. Item 8, United Nations Security Council, Resolution 253 (1968) of 29 May 1968.
35 Brownell, *Collapse of Rhodesia*, pp. 121–2.
36 United Nation Security Council Official Records, Twenty-Seventh Year, 1640th Meeting: 16 February 1972, New York, Item 19, p. 3. Luise White, '"Normal Political Activities": Rhodesia, The Pearce Commission, and the African National Council', *Journal of African History* 52 (2011), 326.
37 TNA, FCO 36/1463, Sir A. Snelling's Despatch on Rhodesia, p. 30.
38 Brownell, *Collapse of Rhodesia*, p. 92.
39 TNA, FCO 36/1634, D.R. Upton, Memorandum, 15 October 1974.
40 Brownell, *Collapse of Rhodesia*, p. 93.
41 TNA, FCO 36/1634, D.R. Upton, Memorandum, 'Encouraging White Emigration from Rhodesia', 18 July 1974.
42 Brownell, *Collapse of Rhodesia*, pp. 97–131.
43 UN General Assembly, Resolution 2396, 'The policies of apartheid of the Government of South Africa', 2 December 1968, p. 20. For more on the role of

the United Nations in the struggle against see Dubow, *Apartheid*, pp. 47–50, 83, 191, 278; Newell M. Stultz, 'Evolution of the United Nations Anti-Apartheid Regime', in *Readings in the International Relations of Africa*, ed. Tom Young (Bloomington: Indiana University Press, 2016).

44 Jérôme Elie, 'The Historical Roots of Cooperation Between the UN High Commissioner for Refugees and the International Organization for Migration', *Global Governance: A Review of Multilateralism and International Organizations* 16:3 (2010), 360. RP 46/1981, Department of Internal Affairs, *Annual Report for the Calendar Year 1980*, p.8.

45 R.P. 17/1979, *Report of the Department of Immigration 1976–1978*, pp. 3–4. The Netherlands, which in this period subsidised emigration, also removed the subsidy for emigration to South Africa. British Council of Churches, *Emigration to South Africa* (London: The British Council of Churches, 1973), p. 8.

46 *First Report of the Commission for Racial Equality, June 1977–December 1977* (London: HMSO, 1978), pp. 114–15. See also TNA, CK 2/148, 'Memorandum Ref IC/29', 14 March 1977.

47 The Department called for companies to work with the government on overseas recruitment and emphasised the importance of 'a discreet approach'. R.P. 21/1971, *Report of the Department of Immigration for the period 1 July 1968 to 30 June 1970* (Pretoria: The Government Printer, 1971), p. 1.

48 International Defence and Aid Fund, *Southern Africa: Immigration from Britain* (Geneva: Centre Europe Tiers Monde, 1975), pp 14–15.

49 Ibid., p. 15.

50 *Emigrating to South Africa: A Guide to Procedure and Introduction to Life in the Republic* (London: Barclays Bank DSO, 1971).

51 Christabel Gurney, 'The 1970s: The Anti-Apartheid Movement's Difficult Decade', *Journal of Southern African Studies* 35:2 (2009), 474; Nerys John, 'The Campaign against British Bank Involvement in Apartheid South Africa', *African Affairs* 99:396 (2000), 415–33; Jodi Burkett, '"Don't Bank on Apartheid": The National Union of Students and the Boycott Barclays Campaign', in *Students in Twentieth-Century Britain and Ireland*, ed. Jodi Burkett (London: Palgrave Macmillan, 2018).

52 For more on the wide range of Christian responses to apartheid in the United Kingdom see Gurney, 'The 1970s', pp. 477–80.

53 British Council of Churches, *The Future of South Africa: A Study by British Christians* (London: SCM Press, 1965), pp. 79, 89.

54 British Council of Churches, *Emigration to South Africa*.

55 Gurney, 'The 1970s', p. 479; The Christian Institute of South Africa, *White Immigration to South Africa* (Johannesburg: Zenith Printers, 1974).

56 *The Case Against Immigration to South Africa: The Ugly Reality of Apartheid* (Dublin: Dominican Publications, 1983).

57 Dummett and Nicol, *Subjects, Citizens*, pp. 232–52; Evan Smith and Marinella Marmo, 'Uncovering the "Virginity Testing" Controversy in the National Archives: The Intersectionality of Discrimination in British Immigration History', *Gender & History* 23:1 (2011); Hansen, *Citizenship and Immigration*.

58 'Dealing with Immigration Problems', Letter to the editor from Mr John Stokes, MP, *The Times*, 27 May 1976, p. 17.
59 The London School of Economics Archive, LONGDEN/3/11, Monday Club, *Right Reason: A Monday Club Policy Document*, 1974.
60 Duncan Bell and Srdjan Vucetic, 'Brexit, CANZUK, and the legacy of empire', *The British Journal of Politics and International Relations* 21:2 (2019).
61 Monday Club, *Right Reason: A Monday Club Policy Document*.
62 Conservative Party, *A Better Tomorrow: The Conservative Party General Election Manifesto 1970* (London: Conservative Party, 1970).
63 A similar mechanism for funding the voluntary return of Commonwealth migrants under the National Assistance Board had also existed previously. Hansen, *Citizenship and Immigration*, p. 194.
64 According to a statement in Parliament, only 139 people were voluntarily repatriated in 1980–81. *Parliamentary Debates, Commons*, 6th Ser., Vol. 24, 22 May 1982, Col. 461.
65 Quoted in Camilla Schofield, *Enoch Powell and the Making of Postcolonial Britain* (Cambridge: Cambridge University Press, 2013), p. 270.
66 Nigel Copsey, *Contemporary British Fascism: The British National Party and the Quest for Legitimacy* (London: Palgrave Macmillan, 2008), pp. 26, 32, 71, 74, 89–90, 104, 123.
67 Bo Särlvik and Ivor Crewe, *Decade of Dealignment: The Conservative Victory of 1979 and Electoral Trends in the 1970s* (Cambridge: Cambridge University Press, 1983), p. 243.
68 El-Enany, *Bordering Britain*, pp. 125–32.

7

'I still don't have a country': The southern African settler diaspora after decolonisation

This chapter traces the impact of decolonisation on the trajectories and sense of identity of British migrants to South Africa and Rhodesia in the second half of the twentieth century. Based on oral history interviews, it explores the disorienting effects of decolonisation and the serial migrations to which it often led. These migrants experienced a double dislocation, both when South Africa declared itself a republic and left the Commonwealth in 1961 and Rhodesia declared independence from Britain in 1965, and again when these white minority regimes ended with the advent of the 'new' South Africa in 1994 and independent Zimbabwe in 1980. The first instance called into question ideas of 'Britishness' or 'Englishness', with new emphasis on Rhodesian or South African identities, though some, especially in South Africa, asserted a British identity, often in critique of their government's actions. At the onset of majority rule, when Rhodesia and apartheid South Africa no longer existed, these Rhodesian or South African identities were also called into question.

Like recent scholarship on 'orphans of empire', this chapter broadens the work on French and Portuguese imperial 'repatriates' to include the British experience, focusing attention on southern Africa and, importantly, on those who did not return to Britain.[1] Close attention to these alternate sites demonstrates that although British South Africans and ex-Rhodesians are far more scattered, they have much in common with other 'colonials' after the end of empire including a sense of exile, exclusion and a loss of status.

The experience of these migrants is similar to their counterparts earlier in the history of the British Empire in many ways, though the added complication of decolonisation meant that not only did they have to adapt to the settler colonial nations to which they moved, but they had to adapt again when these nations severed ties with the United Kingdom and then again at the onset of majority rule. David Lambert and Alan Lester's examination of nineteenth-century imperial migrations found that such travels could leave migrants with a feeling of 'double exile' from both their place of origin and other locations where they had lived.[2] Lambert and Lester also consider the 'reformulations of identities' and 'changes in personhood that came from dwelling in different spaces'.[3] Post-war British migrants underwent similar experiences as they changed physical location and as the changing political circumstances of decolonisation transformed the nations in which they lived. Like Britons who returned to the United Kingdom from India after decolonisation these migrants often felt like exiles and struggled to feel at home in British society.[4] Looking beyond the British case, there are parallels in other European empires, who, as Andrea L. Smith argues, formed 'diasporas of decolonisation' focused on more than one homeland including one that no longer exists.[5] Like the *retornados* from Portuguese colonies and *pieds noirs* from Algeria, ex-Rhodesians and other British migrants form part of a diaspora with multiple homelands, including both the settler colonial society in which they lived, but which no longer exists and the United Kingdom or some imagined version of it.

Here it is important to stress the wide range of responses and identities expressed by British migrants to South Africa and Rhodesia. These depended on a wide range of factors including their own political beliefs, their reasons for migration, how long they stayed, whether they intended to move permanently, their age at migration and their experiences in Africa. While many viewed Rhodesia and apartheid South Africa with fond nostalgia, others were ardent supporters of independent Zimbabwe and the 'new' South Africa.

This chapter's analysis of individual accounts provides a way to explore the impact of multiple instances of decolonisation on British migrants through specific cultural practices and performances of identity and nationalism such as accent, self-presentation, interior design, dress, outdoor leisure in the 'bush,' support of a national sports team, and even attendance at a Rhodesian reunion in Las Vegas. Through focusing on individual narratives, this account highlights the complex and varied impact of decolonisation on the ways in which British migrants understand themselves. To this end, the chapter is based on close readings of self-narrations of ten migrants. Most are oral histories conducted by the author in the United Kingdom, South Africa and the United States from 2009 to 2012, but they also include written questionnaires gathered by Patricia Lin in the 1990s and held at the Imperial War Museum.

Oral history is used here as a unique means to gain insight into subjectivity, to better understand how migrants present their stories and what meanings they attribute to decolonisation in the larger narrative of their lives. As Alessandro Portelli has argued, whether the oral histories are precise recollections is less important than the meaning the narrator attributes to particular events.[6] Because these interviews were undertaken decades after many of the events under consideration and in a very different political context, this is likely to have shaped their content and therefore it is this retrospective appraisal that is the subject of analysis. To convey the often complex ways that these migrants made sense of their experiences, the chapter relies on extended quotations.[7]

The first section describes the way in which the identity and self-presentation of post-war British migrants evolved through the sequential decolonisations of South Africa and Rhodesia and the serial migrations they provoked. The second describes the way in which nostalgia for the landscape and the wildlife of southern Africa both formed part of the material culture of decolonisation and became a seemingly apolitical way to express the loss of the status and way of life accorded to members of the ruling white minority in South Africa and Rhodesia. Both highlight the pervading theme of dislocation experienced by these post-war migrants because of their own movements as well as the political changes that often prompted them.

Serial migration and dislocation

A primary theme threading through the oral histories of British migrants is that of dislocation, of not really belonging to any specific nation or group. For those who have lived in more than one country, their primary identity often becomes that of a migrant.[8] In the case of British migrants to southern Africa this dislocation was intensified by the turmoil of decolonisation and the serial migrations spurred by the end of empire. As discussed in prior chapters, many of the white migrants to both Rhodesia and South Africa in the 1960s and 1970s had lived in other parts of Africa, often leaving in the run-up to independence or thereafter. While many moved directly, others came after spending some time in the United Kingdom.[9] Many left South Africa after the onset of majority rule in 1994, often going to Australia, so that 'packing for Perth' became a cliché, although New Zealand, the United States and the United Kingdom were also popular destinations. Such multiple migrations combined with the redefinition of post-colonial nations meant that many post-war migrants did not feel that they belonged fully in any of the places where they had lived and their self-presentation often shifted in response to their changing circumstances.[10]

Andrew Smith moved from England to what was then Northern Rhodesia (now Zambia) as a child, went to school in Southern Rhodesia (now Zimbabwe), subsequently migrated to South Africa and later returned to England. His movements loosely followed the progress of decolonisation, from Zambian independence in 1964 to majority rule in South Africa in 1994. His account illustrates this complicated trajectory of migration, corresponding changes in his perception of his own identity and the resulting sense of not really belonging anywhere:

> And, the first time I came [to England] in 1969, the guy said, 'Welcome home, sir.' I thought okay well I s'pose I'm English. You have a kind of, well … a crisis of identity. I actually still don't have a country. One of the reasons I want to go back to Zambia is I want to see if that's my country. I don't feel at home anywhere. I feel at home with people and I like being with people of many races. And I guess I am a citizen of the world or whatever but I don't have a country. When I was growing up in what was then Northern Rhodesia, I said to my Dad, 'We're Rhodesian.' He said, 'No you're not, you're English.' I said, 'We're Rhodesian.' He said, 'No you're English.' … I thought I was Rhodesian. That was the only country I knew, I had been there since I was a baby so I thought this was what I am. Then of course it became Zambia and we had a choice, you could either give up your British passport, you weren't allowed to have dual nationality. I was advised not to give up my British passport so I couldn't become a Zambian. So, I wasn't a Zambian. And by that stage anyway, I then moved to South Africa. When I got to South Africa, I found out I was an Englishman, or an Engelsman, not an Afrikaner so I was not a South African. And, then of course when independence came, I was white not black, so I, you know, I wasn't really the real thing either … So, I have never had a country. So, I always used to, perhaps to the disappointment of my sons particularly, I always used to support English sports teams. So, I said, 'Well, I'm English, I must be English. I was born in England. I'm English. I'll support the English sports teams.' But then I came to England and I've been here for eight years and I'm not English and I don't mind living here. I enjoy what I do. I enjoy being with all kinds of people but I am not English.[11]

Multiple instances of decolonisation shaped both the physical trajectory of Smith's life and his perceptions of himself. Decolonisation meant that Smith could no longer be Rhodesian and he did not feel that he was really a South African either. In what became a recurring theme in oral history interviews, this sense of not belonging led Smith to define himself as English, but only while he remained in southern Africa. For example, supporting English sports teams provided a way to signify an English identity in South Africa, but the instability of this affiliation was evident on his return to the United Kingdom, when it became clear that he was not considered to be, nor did he feel himself to be, English once he had returned to England. Not feeling that he was really South African or English, while being considered by others to be English in South Africa and South African in England, Smith describes himself as both a 'citizen of the world' and a man without a country.

A series of migrations and the end of Rhodesia also meant shifts in the identity of William Jervois. Jervois moved to Southern Rhodesia in the late 1940s on the Fairbridge Memorial College child migration scheme discussed in Chapter 3.[12] Unhappy at school, he joined the Rhodesian Air Force in his teens and although he travelled to England for training in his twenties, he returned to Rhodesia and remained there, continuing to work for the newly independent government in Zimbabwe until the mid 1980s. Though initially hopeful about independent Zimbabwe, he later become disillusioned and he and his wife moved to South Africa in the 1980s, eventually settling in Grahamstown, where I interviewed him in 2011. He and his wife Helen returned to the United Kingdom a few years later. When asked about his identity, Jervois replied,

> I have always thought of myself as British. Because now I can't claim ... I did feel quite strongly that I was a Rhodesian, certainly ... But, when Rhodesia ceased to exist, then I just think of myself as British. I am not a South African citizen. I took an oath of loyalty to the Queen when I joined the Air Force.

For Jervois, the end of Rhodesia meant the end of that identification. His phrasing that after the end of Rhodesia 'I just think of myself as British' and his mention of the oath of loyalty to the Queen suggests that even before 1980 he had thought of himself as both Rhodesian and British.[13]

This is borne out in his discussion of his childhood and young adulthood. Jervois described a sense of being stuck between two identities as he moved between southern Africa and the United Kingdom. In a sense this perception was also heightened by the ideology of the institution where he was raised, the Fairbridge Memorial College, which brought British children to Rhodesia explicitly to supplement the settler colony's white British population. Jervois mentioned that the reason that Fairbridge Memorial College, like many other imperial immigration schemes, focused on children was that they were 'considered to be more adaptable and more malleable'. He went onto say that generally this was true, although not entirely, as many Fairbridge students 'maintained our sense of British identity very strongly' and were 'very slow to adopt Rhodesian mannerisms or southern African mannerisms and dialect'. This idea of being caught between two nationalities, belonging fully to neither is also evident in his reflection of how he was perceived by others, which shifted depending on the context. As he explained, 'when I go to England now I am regarded as some sort of colonial just by the way I speak and coming back here I am regarded as some sort of Englishman.'[14] Accent here serves as a marker of identity and contributed to how Jervois was perceived by others. The fact that in England he was considered to be a 'colonial' rather than an Englishman may also have contributed to his self-described identity as British, rather than English, and his mention of his oath of loyalty to the Queen was also broader than a specific geographically based identity.

It follows that Jervois would feel a connection to the United Kingdom: he was born there, spent his early childhood there, returned several times as an adult, eventually retiring there, and grew up in an institution with a very British and indeed imperial ethos. However, it was also related to the nature of settler culture in Rhodesia; British settlement and colonisation was relatively recent (in the 1890s) and there were still close cultural affiliations with the United Kingdom.[15] As he describes:

> everybody in Rhodesia in those years, even the ones whose grandparents had immigrated there in the 1890s, we all still talked about Britain as 'home'. There was a very strong sense of identity with the Empire, right up ... to UDI in fact. There was still this very strong loyalty to the Crown and to the British way of life, generally. Remember of course, most Rhodesians were totally unaware of the rapid social changes that were taking place in Britain and uh, all sorts of things, people came out to visit Rhodesia, often said it was like stepping back fifty years. The clothing that we wore, the suits that men wore were maybe twenty years out of fashion with what was happening overseas or more. From here, when Helen and I first got married, I would wear a suit to go to town. Helen would wear a hat and gloves. It was the done thing. I remember in the tiny little town of Gwelo, when I first went there, people going to the cinema; a lot of them would wear evening dress. Black coat and bow tie and all the rest of it, simply to go the pictures. It was a social occasion and there were things like Mrs Antoniadus' musical evenings and the schools would put on Gilbert and Sullivan as a standard thing. So, it was a very, very, imperial mindset that a lot of people had. In fact, one of the only really socialist people we had were a small bundle of people who came out from Britain to join our Air Force and uh, that was the first time that I ever heard any hostility expressed towards the Queen and I was absolutely staggered by this chap.[16]

This quote illustrates not only the 'Britishness' of Rhodesian settler culture, but more specifically the particular conservative version of 'Britishness' that it upheld: allegiance to the empire, to the monarchy and even to social conventions in things such as dress that were increasingly outdated in the United Kingdom itself. This idea of Rhodesia as an outpost of imperial values in a rapidly changing world became stronger after the Rhodesian government declared itself independent in 1965. Jervois mentions UDI, the Unilateral Declaration of Independence, as a potential rupture for this affiliation with Britain, a moment of decolonisation addressed in more detail below.

The way that identities might shift over time in response to the politics of decolonisation and the personal moves they often led to is also clear in Brien Bonnynge's story. Born in South Africa to Irish parents who came out after the war, Bonnynge moved as a young child to what was then Southern Rhodesia. After serving in the British South Africa Police, including during the war for independence, Bonnynge, who had married Anne, a woman he met on a trip to England in the 1970s, moved back to South Africa, where he lived until 2012 when he and his wife moved to Liverpool to be closer to her family. Bonnynge described a strong sense of being Rhodesian as a child and young adult, heightened by the experience of the Unilateral Declaration of Independence in 1965. When asked about his identity growing up Bonnynge described the coexistence of distinctive national identities within an overriding sense of being Rhodesian. He reflected on his childhood in Southern Rhodesia when everyone would attend various events hosted by patriotic societies:

> *Brien Bonnynge*: Well everybody there had this Rhodesian sense, okay, everyone was in it together. Okay? ... You had the Mashonaland Irish Association, you had the Greek Association, you had all these different associations ... everybody just got together, you just happened to be of Irish descent but the overriding feeling was [pause] Rhodesia was all-important. But we would be Irish within that and be very good friends with the Scots and the Welsh and a few of the English, you know ... My parents actually ended up being on the committee ... of the Mashonaland Irish Association ... they used to have St Patrick's nights, but everyone came to them and the Scots would have Burns nights and everyone would go to them. So, it was just an excuse for a party ... So the Irish made a party and then the Scots made a party and the English made a party and whatever ...
> *Jean Smith*: So ... you have more than one identity, more than one affiliation?
> *Brien Bonnynge*: Yes, definitely, yes, the overriding one was the country you were in, but within that you had your own because you had to cling to something. Because it was all so new, you couldn't be, there's no history so you tend to go back to your roots to be what you are, well ... I don't have an Irish accent and I have never lived there but I have an Irish passport so I suppose that makes me Irish. But I have never lived there.[17]

Here Bonnynge describes a sense of needing another identity, beyond that of being Rhodesian, attributing this to the idea of Rhodesia as a country without history. While this could be interpreted as the stereotypical colonial view of African history beginning only with the arrival of Europeans, it also reflects Bonnynge's own personal sense that his roots lay outside of Rhodesia. Yet although he does come to the eventual conclusion that he must be Irish based on his passport and his family, he does so with ambivalence, with numerous caveats about how he has never lived there and does not speak with an Irish accent.

These multiple national affiliations subsumed by the umbrella identity of Rhodesian, would also provide a possible alternate form of belonging, especially after the collapse of Rhodesia. Before that and especially after UDI, the sense of community Bonnynge describes is one of a *white* Rhodesia, which in reflected in his assertion that, everyone, regardless of national origin would attend the events of the various patriotic societies and that 'Rhodesia was all-important'. His discussion of UDI in 1965 highlights this and illustrates the way that political events could crystallise a sense of identity, even if it might change again later.[18] UDI, like the South African declaration of republic in 1961, was a moment of decolonisation in that it resulted in the severing of ties between metropole and colony. Yet, both were distinctive moments of decolonisation because they preserved settler colonial rule rather than end colonial domination. UDI therefore was a moment of decolonisation that promoted and strengthened settler colonial identity and culture.

Bonnynge describes watching television coverage of the announcement of UDI at Plumtree, the boarding school he attended, and the way that it reinforced his Rhodesian identity:

> I remember seeing it on TV. Everyone told me this was important. Look, I was, I was, about 15, 16 so ja, you know, it was going to affect me. I knew it was going to affect me. Of course, we were all imbibed with the spirit of [holds up his middle finger] 'Up yours!' okay. Because that's how we all felt about UDI. So, we thought, yeah, bring it on. You know what I mean? Not understanding the full, impact ... Because you don't know. I had no clue about politics, or politicians. But I knew that something momentous had happened. For the next two years of school nothing really changed. Nothing in my life really changed. Because Rhodesia still maintained. They were still doing the politics with the UDI and everything else. So, there was a bit of bravado because I was a youngster and ... Ja come here, I thought, we'll go and sort out these pommie bastards. Ja.

For Bonnynge as a schoolboy, UDI cemented a strong sense of Rhodesian unity and identity.[19] His memory of aggression against 'pommie bastards' shows a clear division between himself and the 'English', which may also have been informed by his Irish ancestry. His strong sense of being Rhodesian was also further cemented by his service in one of the most Rhodesian of all institutions, the British South Africa Police, including during the war against anti-colonial forces in the 1970s, a period of his life that he was not willing to speak about in the interview.

Despite this strong affiliation with Rhodesia, another moment of decolonisation, Zimbabwean independence, and Bonnynge's move to South Africa in the 1980s meant another shift in identity presentation. In a similar way to Smith's recollection of not being a South African because he was not an Afrikaner, Bonnynge described a shift to a more British identity in the South African context. He was hired by the cigarette company, Rothmans of Pall Mall, to drive a Rolls Royce as their sales representative, with the persona of 'Mr Dunhill'. He believed that he got the job in part because of his Rhodesian accent, which meant that he fit better with Dunhill's image:

> So here I was going around in two- or three-piece suits, oooh, with little fob pockets and everything. Yes, from all accounts I did it very well. Well, you see the accent is good too. They wanted people who didn't have a, [puts on a strong Afrikaans accent] 'Ja sommer, you know I am from Dunhill,' I mean it would never have worked you understand. You had to have someone who had an English feeling to it. And the colonial accent was considered quite English, so okay ... So yes, I ended up being Mr Dunhill.

Though the display of Englishness was in part the gimmick of being 'Mr Dunhill' and perhaps connected to his marriage to a woman from England, it also became a way of differentiating himself from Afrikaners. Bonnynge describes a party he threw in Durban for Prince Andrew and Sarah Ferguson's wedding in 1986:

> We got a meal with silver service from the Royal Hotel, which is, I mean really top-notch. It was a five-star hotel. So silver service laid out there with everything. All the different glasses in ascending and descending order. And you get confused because of all the knives and forks you have. We all took the day off and we got the British Embassy to give us a flag. And we got a flagpole and we put up the flag and saluted the flag and pulled it up and pulled it down at night. And all the rest. And everyone came and had a party with us. It was ... it was a good reason for a party. But it was also, that was what Dunhill was all about, it was very British, very English. Wonderful time. Yes.

Holding a party to celebrate the royal wedding and saluting the Union Jack in the Republic of South Africa even in the context of a promotion for Dunhill cigarettes made a definite statement, very much in line with the idea of Natal as 'the last outpost of the British Empire'.[20] Looking at this anecdote alongside the desire to get the 'pommie bastards' after UDI illustrates the complexity of national identity and its presentation and how this could shift in relation to the politics of decolonisation and personal circumstances.[21]

As Bonnynge's discussion of 'Mr Dunhill' illustrates, accent acted as an important marker of identity. Aside from how he perceived his own national identity, Jervois' accent marked him as an outsider both in South Africa and in the United Kingdom. Bonnynge specifically mentions his lack of an Irish accent when discussing his claim to an Irish identity and how his Rhodesian accent in South Africa allowed him to play the role of the English 'Mr Dunhill'. The writer Alexandra Fuller also notes the importance of accent in her memoir. Her British-born mother, Nicola Fuller, returned from Kenya to London for secretarial school in the 1960s. She describes how her mother turned down the offer of a coming-out ball with characteristic flair, 'the sort of Englishman who went to those balls would have sneered at me because I was a colonial ... They'd all have been terribly snobbish and listened like hawks for a slip in my accent; if I made the slightest mistake with my pronunciation, they would have pounced.' Despite this criticism of English snobbery, Fuller also describes her mother's attempts to teach her children received pronunciation, to bring down the pitch of their voices and avoid Rhodesian slang, illustrating her keen awareness of the importance of accent as a marker of identity and social standing.[22] This is also tied into the importance of the formative years, when one's way of speaking is generally established, to identity, both in terms of self-perception and the ways in which a person is perceived by others.

The complex effect of migration on identity, especially migration at a young age is evident in many of the reminiscences of children evacuated to South Africa during the Second World War. Alfred Reid, evacuated to stay with his aunt and uncle in Johannesburg at the age of fourteen, returned to the United Kingdom after the war, beginning a pattern of migration that would span much of the Commonwealth. Returning to the United Kingdom in December 1947 after completing an apprenticeship, he stated:

> I regarded my return to Britain as a holiday and returned to S.A. by 18 months. I stayed in my hometown for 3 weeks immediately on my return and only made 2 brief return visits before returning to S.A. I was completely estranged from my family and did not feel, nor did I wish to fit in. I also had nothing in common with former friends. S.A. was now my country and I felt a closer attachment to my Aunt and Uncle.

This sense of estrangement upon return to the United Kingdom was a common theme in these accounts. Yet Reid's return to South Africa in 1949 did not result in his permanent settlement as his 'host-uncle' died shortly after his return. Reid didn't feel at home in South Africa or England, a common experience of many migrants, especially those who moved at a young age. Reid set off on a long series of migrations around the Commonwealth:

> Having broken friendship ties by my absence from S.A. for 18 months and also having a different outlook on the internal political situation there caused I believe by an 18-month absence, I decided to go to Australia where I spent 1 year. Then on to New Zealand also for 1 year. I then travelled to Canada meeting my future and present wife on the voyage.

Reid married in 1953, moving to the United States in 1959 for five years and then back to England for a further five years before returning to Canada in 1969.[23]

For another child evacuee, Laura Wynn, her voyage to South Africa was also the first of many. She reluctantly returned to the United Kingdom in January 1946, 'because I felt I had no alternative, my parents had sacrificed a lot to send us away and I felt I must return to them, though I didn't really want to'. Wynn recounts, 'Britain seemed very grey and the people very dull to an 18 year old's eyes. My poor parents seemed very stodgy, father too strict and mother too condemning of behaviour and attitudes. Could not really adjust and joined the WRENS.' After three years in the Women's Royal Navy Service and then later in the Foreign Office working as a cipher clerk, she married an Australian-born Royal Navy officer. After a series of moves dictated by her husband's naval career, they relocated to Australia following his retirement from the navy in 1960.[24]

Henry Henderson was evacuated to South Africa at the age of five and his sense of not belonging and restlessness is even more strongly expressed. When he returned after the war, his parents had split up and 'England seemed drab, cold, austere, old fashioned. Having spent 5 years longing to return the reality was devastating ... I was now in a position where I felt I belonged nowhere.' This had a profound impact on the rest of his life: 'I have spent most of my life on the move – Never felt settled after the war – lived in Australia, Bahrain, Tanzania, England ... I don't (to this day) feel that I belong anywhere. Nothing seems permanent to me ... I always feel as though I'm about to move on ... To this day I feel like a refugee.'[25]

While Henderson's sense of loss was tied to the idea that he didn't belong anywhere, the theme of loss took on a slightly different tone for those who had felt rooted in Rhodesia or South Africa but had left after independence. Smith, Bonnynge and Jervois all moved to South Africa from Zambia and Rhodesia as those countries gained or were close to gaining independence. Despite differences in their experience, they illustrate the compounding sense of dislocation engendered by the repeated migrations undertaken by many Britons who came to South Africa and Rhodesia in the decades after the Second World War. As they describe, because of family influence or in the case of Jervois the institution that he grew up in, this idea that they were not Rhodesian or not only Rhodesian but also English or British or Irish was reinforced. But, because their formative experiences were spent away from the United Kingdom, this identity was not secure. They might consider themselves English or British and then find that they were not accepted as such when they visited the British Isles. This was a common experience for those who travelled to the United Kingdom from the settler empire, as Angela Woollacott in her study of Australian women travelling to Britain in an earlier period has shown.[26] Here the dislocating effects of migration were compounded by decolonisation.

Nostalgia and the southern African landscape

As well as dislocation, the theme of loss and nostalgia came through strongly in many of the interviews. Yet, this was not uniformly the case. Some experienced settler society as suffocating and welcomed the end of settler rule. Regardless of their political perspective, most expressed a love of the southern African landscape and an appreciation for its beauty. Many specifically mentioned the houses and gardens that they had left behind when leaving Rhodesia or South Africa. Another expression of nostalgia came in the form of memories about spending time in the outdoors and the freedom and adventure this represented.[27] The 'bush' was a common feature in these oral histories and memoirs. It could serve as a seemingly neutral way to explain the attraction of moving to and living in the minority settler colonial regimes of southern Africa without condoning or even addressing the racial policies of those states. As David Hughes has argued, an important locus of a distinctive white Rhodesian identity was the landscape and wildlife, and a similar trend is evident among many white South Africans.[28]

Thelma and Harold Robson, living in the United States when interviewed, had both moved to Southern Rhodesia from England in the 1940s, Thelma as a child and Harold as a young adult. They moved to the United States first in the 1970s and later returned for a time to Rhodesia before permanently settling in California. Though they were convinced that they had made the right decision in leaving, especially for their sons' prospects, their discussion of their time in Rhodesia was tinged with a sense of loss. After gaining the green card that would allow them entry to the United States, they had to leave Rhodesia in three months and consequently abandoned their house in Harare:

> *Harold Robson*: So, imagine, three months, we got to get rid of this, get rid of that ... We still have a house sitting there. Can't do nothing about it. Sitting in Harare. Still got a house. Don't get no money from it. Nothing. But it's sitting there ...
> *Thelma Robson*: Fully furnished.
> *Harold Robson*: Got the title deeds. Everything.
> *Thelma Robson*: But there's an African woman in there with her daughter.
> *Harold Robson*: And the house is as good as this ... [points to the wall of their current home]
> *Thelma Robson*: It's brick.
> *Harold Robson*: Yes, it's brick and it has got a nice garden, everything. In a nice area within the view of Salisbury or Harare. So, anyway that was ... [trails off] Then we got here and we got back on our feet again. So, it's been a battle. So, that's twice I left a country with nothing ...[29]

Their house, made of brick with a 'nice garden' and in a 'nice area' represented the standard of living that they had achieved in Rhodesia. The loss of the house without compensation was the direct consequence of decolonisation. Though they still had the title deed, their house was now occupied by an African family, a microcosm of the collapse of minority rule in Rhodesia.

William Jervois also described his house in Harare, explaining that it was part of his reluctance to leave after independence. As he put it: 'we had a very comfortable house with three acres of balancing rocks and bushmen paintings and such like and a very pleasant way of life, living in Salisbury'.[30] This description strongly evokes not only the lifestyle available to white Rhodesians but also distinctive features of the southern African landscape, again illustrating the connection between nostalgia for the landscape and the way of life it signified.

This comes through even more clearly in the Robsons' reminiscences about Rhodesia. These were largely focused on the 'bush':

> *Thelma Robson*: And I do miss the bush. You could turn the clock back and you could live just like an African and I was quite happy with that ... I love the bush. He really loved the bush. In fact, I introduced him to the bush. When we got to Rhodesia, my dad met this electrician ... Man he was three generation Rhodesian, whoa! Did he show us the bush! Did he show us the bush. Man, oh, man, oh when we used to go and sleep next to a river. All you had was one blanket and a pillow if you were lucky and we dug the sand out.
> *Harold Robson*: With crocodiles, with lions roaring.[31]

This discussion of 'living like an African' in the bush, though it was discussed positively as an exciting adventure, reflects the common imperial trope of Africans as primitive, as stuck in the past, living outside of civilisation. It also provided a way to express a sense of belonging in Africa. Sleeping under the stars undeterred by the threat of crocodiles and lions was a way of claiming and mastering the landscape. This is like the preference of many ex-Rhodesians to call themselves 'white Africans' that Kate Law has found, a way of claiming belonging in Africa.[32] Professing a love for the outdoors and camping also provided a way to express the sense of loss entailed by leaving Rhodesia without explicitly addressing racial politics or the economic and social privileges of the ruling white minority.

The interior decor of the Robsons' home also reflected this nostalgia.[33] The house, filled with depictions of African wildlife and scenes, reflected their love of the African landscape. As well as copper hammered art depicting lions and elephants, they displayed African leatherwork, wood carvings and other curios. This self-presentation and their impressive collection of memorabilia including back issues of Rhodesian magazines suggest a deep-rooted nostalgia for their time in southern Africa, despite decades of living in the United States. The Robsons' identification with Rhodesia and nostalgia about their time there is also connected to their sense of loss, having abandoned their home in Harare to start a new life in the United States. The way they decorated their house suggests that their time in Africa remains an important part of their identity.

Another indication of this ongoing affiliation was the Robsons' involvement with the Rhodesian Association of the USA, which organised annual reunions, usually in Las Vegas.[34] The themes of these events also often focused on the African landscape. In recent years these included Jacaranda Days, with decorations resembling the distinctive purple of the jacaranda tree and Kariba, focused on the Kariba Dam and complete with inflatable crocodiles in the pool.[35] Here representations of the Rhodesian landscape stand in for a vanished homeland.

An affinity for the landscape and animals of southern Africa could also be a justification for moving to southern Africa, especially in the 1960s and afterwards, when Rhodesia and South Africa were coming under more international criticism. It is a seemingly apolitical reason, which eludes the question of whether, by moving to South Africa or Rhodesia in the 1960s and 1970s, often as part of government-sponsored schemes to increase the white population described in Chapters 5 and 6, migrants were complicit in supporting the systems of racial discrimination and dispossession in these countries. Ian Jones, for instance mentioned his interest in African animals based on watching nature programmes on television when explaining his decision to move in the late 1960s and continued to express a strong affiliation with the South African landscape and the lifestyle that it represented.[36] He moved as a young man in the late 1960s from England to South Africa on the subsidised migration scheme. Though his children, grandchildren and ex-wife had all moved to Australia, he remained in South Africa and was the only oral history interviewee to state clearly that he felt he was South African.[37] When asked whether he considered himself British he replied:

> No, I don't. Now I have my English accent, which was being mentioned by some friends last night. They say, 'Ian is never getting rid of his accent. He has always got an English accent.' But that of course isn't what they say when I used to go back to England ... Then I would have a South African accent. So, no, I am happy to say, I'm not proud but I am happy to say I am South African. That's what I feel like. I couldn't go back to England. In fact, I won't dare do that in case somehow, I get trapped there and my nightmare comes true.

Here again accent acts as a signifier of identity and the influence of migration means that Jones' accent is neither completely English nor completely South African. Though Jones noted a similar phenomenon to Jervois that in England he is considered South African and in South Africa he is considered English, he is clear in his own self-identification as South African. In part, this was because he was so much happier in South Africa than in England, but it also seems that his age at migration was also a factor. Having made the decision to move to a new country as an adult, for Jones it was a conscious rejection of his home country and a wholesale adoption of his adopted one.

His strong identification with South Africa and consequent rejection of England were explicitly tied to the landscape and climate of these countries and the different lifestyles available to him. The nightmare that he refers to above dates from a time when his English-born wife was pressuring him to return to the United Kingdom. His refusal to return was a large part of the reason for their subsequent divorce:

> I used to have a nightmare, when Janice was putting the pressure on me to go back. I was an, I was an old, I mean a doddery, shaky old man and I was sitting in, like a bath chair sitting in a little room, with a washroom and a sink in the corner, in front of the window, with the curtain drawn. The window was covered in rain and you couldn't see anything anyway because a couple of metres beyond the window was a brick wall. And which point I would wake up in hot sweats. [laughs] And I had that recurring for a long, long time. But it finally stopped. So, ja, I suppose I buried my roots fairly deeply. The only thing was that I didn't marry a South African. I should have married a South African.

Here he mentions not only the rainy English climate as part of his nightmare but also the cramped living conditions he might expect if he returned, signifying the different lifestyle available to him there.

For Jones, England was crowded and congested in contrast to the wide, open spaces of South Africa. He described the traffic in Guildford, where he lived, and the long commute into central London when he would leave home at seven o'clock in the morning and return by half past six in the evening. As he put it:

> Years and years of that was just too much. Too much out of one's life. All that travelling. I suppose that was also a bit of a factor. Because Johannesburg was drivable in those days. Not like now when virtually the whole city is gridlocked all day long. But you could drive and ja, it was different. Much more free. And just beyond Johannesburg, there wasn't much for miles and miles. You could go out there, I think it's completely surrounded by suburbia now, there was the Lion Park. The famous Lion Park, a favourite place ... you could

drive the little hill and just over the hill there was buck and lots of birds and you could go and play with the little baby lions. It was a great adventure for us. You can't do that in England. So, ja. Ja [sighs] ... I remember my mother sort of saying to me when I had to visit back because my father was ill, 'Well you have had your trip and seen Africa now. When are you back?' 'I am not coming back!' ... Perhaps it isn't about the place being so different but it's about getting out and being an individual on your own. Doing your own sort of thing ... [pause] It was easier to come here than it was to, sort of, move to another town or city in England. That would have been, 'Why do you want to leave home? What's wrong with us? With our home? Here in Guildford?' If you were going to emigrate, you can't ask that because of course you are going to get so much more by going to a complete and total new country. New Job. New people. New scenery. New everything.[38]

His mention of the hills, the animals in the Lion Park and the birds echo the affinity with the landscape and wildlife of southern Africa in the Robsons' narrative. The passage also makes clear that Jones moved because of a strong desire to begin a new life and to escape the constraints of his family and of life in England. Given these circumstances, it follows that he would strongly identity himself as a South African.

By contrast, Marieke Clarke came to Rhodesia not because she had chosen to, but rather because the London Missionary Society assigned her there rather than to what would soon be independent Botswana, which was her preferred choice. Coming from a progressive, anti-racist background, Clarke did not identity at all with white Rhodesian culture. She described most white Rhodesians as coming from 'very limited white English backgrounds who had come out for the sun and the servants, you know'. She described her time in Southern Rhodesia through a long list of the like-minded anti-colonial activists that she spent time with, noting that she was 'insulated really against white Rhodesia ... by good contacts'. Because of the company she kept, she noted, 'It was very rare that I met anyone who didn't believe that Zimbabwe had to be free as soon as possible and that it was following in the steps of Zambia and that the Federation was doomed long ago.'

As a feminist, she was particularly critical of constructions of gender she encountered while there,

> The construction of white womanhood in Rhodesia was of course that she propped up her man and looked after the servants and bossed the servants around and this sort of thing. I just didn't believe in that sort of thing at all. I mean we had somebody who cleaned in my family home. But not the sort of ridiculous propping up they had in Rhodesia. I thought that, what nowadays we would call the construction of white femininity was one of the most depressing in the world and probably worse than in South Africa. Because of the distances, I mean the white suburbs were miles away [from the centre of

town] ... It was almost impossible to stay there and have any kind of reasonable life ... I suppose lots of the white men would go off to their business and leave the women imprisoned at home. I mean it was a terrible construction for women.[39]

Clarke only stayed for just over a year before she was deported by the Rhodesian government, and it is clear she never felt herself to be Rhodesian. Rather she identified with those who shared her anti-racist and feminist ideologies. Her story is a very particular one, however, after returning to the United Kingdom, she continued to be involved in anti-colonial politics and eventually ended up working for Oxfam. She returned to Zimbabwe after independence in the late 1980s and wrote a biography of Lozikeyi Dlodlo, Queen of the Ndebele in the nineteenth century.[40]

More typical was Carolyn Hastings, who spent two years in South Africa from 1970 working as a nurse. Hastings was less focused on politics, although she did express her discomfort with apartheid.[41] Despite these misgivings, she made it clear that she had a wonderful time in South Africa, highlighting the warm welcome she received from colleagues and her love of the South African landscape. She went in her early twenties with a friend and very much saw the move as a chance for travel rather than a permanent migration. Though she clearly felt a strong affinity for the landscape and described her travels around the region to game reserves and Victoria Falls, her account largely took the form of a travel narrative. Unlike those who mentioned their lost gardens or houses, Hastings made no claim to belong to South Africa. In her discussion of her disagreements with a South African boyfriend over the racial politics of apartheid, she makes a point of noting how it was easy for an outsider who had grown up in South Africa to criticise apartheid.

By contrast, in the accounts of those who spent more time in South Africa and Rhodesia and had the intention to stay permanently, the discussions of time spent in the southern African landscape took on a different meaning. In these narratives the sense of freedom and adventure that the African landscape signifies functions in two primary ways. One is to serve as a claim-making device. In a twist in the way Bill Schwarz shows that the 'incessant claim' to 'know the native' reflected the self-justified authority of settlers to rule during the colonial period, to state that you could live 'like an African' or to identify as a 'white African' is to say that you possess a deep understanding of Africa and its wildlife and that you belong there even after the colonial order has collapsed.[42] The other is to express nostalgia for Rhodesia and apartheid South Africa in a way that obscures the racial politics and exploitation that enabled the privileged lifestyle of the ruling minority in those states including the opportunity for outdoor leisure.[43]

Conclusion

British post-war migrants are more scattered around the globe and more likely to have remained in Africa than other 'orphans of empire', even if not necessarily the place to which they originally moved. Even so, British people who moved to Africa in the mid twentieth century, though less visible than the Portuguese *retornados* or other groups such as the *pieds noirs* of Algeria, share much in common with them. As these oral histories reflect, many felt displaced and unmoored. Their sense of identity is fluid, influenced by both large-scale political events such as UDI and personal ones such as a move from Rhodesia to South Africa or the United States as well as the political views of each migrant, how long they had spent in southern Africa, their age on migration and whether they intended to stay permanently. Many expressed nostalgia for the landscape and wildlife of southern Africa, which became a way to discuss the losses entailed by decolonisation and to mourn the end of the privileged lifestyle of the white minority without addressing race or politics explicitly. The material culture of decolonisation often focused on signifiers of 'the bush', whether the inflatable crocodiles in the Las Vegas pool at the Rhodesian reunion or paintings of elephants and lions and baobab trees. While much of the ambivalence and fluidity in identity described above comes from the individual experience of migration, it was also shaped, though often in unexpected ways, by decolonisation.

Examining the experiences of white settlers in southern Africa illustrates the complex personal consequences of political decolonisation, which, in South Africa and Zimbabwe, occurred twice, with very different implications for the populations of these countries: first, reinforcing white settler identities, and then diminishing them. This layered process of decolonisation and especially the first stage which served to disassociate British migrants in southern Africa from the United Kingdom has served to obscure their experience of decolonisation. That many continued to relocate as a result means that their experience of and contribution to shaping cultures of decolonisation is difficult to perceive without attention to the individual stories and reflections provided by oral history. The material presented here highlights decolonisation as an identity-making process, in which some people and practices are included in the new order and others rejected. Identities are performed through cultures of association, sociability, ceremony, accent and interior decoration, therefore oral history evidence can help us to understand the ways in which decolonisation was experienced, negotiated and contested by different communities and individuals caught up in the political transitions that marked the end of empire.

Notes

1 See Bickers, *Settlers and Expatriates: Britons over the Seas*, especially the chapters by Elizabeth Buettner and John Darwin. For work on French and Portuguese 'repatriates' see Andrea L. Smith, ed., *Europe's Invisible Migrants* (Amsterdam: Amsterdam University Press, 2003).
2 Lambert and Lester, 'Imperial Spaces', p. 27.
3 Ibid., p. 26.
4 Elizabeth Buettner, *Empire Families: Britons and Late Imperial India* (Oxford: Oxford University Press, 2004), pp. 188–251.
5 Andrea L. Smith, 'Introduction', in *Europe's Invisible Migrants*, ed. Andrea L. Smith (Amsterdam: Amsterdam University Press, 2003), p. 25. See also Stephen C. Lubkemann, 'Race, Class and Kin in the Negotiation of 'Internal Strangerhood' among Portuguese Retornados, 1975–2000', in *Europe's Invisible Migrants*, ed. Andrea L. Smith (Amsterdam: Amsterdam University Press, 2003), pp. 75–94; Stephen C. Lubkemann, 'Unsettling the Metropole: Race and Settler Reincorporation in Postcolonial Portugal', in *Settler Colonialism in the Twentieth Century*, eds Caroline Elkins and Susan Pederson (Routledge: New York and London, 2005), pp. 257–70; Keith Middlemas, 'Twentieth Century White Society in Mozambique', *Tarikh* 6:2 (1979), 44; Ricardo E. Ovalle-Bahamón, 'The Wrinkles of Decolonization and Nationness: White Angolans as Retornados in Portugal', in *Europe's Invisible Migrants*, ed. Andrea L. Smith (Amsterdam: Amsterdam University Press, 2003), pp. 147–68.
6 Portelli, 'What Makes Oral History Different' See also Miescher, *Making Men in Ghana*, p. 14.
7 I left the decision about whether to use a pseudonym up to the individual interviewee and have indicated where this is the case.
8 Hammerton and Thomson, *Ten Pound Poms*, p. 341.
9 For instance, more than a quarter of recent migrants from the United Kingdom to Durban surveyed in 1967 had spent time in Africa previously and 'many ... had lived in Kenya, returned to Great Britain and subsequently migrated to South Africa'. Johnston, *British Emigration to Durban*, pp. 30, 39.
10 Ellen Boucher described a similar sense of dislocation in relation to child migrants to Rhodesia, Boucher, *Empire's Children*, pp. 236–41, 249–58.
11 Interview with Andrew Smith, London, United Kingdom, 22 July 2009.
12 Boucher, *Empire's Children*; Sherington and Jeffery, *Fairbridge*.
13 The post-UDI relationship between Rhodesia and the Queen was complex and many white Rhodesians, like Jervois, continued to feel an affiliation to the monarchy even after the declaration of republic in 1970. Kenrick, 'Settler Soul-Searching and Sovereign Independence: The Monarchy in Rhodesia, 1965–1970'.
14 Interview with William Jervois, Grahamstown, South Africa, 20 April 2011.
15 Alois Mlambo attributes this to the proximity of Afrikanerdom, that in Rhodesia settler nationalism took on a distinctly British character in opposition to an expansionist South Africa. Mlambo, *White Immigration*, p. 51.

16 Interview with William Jervois, Grahamstown, South Africa, 20 April 2011.
17 Interview with Brien Bonnynge, Randburg, South Africa, 3 April 2011.
18 Kate Law found a similar reaction to UDI when interviewing women she located on 'Rhodesians Worldwide'. Kate Law, *Gendering the Settler State: White Women, Race, Liberalism and Empire in Rhodesia, 1950–1980* (Abingdon: Routledge, 2016), pp. 144–5.
19 On the coalescence of white Rhodesian national identity after UDI, see Brownell, *Collapse of Rhodesia*, p. 16.
20 This refers to Tommy Bedford, a well-known rugby player from Natal, who welcomed the New Zealand All Blacks team at a banquet given for them in 1970 in Durban, to 'the last outpost of the British Empire', a phrase that entered into popular use among the English-speaking population of Natal thereafter. Lambert, 'The Last Outpost', pp. 150, 174–5.
21 Interview with Brien Bonnynge, Randburg, South Africa, 3 April 2011. This kind of affiliation to the monarchy, even after republic, was an important aspect of British South African identity. Lambert, 'An unknown people', p. 604.
22 Alexandra Fuller, *Cocktail Hour Under the Tree of Forgetfulness* (London: Simon and Schuster, 2011), p. 159.
23 IWM, 91/33/2, No. 50, Alfred Reid. These questionnaires were completed in the 1990s so reflect some chronological distance from the events they describe.
24 IWM, 91/33/2, No. 111, Laura Wynn.
25 IWM, 91/33/2, No. 113, Henry Henderson.
26 Angela Woollacott, *To Try Her Fortune in London: Australian Women, Colonialism and Modernity* (Oxford: Oxford University Press, 2001), p. 14.
27 Ellen Boucher found a similar trend in the memoirs of child migrants to Rhodesia. Boucher, *Empire's Children*, pp. 228–9.
28 David McDermott Hughes, *Whiteness in Zimbabwe: Race, Landscape and the Problem of Belonging* (New York: Palgrave Macmillan, 2010).
29 Interview with Harold and Thelma Robson, Santa Barbara, USA, 3 October 2009. At the interviewees' request, these names are pseudonyms. Here Harold refers also to his initial migration to Rhodesia as a young man in the 1940s.
30 Interview with William Jervois, Grahamstown, South Africa, 20 April 2011.
31 Interview with Harold and Thelma Robson, Santa Barbara, USA, 3 October 2009.
32 Law, *Gendering the Settler State*, pp. 7, 153.
33 For more on the connection between domestic decoration and display and self-presentation and identity, see Claire Wintle, 'Career Development: Domestic Display as Imperial, Anthropological and Social Trophy', *Victorian Studies* 50:2 (2008); Deborah Cohen, *Household Gods: The British and their Possessions* (New Haven and London: Yale University Press, 2006).
34 The 'July Braai' organised annually in Derby by the Rhodesian Pioneer Club provides a similar forum for ex-Rhodesians in the United Kingdom. Zembe, 'Migrating', pp. 45–7. There were similar events in South Africa, for instance the Rhodesia Association of South Africa celebrated the centenary of British settlement in Rhodesia in 1990 at a resort near Messina close to the Zimbabwean

border renamed 'Rhodesianaland' for the occasion. Godwin and Hancock, *Rhodesians Never Die*, p. 316.
35 Events described in the November 2009 and November 2011 newsletters of the Rhodesian Association of the USA. In the personal collection of the author.
36 At the interviewee's request, this name is a pseudonym. See also the discussion of Jones in Chapter 5.
37 Interview with Ian Jones, Grahamstown, South Africa, 16 April 2011.
38 Interview with Ian Jones, Grahamstown, South Africa, 16 April 2011.
39 Interview with Marieke Clarke, Oxford, United Kingdom, 5 June 2012.
40 Marieke Clarke and Pathisa Nyathi, *Lozikeyi Dlodlo: Queen of the Ndebele* (Bulawayo: AmaGugu Publishers, 2011).
41 Interview with Carolyn Hastings, Cambridge, United Kingdom, 2 September 2011. See more details in Chapter 5.
42 Schwarz, *White Man's World*, p. 22.
43 Will Jackson has identified a similar phenomenon in relation to nostalgia for colonial Kenya. Will Jackson, 'White man's country: Kenya Colony and the making of a myth', *Journal of East African Studies* 5:2 (May 2011).

Epilogue

The way that decolonisation unfolded in South Africa and Rhodesia has shaped how the relationship between those nations and the United Kingdom has been understood. Because both settler colonial regimes cut all formal political ties with the United Kingdom and left the Commonwealth to continue white minority rule, this separation has come to define their relationship with the United Kingdom in the second half of the twentieth century. Just as emphasis on Britain's role in the abolition the slave trade created a humanitarian narrative that obscures culpability in that same slave trade, by the mid twentieth century emphasis on British opposition to apartheid and minority rule in Rhodesia has worked to diminish both racism in Britain and the ongoing connections between the United Kingdom and both apartheid South Africa and Rhodesia. Both ideas contribute to the mythology of benevolent imperialism and orderly decolonisation, to which many Britons still adhere.

Kennetta Hammond Perry has termed these 'collective narrative myths' the 'mystique of British anti-racism': the idea that there is no native racism in Britain, it exists elsewhere and comes from elsewhere.[1] This perception is reinforced by a flattering comparison between the United Kingdom and the United States as well as Rhodesia and apartheid South Africa with their explicit systems of legal segregation and discrimination. It draws on long-running tropes positioning British liberalism against Afrikaner racism, dating back to the abolition of slavery in the Cape in the early nineteenth century. This contrast operated as a kind of alibi, minimising and obscuring racist policies, attitudes, and discrimination in the United Kingdom as well as ongoing connections to Rhodesia and South Africa throughout the second half of the twentieth century.

In part because of the moral force of the anti-apartheid movement in Britain, the apartheid regime came to represent precisely the kind of unbending racist sentiment incompatible with emerging moral sensibilities within Britain. Yet these contrasting perceptions of ever-more tolerant multicultural Britain with racist Rhodesia and apartheid South Africa overlook high levels of British migration in the 1960s and 1970s to those nations and the continued attraction of the settler colony for British people. They also overlook the ways in which, by the 1960s, all three states implemented migration policies designed to bolster their white populations. Increasing incentives were offered to white migrants by the Rhodesian and South African states just as the United Kingdom began to implement increasingly racialised immigration policies, removing the rights of Commonwealth citizens to live and work in the United Kingdom that had been enshrined into law by the British Nationality Act of 1948.

The 1981 British Nationality Act completed in legal terms the shift from empire to racialised nation in the United Kingdom. White minority rule ended in Rhodesia and South Africa in 1980 and 1994 respectively. While white nationalist ideology persists in both nations and among their expatriates and other supporters abroad, it no longer has the power of state endorsement, though the political and economic legacies of both apartheid and colonial Rhodesia remain. The ideology of white nationalism has also persisted in the United Kingdom, taking on greater and lesser importance over time, depending on the fluctuations of the economy and the ebb and flow of politics. It is not the only nationalist ideology and was challenged by and coexisted with others at various points, notably multiculturalism. Despite the increasing diversity of British society, in religious, ethnic and cultural terms, an essential 'common sense' understanding of the nation as white remains and is still reflected in the politics of migration today.

The 'hostile environment' policy introduced by the Home Secretary, Theresa May, under the coalition government, which came into effect in 2012, was not specifically aimed at people of colour. It had a disproportionate impact on people of colour, however, as revealed by the Windrush scandal, because by the racial logic of the white nation, it was disproportionately people of colour whose right to be in the United Kingdom was challenged by the outsourcing of border control to landlords, doctors and employers.[2] Though the independent review of the scandal by Wendy Williams, released in March 2020, stopped short of finding the Home Office to be institutionally racist, it did find that the failings of the Home Office, described as a 'culture of carelessness and disbelief', were evidence of 'an institutional ignorance and thoughtlessness towards the issue of race and the history of the Windrush generation ... which are consistent with some elements of the definition of institutional racism'.[3] The notorious 'Go Home' vans, meanwhile, deployed by 'Operation Vaken' in 2013 to the most ethnically diverse areas of London, echo the repatriation campaigns of earlier decades.

To be sure, race is not the only criterion for national belonging, now or in the past, in the United Kingdom, as the Brexit referendum campaign and opposition to the immigration of largely, although not entirely, white migrants from the European Union illustrates. Neither was it the only criterion in Rhodesia or apartheid South Africa, who both implemented selective immigration policies even as they sought to increase their white populations. But often implicit ideas about race continue in perceptions of what kind of migration is desirable, who has the right to mobility, and the terms used for people who cross borders whether migrant, immigrant, or expatriate. That the volume of emigration from the United Kingdom both in the decades after the Second World War and today including to South Africa and Rhodesia has largely been ignored or taken for granted and is seen as the natural order of things, is itself a testament to the persistence of racial ideology in perceptions of migration.

Notes

1 Perry, *London is the Place for Me*, pp. 19, 92, 101, 108, 133.
2 Maya Goodfellow, *Hostile Environment: How Immigrants Became Scapegoats* (London: Verso, 2019); Amelia Gentleman, *The Windrush Betrayal: Exposing the Hostile Environment* (London: Faber, 2019).
3 Wendy Williams, *Windrush Lesson Learned Review* (London: HMSO, 2020), p. 7.

Select bibliography

Media

Die Burger
Cape Argus
The Cape Times
The Christian Science Monitor
Daily Mail
Daily Sketch
Daily Telegraph
Evening Standard (London)
Financial Times
Liverpool Post
Manchester Guardian
The Natal Mercury
Pretoria News
The Scotsman
The Star
The Sun
The Times (London)
Die Volkstem
'Should 20 Million Emigrate?' Pathé Newsreel, Issued 18 October 1948.
'Royal Tour of South Africa, 1947', BBC Television Service, First Broadcast 2 June 1947.
'South Africa's Royal Visit Reel 1', Pathé Pictures, 1947.
'South Africa's Royal Visit Reel 2', Pathé Pictures, 1947.

Archives – South Africa

Cory Library, Rhodes University, Grahamstown

The Ian Smith papers were consulted in 2011. They have since been returned to Zimbabwe.
1/78/002, Southern Rhodesia Cabinet Minutes and Memoranda, 1953.
1/78/004, Southern Rhodesia Cabinet Minutes and Memoranda, 1955.
1/78/006, Southern Rhodesia Cabinet Minutes and Memoranda, 1957–58.
1/78/019, Rhodesia Cabinet Minutes and Memoranda, 1965.

1820 Memorial Settlers' Association, *The 1820 Memorial Settlers' Association, its aims, objects, constitution, organisation, etc.*, 1920.

National Archives of South Africa

A2, File 158, Files of J.G Strijdom, Koerant Uitknipsnels (Press clippings), 1927–52.
A326, F.G. Brownell Collection.
BNS 1/1/365, Ref. 117/74, Vol. 5, Immigration Laws: Southern and Northern Rhodesia, 1950–59.
BNS 1/1/401, Ref. 301/74, Vols 1–3, Post-war Immigration of British and Allied Soldiers, 1942–45.
BNS 1/1/402, Ref. 301/74, Vols 4–7, Post-war Immigration of British and Allied Soldiers, 1945–46.
BNS 1/1/410, Ref. 336/74, Vol. A, Immigration of British Subjects to South Africa, 1946.
BNS 1/1/411, Ref. 336/74, Vols B–D, Immigration of British Subjects to South Africa, 1946–47.
BNS 1/1/412, Ref. 336/74, Vol. E, Immigration of British Subjects to South Africa, 1948–50.
BTS Ref. 59/3 Vol. 1, Union Government Policy Re: Immigration 1957–61.
BTS Ref. 59/5, Vol. 44, Applications to Immigrate into the Union, General 1958–60.
BTS Ref. 59/6, Vol. 51, Info Office for Immigrants in London, 1944.
BTS Ref. 59/6C, Vol. 1, Child Immigration Scheme, 1946–51.
DGD Vol. 195, Ref. 57/3, Immigration. Post-war Enquiries from members of the Allied Forces, 1944 to 1948.
GG 1313, Ref. 36.390, Enquiries regarding a scheme of immigration to South Africa: possibility of settling men of RAF in S.A. after the war, 15 January 1941.
MBN 1, Ref. MIN 2/1, Immigrasiebeleid (Immigration Policy), 1948–54.
MBN 2, Ref. MIN 2/14, Vol. 1 Algemeen Immigrasie (General Immigration), 1948–56.
MBN 2, Ref. MIN 2/14, Vol. 2, Immigrasie – Algemeen (Immigration – General) 1957–58.
MSK Vol. 576, Ref. 9/9/16/02, 'Ander Departmentes, Departement van Immigrasie' (Other Departments, Department of Immigration), 1969–78.
TES 6373, Ref. 48/45/3, Immigration. European Immigration Scheme: Transit Accommodation Centres, 1947–64.
VWN Vol.1117, Ref. SW483/1, Vol. I, Child Immigration Scheme General, 1945–46.
VWN Vol.1117, Ref. SW483/1, Vol. II, Child Immigration Scheme, 1946.
VWN Vol. 1117, Ref. SW483/1–2, Union Immigration Scheme, Child Immigration Scheme, Applications for Adoption of Children, 1945–48.
VWN Vol. 1118, Ref. SW483/1–4, Union Immigration Scheme – Dietse Kinderfonds (Teutonic Children's League), 1945–63.

Select bibliography 197

South African Military Archives Depot, Pretoria

AG (3) 154, Box 57, Ref. AG (3) 154X/591, Immigration Policy, 1943.
AG (3) 154, Box 132, Ref. 1158, Members of Imperial Forces wishing to Reside in Union, 1945.
WR Box 242, File 124/3, Repatriation of Wives of Service Men and Evacuation of Fiancées, 1945–47.

Western Cape Archival Repository

1/BIZ Vol. 6/46, Bizana The Overseas Children's Reception Administration.
1/BW Vol. 12/36, Beaufort West The Overseas Children's Reception Administration.
1/CT Vol. 420, Cape Town National Child Refugee Administration.
3/ELN Vol. 893, Ref. 1975/3, Refugee and Evacuee Children from Overseas Refugee Camps, 1940–49.
1/HFD Vol. 7/1/13, Hopefield National Child Refugee Administration.
1/IWE Vol. 4/1/25, Ingwe National Child Refugee Administration.
1/KNT Vol. 95, Kentani National Child Refugee Administration.
1/KNY Vol. 8/25, Knysna National Child Refugee Administration.
1/LBG Vol. 38, Laingsburg The Overseas Children's Reception Administration.
1/LSK Vol. 66, Lusikisiki National Child Refugee Administration.
1/LSM Vol. 50, Ladismith The Overseas Children's Reception Administration.
1/MDB Vol. 73, Middelburg National Child Refugee Administration.
1/NKE Vol. 38, Nqamakwe National Child Refugee Administration.
1/PKB Vol. 32, Piquetburg National Child Refugee Administration.
1/PTA Vol. 13, Port Alfred National Child Refugee Administration.
1/RMD Vol. 31, Richmond National Child Refugee Administration.
1/STG Vol. 10, Steynburg National Child Refugee Administration.
1/WIL Vol. 4/6, Ref. 33/1/2/3, Evacuee Child Williston.
PAE Vol. E806, Ref. Z/709, 1940, Evacuee Children from Overseas.

Archives – United Kingdom

Caird Library, National Maritime Museum, London

UCM/1/7, Union-Castle Mail Steamship Company, Directors Meetings Minute Book No. 7, April 1942–September 1947.
UCM/1/8, Union-Castle Mail Steamship Company, Directors Meetings Minute Book No. 8, October 1947–October 1951.

Imperial War Museum, London

03/33/1, Personal Papers of K.A.C. Melvin.
08/29/1, Personal Papers of W.J. Malone.
11/13/1, Personal Papers of F. Dane.
11/35/1, Personal Papers of P. Salter.
85/19/1, Personal Papers of G.M. Ball.

91/33/2, Private Papers of Miss P.Y. Lin, Questionnaires of Overseas Evacuees.
Item 1375, Misc. 92, Letters concerning the South African Women's Auxiliary Services during the Second World War.

The London School of Economics Archive, London

LONGDEN/3/11, Monday Club, *Right Reason: A Monday Club Policy Document*, 1974.

National Archives of the United Kingdom

ADM 1/11778, Naval Training, HMS Assegai, 1942–43.
AIR 20/9051, West Indians serving in RAF – Demobilisation and Repatriation, 1945–50.
CAB 66/30/28, War Cabinet, Demobilisation and Resettlement, 1942.
CAB 124/2731, Emigration of Scientists, 1952–57.
CK 2/148, Race Relations Board, Counsel's Opinions and Court Judgements, 1975–77.
CO 1015/1248, Control of immigration into the Federation of Rhodesia and Nyasaland, 1957–59.
DO 35/1133/20–27, Schemes and Suggestions for Overseas Settlements, 1943–46.
DO 35/1135, Post-war Migration, 1943–46.
DO 35/10184, Migration to the Federation of Rhodesia and Nyasaland: brief for Secretary of State's meeting with Mr B.D. Goldberg, 1958.
DO 35/10220, The Migration Council, 1952–56.
DO 131/4, Minutes of the Advisory Council to the Children's Overseas Reception Board, 1940–45.
DO 131/6, CORB: Reception Arrangements – Southern Rhodesia, 1940.
DO 131/28, Children's Overseas Reception Scheme: Speeches and General Surveys, 1942–45.
DO 131/36, Proposals for post-war settlement: South Africa, 1941–45.
DO 131/43, History of the Children's Overseas Reception Board, 1940–44.
DO 131/50, R. Haldane Murray and Miss Murray of Graff-Reinet, South Africa: Scheme to provide free transport, accommodation and education for English children in South Africa, 1940–41.
FCO 36/1463, Prospects for Encouraging European Migration from Rhodesia to Further Settlement between United Kingdom and Rhodesia, 1973.
FCO 36/1634, Prospects for Encouraging European Migration from Rhodesia to Further Settlement between United Kingdom and Rhodesia, 1974.
LAB 13/985, Federation of Rhodesia and Nyasaland Immigration Policy, 1953–58.
LAB 8/2736, British Emigration Policy, 1961–67.
T 334/13, Measures to Encourage Scientists to Remain in the United Kingdom and to attract back those who have already left (the Brain Drain), 1963–67.

Select bibliography

Archives – Zimbabwe

National Archives of Zimbabwe

FG-P/HIG, 'There's a Welcome for you in Rhodesia and Nyasaland', 1955.
ORAL/232, Interview of Mark Edward Dawson, by I.J. Johnstone, London, 1983.
S482/132/49, HD (49) Imm/2, 'Memorandum: The Impact of Immigration on the Southern Rhodesian Economy', 1949.
S3285/14/147/3, Executive Sub-Committee on Immigration, 1970.
S3609142, Local Advisory Immigration Committees, 'Welcome to Rhodesia and Nyasaland'.

Official Publications

Government Publications – South Africa

Union of South Africa, *Statistics of Migration 1948* (Pretoria: The Government Printer, 1950).
Republic of South Africa Bureau of Statistics, *Report No. 286: Statistics of Immigrants and Emigrants 1924–1964* (Pretoria: The Government Printer, 1964).
Republic of South Africa Department of Statistics, *Report No. 19–01–01, Migration Statistics: Immigrants and Emigrants, 1966 to 1969* (Pretoria: The Government Printer, 1969).
R.P. 31/1969, *Report of the Department of Immigration for the period 1 April 1961 to 30 June 1968* (Pretoria: The Government Printer, 1968).
R.P. 21/1971, *Report of the Department of Immigration for the period 1 July 1968 to 30 June 1970* (Pretoria: The Government Printer, 1971).
R.P. 21/1973, *Report of the Department of Immigration for the period 1 July 1970 to 30 June 1972* (Pretoria: The Government Printer, 1973).
R.P. 41/1975, *Report of the Department of Immigration for the period 1 July 1972 to 30 June 1974* (Pretoria: The Government Printer, 1975).
R.P. 18/1977, *Report of the Department of Immigration for the period 1 July 1974 to 30 June 1976* (Pretoria: The Government Printer, 1977).
R.P. 17/1979, *Report of the Department of Immigration for the period 1 July 1976 to 30 June 1978* (Pretoria: The Government Printer, 1979).
R.P. 21/1980, Department of the Interior, *Annual Report for the Calendar Year 1979* (Pretoria: The Government Printer, 1980), p. 26.
R.P. 46/1981, Department of Internal Affairs, *Annual Report for the Calendar Year 1980* (Pretoria: The Government Printer, 1981).
Union of South Africa, Debates of the House of Assembly.
Union of South Africa, Debates of the Senate.

Government Publications – Southern Rhodesia/Rhodesia

The Statute Law of Southern Rhodesia 1946 (Salisbury: The Government Printer, 1947).
The Statute Law of Southern Rhodesia 1948 (Salisbury: The Government Printer, 1949).

Republic of Rhodesia, *Monthly Migration and Tourist Statistics for March 1970* (Salisbury: Central Statistics Office, 1970).

Southern Rhodesia, Debates of the Legislative Assembly.

Government Publications – United Kingdom

Cd 7111, Union of South Africa, *Correspondence relating to the Immigrants Regulation Act and other matters affecting Asiatics in South Africa* (London: HMSO, 1913).

Cmd 2738, Board of Trade, *Statistical Abstract for the Several British Oversea Dominions and Protectorates in each from 1909 to 1923*, Fifty-Seventh Number (London: HMSO, 1923).

Cmd 6658, *Migration within the British Commonwealth. Statement by His Majesty's Government in the United Kingdom* (London: HMSO, 1945).

Cmnd 336, Commonwealth Relations Office, *Third Report of the Oversea Migration Board December 1957* (London: HMSO, 1957).

Cmnd 619, Commonwealth Relations Office, *Fourth Report of the Oversea Migration Board December 1958* (London: HMSO, 1958).

Cmnd 975 *Fifth Report of the Oversea Migration Board* (London: HMSO, 1960).

Cmnd 1586, Commonwealth Relations Office, *Seventh Report of the Oversea Migration Board December 1961* (London: HMSO, 1961).

Cmnd 2217, Commonwealth Relations Office, *Oversea Migration Board. Statistics for 1962* (London: HMSO, 1963).

Cmnd 2861, Commonwealth Relations Office, *Oversea Migration Board. Statistics for 1964* (London: HMSO, 1965).

Commonwealth Relations Office, *Oversea Migration Statistics 1955* (London, HMSO, 1956).

First Report of the Commission for Racial Equality, June 1977–December 1977 (London: HMSO, 1978).

Series MN, Office of Population, Censuses and Statistics, *International Migration: Migrants Entering or Leaving the United Kingdom, 1964–2000*.

House of Commons Debates.

House of Lords Debates.

United Nations

United Nations Security Council, Resolution 253 (1968) of 29 May 1968.

UN General Assembly, Resolution 2396, 'The policies of apartheid of the Government of South Africa', 2 December 1968.

United Nation Security Council Official Records, Twenty-Seventh Year, 1640th Meeting: 16 February 1972, New York, Item 19.

Published Works

Ahonen, Pertti, Gustavo Corni, Jerzy Kochanowski, Rainer Schulze, Tamás Stark and Barbara Stelzi-Marx. *People on the Move: Forced Population Movements in Europe in the Second World War and Its Aftermath*. Oxford: Berg, 2008.

Allport, Alan. *Demobbed: Coming Home After World War Two*. New Haven: Yale University Press, 2009.
Anderson, Clare. *Subaltern Lives: Biographies of Colonialism in the Indian Ocean World, 1790–1920*. Cambridge: Cambridge University Press, 2012.
Appleyard, Reg. *The Ten Pound Immigrants*. London: Boxtree Limited, 1988.
Bailey, E.A.S., ed. *SAWAS 1938–1947: Book of Thanks*. Edinburgh: Macdonald Printers, 1981.
Bailkin, Jordanna. *The Afterlife of Empire*. Berkeley: University of California Press, 2012.
Barber, Marilyn, and Murray Watson. *Invisible Immigrants: The English in Canada since 1945*. Winnipeg: University of Manitoba Press, 2015.
Bashford, Alison. 'At the Border: Contagion, Immigration, Nation'. *Australian Historical Studies* 33:120 (2002), 344–58.
———. 'Immigration restriction: rethinking period and place from settler colonies to postcolonial nations'. *Journal of Global History* 9:1 (2014), 26–48.
———. *Imperial Hygiene: A Critical History of Colonialism, Nationalism and Public Health*. Basingstoke: Palgrave Macmillan, 2003.
Basner, Miriam, and Hymnan Basner. *Am I an African? The Political Memoirs of H.M. Basner*. Johannesburg: Witwatersrand University Press, 1993.
Bean, Lucy. *Strangers in our Midst*. Cape Town: Howard Timmins, 1970.
Bean, Philip, and Joy Melville. *Lost Children of the Empire*. London: Unwin Hyman Limited, 1989.
Beinart, William, and Saul Dubow. 'Introduction: The Historiography of Segregation and Apartheid'. In *Segregation and Apartheid in Twentieth Century South Africa*, edited by William Beinart and Saul Dubow, pp. 1–24. London: Routledge, 2002.
Beissinger, Mark R. 'Soviet Empire as "Family Resemblance"'. *Slavic Review* 65:2 (2006), 294–303.
Belich, James. *Replenishing the Earth: The Settler Revolution and the Rise of the Anglo-World, 1783–1939*. Oxford: Oxford University Press, 2009.
Bell, Duncan, and Srdjan Vucetic. 'Brexit, CANZUK, and the legacy of empire'. *The British Journal of Politics and International Relations* 21:2 (2019), 367–82.
Bickers, Robert, ed. *Settlers and Expatriates: Britons over the Seas*. Oxford: Oxford University Press, 2010.
Bickford-Smith, Vivian. *Ethnic Pride and Racial Prejudice in Victorian Cape Town: Group Identity and Social Practice, 1875–1902*. Cambridge: Cambridge University Press, 1995.
Bickford-Smith, Vivian, Elizabeth Van Heyningen and Nigel Worden. *Cape Town in the Twentieth Century: An Illustrated Social History*. Claremont: David Philip Publishers, 1999.
Bilson, Geoffrey. *The Guest Children: The Story of the British Child Evacuees Sent to Canada During World War II*. Saskatoon: Fifth House, 1988.
Bishi, George. 'Immigration and Settlement of "undesirable" whites in Southern Rhodesia, c. 1940s–1960s'. In *Rethinking White Societies in Southern Africa, 1930s–1990s*, edited by Duncan Money and Danelle van Zyl-Hermann, pp. 59–77. London: Routledge, 2020.
Black, Peter. *Poms in the Sun*. London: The Travel Book Club, 1965.
Blakely, Brian L. 'Women and Imperialism: The Colonial Office and Female Emigration to South Africa, 1901–1910'. *Albion: A Quarterly Journal Concerned with British Studies* 13:2 (1981), 131–49.

Boucher, Ellen. *Empire's Children: Child Emigration. Welfare, and the Decline of the British World, 1869–1967*. Cambridge: Cambridge University Press, 2014.

———. 'The Limits of Potential: Race, Welfare, and the Interwar Extension of Child Emigration to Southern Rhodesia'. *Journal of British Studies* 48:4 (2009), 914–34.

Bowen, Lynne. *Muddling Through: The Remarkable Story of the Barr Colonists*. Vancouver: Douglas & McIntyre, 1992.

Bradlow, Edna. 'Empire Settlement and South African Immigration Policy, 1910–1948'. In *Emigrants and Empire: British Settlement in the Dominions Between the Wars*, edited by Stephen Constantine, pp. 174–201. Manchester: Manchester University Press, 1990.

———. 'Immigration into the Union, 1910–1948: Policies and Attitudes'. PhD dissertation, University of Cape Town, 1978.

Bridge, Carl, and Kent Fedorowich. 'Mapping the British World'. In *The British World: Diaspora, Culture, and Identity*, edited by Carl Bridge and Kent Fedorowich, pp. 1–15. London: Frank Cass Publishers, 2003.

British Council of Churches. *Emigration to South Africa*. London: The British Council of Churches, 1973.

———. *The Future of South Africa: A Study by British Christians*. London: SCM Press, 1965.

Brownell, F.G. *British Immigration to South Africa, 1946–1970*. Pretoria: The Government Printer, 1985.

Brownell, Josiah. *The Collapse of Rhodesia: Population Demographics and the Politics of Race*. London: I.B. Taurus, 2011.

———. 'The Hole in Rhodesia's Bucket: White Emigration and the End of Settler Rule'. *Journal of South African Studies* 34:3 (2008), 591–610.

———. '"One last retreat": Racial Nostalgia and Population Panic in Smith's Rhodesia and Powell's Britain'. In *Global White Nationalism: From Apartheid to Trump*, edited by Daniel Geary, Camilla Schofield and Jennifer Sutton, pp. 157–86. Manchester: Manchester University Press, 2020.

Bryant, Margot. *As We Were: South Africa 1939–1941*. Johannesburg: Keartland Publishers, 1974.

Buettner, Elizabeth. *Empire Families: Britons and Late Imperial India*. Oxford: Oxford University Press, 2004.

———. *Europe After Empire: Decolonization, Society, and Culture*. Cambridge: Cambridge University Press, 2016.

Bull, Esme. *Aided Immigration from Britain to South Africa, 1857–1867*. Pretoria: Human Sciences Research Council, 1991.

Burkett, Jodi. '"Don't Bank on Apartheid": The National Union of Students and the Boycott Barclays Campaign'. In *Students in Twentieth-Century Britain and Ireland*, edited by Jodi Burkett, pp. 225–45. London: Palgrave Macmillan, 2018.

Bush, Julia. '"The Right Sort of Woman": Female Emigrators and the Emigration to the British Empire, 1890–1910'. *Women's History Review* 3:3 (1994), 385–409.

Byfield, Judith A. 'Preface'. In *Africa and World War II*, edited by Judith A. Byfield, Carolyn A. Brown and Timothy Parsons, pp. xvii–xxiii. Cambridge: Cambridge University Press, 2015.

Cain, P.J., and A.G. Hopkins. *British Imperialism: Crisis and Deconstruction 1914–1990*. London and New York: Longman, 1993.

Calcott, Dean, ed. *Windows: Rhodesia Fairbridge Memorial College Autobiographies*. Christchurch, New Zealand: Fairbridge Marketing Company Limited, 2001.
Carby, Hazel V. *Imperial Intimacies: A Tale of Two Islands*. London: Verso, 2019.
Carey, Jane. 'White Anxieties and the Articulation of Race: The Women's Movement and the Making of White Australia, 1910s–1930s'. In *Creating White Australia*, edited by Jane Carey and Claire McLisky, pp. 195–213. Sydney: Sydney University Press, 2009.
Carter, Bob, Clive Harris, and Shirley Joshi. 'The 1951–55 Conservative Government and the Racialization of Black Immigration'. In *Inside Babylon: The Caribbean Diaspora in Britain*, edited by Winston James and Clive Harris, pp. 55–71. London: Verso, 1993.
Carter, Gwendolen M. *The Politics of Inequality: South Africa since 1948*. London: Thames and Hudson, 1958.
Castle, Kathryn. *Britannia's Children: Reading Colonialism through Children's Books and Magazines*. Manchester: Manchester University Press, 1996.
Cavanaugh, Edward. 'Settler Colonialism in South Africa: Land, Labour and Transformation, 1880–2015'. In *The Routledge Handbook of the History of Settler Colonialism*, edited by Edward Cavanaugh and Lorenzo Veracini, pp. 291–309. Abingdon: Routledge, 2017.
Centre for Contemporary Cultural Studies. *The Empire Strikes Back: Race and Racism in 70s Britain*. London: Hutchinson, 1982.
Chilton, Lisa. *Agents of Empire: British Female Migration to Canada and Australia, 1860s–1930*. Toronto: University of Toronto Press, 2007.
———. 'A New Class of Women for the Colonies: *The Imperial Colonist* and the Construction of Empire'. *The Journal of Imperial and Commonwealth History* 31:2 (2003), 36–56.
Clarke, Marieke, and Pathisa Nyathi. *Lozikeyi Dlodlo: Queen of the Ndebele*. Bulawayo: AmaGugu Publishers, 2011.
Coetzee, J.M. *White Writing: On the Culture of Letters in South Africa*. New Haven: Yale University Press, 1988.
Cohen, Deborah. *Household Gods: The British and their Possessions*. New Haven and London: Yale University Press, 2006.
Collingham, Lizzie. *The Taste of War: World War Two and the Battle for Food*. London: Allen Lane, 2011.
Conservative Party, *A Better Tomorrow: The Conservative Party General Election Manifesto 1970*. London: Conservative Party, 1970.
Constantine, Stephen. '"Bringing the Empire alive": the Empire Marketing Board and imperial propaganda, 1926–33'. In *Imperialism and Popular Culture*, edited by John M. MacKenzie, pp. 192–231. Manchester: Manchester University Press, 1986.
———. 'British Emigration to the Empire-Commonwealth since 1880: From Overseas Settlement to Diaspora?'. *Journal of Imperial and Commonwealth History* 31:2 (2003), 16–35.
———. 'The British Government, Child Welfare, and Child Migration to Australia after 1945'. *Journal of Imperial and Commonwealth History* 30:1 (2002), 99–132.
———. 'Waving Goodbye? Australia, Assisted Passages, and the Empire and Commonwealth Settlement Acts, 1945–72'. *Journal of Imperial and Commonwealth History* 26:2 (1998), 176–95.

Conway, Daniel, and Pauline Leonard. *Migration, Space and Transnational Identities: The British in South Africa*. Basingstoke: Palgrave Macmillan, 2014.

Conway, Martin, and José Gotovich, eds. *Europe in Exile: European Exile Communities in Britain 1940–45*. Oxford: Berghahn Books, 2001.

Cooper, Frederick, and Ann L. Stoler. 'Introduction: Tensions of Empire: Colonial Control and Visions of Rule'. *American Ethnologist* 16:4 (1989), 609–21.

Copsey, Nigel. *Contemporary British Fascism: The British National Party and the Quest for Legitimacy*. London: Palgrave Macmillan, 2008.

Crowder, Michael. 'The Second World War: Prelude to Decolonisation in Africa'. In *The Cambridge History of Africa, Vol. 8, From c. 1940 to c. 1975*, edited by Michael Crowder, pp. 8–51. Cambridge: Cambridge University Press, 1984.

Crowley, Mark J., and Sandra Trudgen Dawson, eds. *Home Fronts: Britain and the Empire at War, 1939–1945*. Woodbridge: The Boydell Press, 2017.

Crwys-Williams, Jennifer. *A Country at War 1939–1945: The Mood of a Nation*. Rivonia: Ashanti Publishing, 1992.

Daniels, Stephan, and Catherine Nash. 'Lifepaths: Geography and Biography'. *Journal of Historical Geography* 30 (2004), 449–58.

Davidson, B. 'South Africa and The Second World War'. In *Africa and the Second World War: Symposium: Papers and Report*, edited by Unesco, pp. 107–22. Paris, 1985.

Dubow, Saul. *Apartheid: 1948–1994*. Oxford: Oxford University Press, 2014.

———. 'How British was the British World? The Case of South Africa'. *The Journal of Imperial and Commonwealth History* 37:1 (2009), 1–27.

———. 'Introduction: South Africa's 1940s'. In *South Africa's 1940s: Worlds of Possibilities*, edited by Saul Dubow and Alan Jeeves, pp. 1–19. Cape Town: Double Storey, 2005.

———. *Racial Segregation and the Origins of Apartheid in South Africa, 1919–36*. Basingstoke: Macmillan, 1989.

Dummett, Ann, and Andrew Nicol. *Subjects, Citizens, Aliens and Others: Nationality and Immigration Law*. London: Weidenfeld and Nicolson, 1990.

Edgerton, David. *Britain's War Machine: Weapons, Resources and Experts in the Second World War*. London: Allen Lane, 2011.

———. *The Rise and Fall of the British Nation: A Twentieth-Century History*. London: Allen Lane, 2018.

El-Enany, Nadine. *(B)ordering Britain: Law, Race and Empire*. Manchester: Manchester University Press, 2020.

Elie, Jérôme. 'The Historical Roots of Cooperation Between the UN High Commissioner for Refugees and the International Organization for Migration'. *Global Governance: A Review of Multilateralism and International Organizations* 16:3 (2010), 345–60.

Emigrating to South Africa: A Guide to Procedure and Introduction to Life in the Republic. London: Barclays Bank DSO, 1971.

Fedorowich, Kent. *Unfit for Heroes: Reconstruction and Soldier Settlement in the Empire between the Wars*. Manchester: Manchester University Press, 1995.

Fedorowich, Kent, and Andrew Thompson, eds. *Empire, Migration and Identity in the British World*. Manchester: Manchester University Press, 2013.

Fennell, Jonathan. *Combat and Morale in the North African Campaign: The Eighth Army and the Path to El Alamein*. Cambridge: Cambridge University Press, 2011.

———. *Fighting the People's War: The British and Commonwealth Armies and the Second World War*. Cambridge: Cambridge University Press, 2019.

Fethney, Michael. *The Absurd and the Brave: CORB – The True Account of the British Government's World War II Evacuation of Children Overseas*. Sussex: The Book Guild Ltd, 1990.

Fryer, Peter. *Staying Power: The History of Black People in Britain*. London: Pluto Books, 1984.

Fuller, Alexandra. *Cocktail Hour Under the Tree of Forgetfulness*. London: Simon and Schuster, 2011.

Furlong, Patrick. *Between Crown and Swastika: The Impact of the Radical Right on the Afrikaner Nationalist Movement in the Fascist Era*. Middletown: Wesleyan University Press, 1991.

Gallup, George H., ed. *The Gallup International Public Opinion Polls: Great Britain 1937–1975*. New York: Random House, 1976.

Gann, L.H. *Huggins of Rhodesia the Man and His Country*. London: George Allen & Unwin Ltd, 1964.

Geary, Daniel, Camilla Schofield and Jennifer Sutton. 'Introduction: Toward a global history of white nationalism'. In *Global White Nationalism: From Apartheid to Trump*, edited by Daniel Geary, Camilla Schofield and Jennifer Sutton, pp. 1–27. Manchester: Manchester University Press, 2020.

Gentleman, Amelia. *The Windrush Betrayal: Exposing the Hostile Environment*. London: Faber, 2019.

Gertzel, Cherry. 'East and Central Africa'. In *The Cambridge History of Africa*, edited by Michael Crowder, pp. 383–457. Cambridge: Cambridge University Press, 1984.

Gibson, Perla Siedle. *Durban's Lady in White: An Autobiography*. Northaw: Aedificamus Press, 1991.

Gilroy, Paul. *After Empire: Melancholia or Convivial Culture*. Abingdon: Routledge, 2004.

———. *'There ain't no black in the Union Jack': The Cultural Politics of Race and Nation*. Chicago: University of Chicago Press, 1991.

Godwin, Peter, and Ian Hancock. *'Rhodesians Never Die': The Impact of War and Political Change on White Rhodesia, c. 1970–1980*. Oxford: Oxford University Press, 1993.

Golley, John. *Aircrew Unlimited: The Commonwealth Air Training Plan During World War Two*. Sparkford: Patrick Stephens, 1993.

Goodfellow, Maya. *Hostile Environment: How Immigrants Became Scapegoats*. London: Verso, 2019.

Goulbourne, Harry. *Ethnicity and Nationalism in Post-Imperial Britain*. Cambridge: Cambridge University Press, 1991.

Grant, Colin. *Home Coming: Voices of the Windrush Generation*. London: Jonathan Cape, 2019.

Gunn, Simon. 'Spatial mobility in later twentieth-century Britain'. *Contemporary British History* (2021), 1–22.

Gurney, Christabel. 'The 1970s: The Anti-Apartheid Movement's Difficult Decade'. *Journal of Southern African Studies* 35:2 (2009), 471–87.

Hammerton, A. James. *Emigrant Gentlewomen: Genteel Poverty and Female Emigration, 1830–1914*. London: Croom Helm, 1979.

———. '"I'm a citizen of the world": Late Twentieth-Century British Emigration and Global Identities – The End of the "British World"?'. In *Empire, Migration and Identity in the British World*, edited by Kent Fedorowich and Andrew S. Thompson, pp. 232–46. Manchester: Manchester University Press, 2013.

———. *Migrants of the British Diaspora Since the 1960s: Stories From Modern Nomads*. Manchester: Manchester University Press, 2017.

———. '"Out of their Natural Station": Empire and Empowerment in the Emigration of Lower-Middle-Class Women'. In *Imperial Objects: Essays on Victorian Women's Emigration and the Unauthorized Imperial Experience*, edited by Rita S. Kranidis, pp. 143–69. New York: Twayne Publishers, 1998.

Hammerton, A. James, and Alistair Thomson. *Ten Pound Poms: Australia's Invisible Migrants*. Manchester: Manchester University Press, 2005.

Hampshire, James. *Citizenship and Belonging: Immigration and the Politics of Demographic Governance in Postwar Britain*. Basingstoke: Palgrave Macmillan, 2005.

Hansen, Randall. *Citizenship and Immigration in Post-war Britain: The Institutional Origins of a Multicultural Nation*. Oxford: Oxford University Press, 2000.

Harper, Marjory, and Stephen Constantine. *Migration and Empire*. Oxford: Oxford University Press, 2010.

Hatton, Timothy J. 'Emigration from the UK, 1870–1913 and 1950–1998'. *European Review of Economic History* 8:2 (2004), 149–71.

Heaton, Matthew M. 'Elder Dempster and the transport of lunatics in British West Africa'. In *Beyond the State*, edited by Anna Greenwood, pp. 104–25. Cambridge: Cambridge University Press, 2016.

Hewitt, Gwen. *Womanhood at War: The Story of the SAWAS*. Johannesburg: Frier and Munro, 1947.

Higman, B.W. 'Testing the Boundaries of White Australia: Domestic Servants and Immigration Policy, 1901–45'. *Immigrants and Minorities* 22:1 (2003), 1–21.

Hobsbawm, Eric. 'Mass Producing Traditions: Europe, 1870–1914'. In *The Invention of Tradition*, edited by Eric Hobsbawm and Terence Ranger, pp. 263–307. Cambridge: Cambridge University Press, 1983.

Hoerder, Dick. *Cultures in Contact: World Migrations in the Second Millennium*. Durham and London: Duke University Press, 2002.

Hofstede, B.P. *Thwarted Exodus: Postwar Overseas Emigration from the Netherlands*. The Hague: M. Nijhoff, 1964.

Hopkins, A.G. 'Rethinking Decolonization'. *Past and Present* 200:1 (2008), 211–47.

Horne, Gerald. *From the Barrel of a Gun: The United States and the War Against Zimbabwe, 1965–1980*. Chapel Hill: University of North Carolina Press, 2001.

Howe, Stephen. 'Internal Decolonization? British Politics since Thatcher as Post-colonial Trauma'. *Twentieth Century British History* 14:3 (2003), 286–304.

———. 'When (if ever) did Empire End? "Internal Decolonisation" in British Culture since the 1950s'. In *The British Empire in the 1950s: Retreat or Revival?*, edited by Martin Lynn, pp. 214–37. Basingstoke: Palgrave Macmillan, 2006.

Hughes, David McDermott. *Whiteness in Zimbabwe: Race, Landscape and the Problem of Belonging*. New York: Palgrave Macmillan, 2010.

Hutching, Megan. *Long Journey for Sevenpence: An Oral History of Assisted Immigration to New Zealand from the United Kingdom, 1947–1975*. Wellington: Victoria University Press, 1999.

Hyam, Ronald, and Peter Henshaw. *The Lion and the Springbok: British and South Africa since the Boer War*. Cambridge: Cambridge University Press, 2003.

Hyslop, Jonathan. 'The Lady in White: British Imperial Loyalism and Women's Volunteerism in Second World War Durban'. *Journal of Natal and Zulu History* 32:1 (2018), 38–54.

International Defence and Aid Fund. *Southern Africa: Immigration from Britain*. Geneva: Centre Europe Tiers Monde, 1975.

Jackson, Ashley. *The British Empire and the Second World War*. New York: Hambledon Continuum, 2006.

———. *Distant Drums: The Role of Colonies in British Imperial Warfare*. Brighton: Sussex Academic Press, 2010.

Jackson, Ashley, Yasmin Khan, and Gajendra Singh, eds. *An Imperial World at War: Aspects of the British Empire's War Experience, 1939–1945*. London: Routledge, 2017.

Jackson, Carlton. *Who Will Take Our Children?* London: Methuen, 1985.

Jackson, Will. 'White man's country: Kenya Colony and the making of a myth'. *Journal of East African Studies* 5:2 (May 2011), 344–68.

Jarratt, Melynda. *War Brides: The Stories of the Women Who Left Everything Behind to Follow the Men They Loved*. Stroud: Tempus, 2007.

Jenkinson, Jacqueline. *Black 1919: Riots, Racism and Resistance in Imperial Britain*. Liverpool: Liverpool University Press, 2009.

John, Nerys. 'The Campaign against British Bank Involvement in Apartheid South Africa'. *African Affairs* 99:396 (2000), 415–33.

Johnson, David. 'Settler Farmers and Coerced African Labour in Southern Rhodesia, 1936–46'. *The Journal of African History* 33:1 (1992), 111–28.

Johnston-White, Iain. *The British Commonwealth and Victory in the Second World War*. London: Palgrave Macmillan, 2017.

Johnston, P.H.W. *British emigration to Durban, South Africa*. Durban: Institute for Social Research: University of Natal, 1970.

Jones, Ben. *The working class in mid twentieth-century England: community, identity and social memory*. Manchester: Manchester University Press, 2012.

Jones, Stuart, and Jon Inggs. 'An overview of the South African economy in the 1970s'. *South African Journal of Economic History* 14:1–2 (1999), 1–10.

Jupp, James. *The English in Australia*. Cambridge and New York: Cambridge University Press, 2004.

———. *From White Australia to Woomera: The Story of Australian Immigration*. Cambridge: Cambridge University Press, 2002.

Karatani, Rieko. *Defining British Citizenship: Empire, Commonwealth and Modern Britain*. London: Frank Cass, 2003.

Kauanui, J. Kehaulani, and Patrick Wolfe. 'Settler Colonialism Then and Now: A Conversation Between J. Kehaulani Kauanui and Patrick Wolfe'. *Politica & Società* 2 (2012), 235–58.

Kelley, Ninette, and Michael Trebilcock. *The Making of the Mosaic: A History of Canadian Immigration Policy*. Toronto: University of Toronto Press, 2010.

Kennedy, Dane. 'Imperial History and Post-Colonial Theory'. *Journal of Imperial and Commonwealth History* 24:3 (1996), 345–63.

———. *Islands of White: Settler Society and Culture in Kenya and Southern Rhodesia, 1890–1939*. Durham: Duke University Press, 1987.

Kenrick, David. *Decolonisation, Identity and Nation in Rhodesia, 1964–1979*. London: Palgrave Macmillan, 2019.

———. 'Settler Soul-Searching and Sovereign Independence: The Monarchy in Rhodesia, 1965–1970'. *Journal of South African Studies* 44:6 (2018), 1077–93.

Kershaw, Roger, and Janet Sacks. *New Lives for Old: The Story of Britain's Child Migrants*. Kew: The National Archives, 2008.

Khan, Yasmin. *The Raj at War: A People's History of India's Second World War*. London: The Bodley Head, 2015.

———. 'Sex in an Imperial War Zone: Transnational Encounters in Second World War India'. *History Workshop Journal* 73:1 (2012), 240–58.

Killingray, David, and Martin Plaut. *Fighting for Britain: African Soldiers in the Second World War*. Suffolk: James Currey, 2010.

Killingray, David, and Richard Rathbone, eds. *Africa and the Second World War*. Basingstoke: Macmillan, 1986.

———. 'Introduction'. In *Africa and the Second World War*, edited by David Killingray and Richard Rathbone, pp. 1–19. Basingstoke: Macmillan, 1986.

Klausen, Susanne M. *Abortion Under Apartheid: Nationalism, Sexuality, and Women's Reproductive Rights in South Africa*. Oxford: Oxford University Press, 2015.

———. '"Reclaiming the White Daughter's Purity": Afrikaner Nationalism, Racialized Sexuality, and the 1975 Abortion and Sterilization Act in Apartheid South Africa'. *Journal of Women's History* 22:3 (2010), 39–63.

Kranidis, Rita S. *The Victorian Spinster and Colonial Emigration: Contested Subjects*. New York: St. Martin's Press, 1999.

Kristiansen, Jean G. *Brother Officers on the Sheep's Back: An Account of the Indian Army Officers' Settlement in Victoria in the 1920s*. Camperdown: J.G. Kristiansen, 1993.

Lake, Marilyn, and Henry Reynolds. *Drawing the Global Colour Line: White Men's Countries and the International Challenge of Racial Equality*. Cambridge: Cambridge University Press, 2008.

Lambert, David, and Alan Lester. 'Introduction: Imperial Spaces, Imperial Subjects'. In *Colonial Lives Across the British Empire: Imperial Careering in the Long Nineteenth Century*, edited by David Lambert and Alan Lester, pp. 1–31. Cambridge: Cambridge University Press, 2006.

Lambert, John. '"The Last Outpost": The Natalians, South Africa, and the British Empire'. In *Settlers and Expatriates: Britons over the Seas*, edited by Robert Bickers, pp. 150–77. Oxford: Oxford University Press, 2010.

———. 'South African British? Or Dominion South Africans? The Evolution of an Identity in the 1910s and 1920s'. *South African Historical Journal* 43:1 (November 2000), 197–222.

———. '"Their Finest Hour?" English-speaking South Africans and World War II'. *South African Historical Journal* 60 (2008), 60–84.

———. '"An Unknown People": Reconstructing British South African Identity'. *The Journal of Imperial and Commonwealth History* 37:4 (2009), 599–617.

Law, Kate. *Gendering the Settler State: White Women, Race, Liberalism and Empire in Rhodesia, 1950–1980*. Abingdon: Routledge, 2016.

Legassick, Martin. 'British Hegemony and the Origins of Segregation in South Africa, 1901–14'. In *Segregation and Apartheid in Twentieth Century South Africa*, edited by William Beinart and Saul Dubow, pp. 43–59. London: Routledge, 2002.

Lin, Patricia Y. 'National Identity and Social Mobility: Class, Empire and the British Government Overseas Evacuation of Children during the Second World War'. *Twentieth Century British History* 7:3 (1996), 310–44.

Lindsey, Lydia. 'Halting the Tide: Responses to West Indian Immigration to Britain, 1946–1952'. *The Journal of Caribbean History* 26:1 (1992), 62–96.

Low, D.A. *Eclipse of Empire*. Cambridge: Cambridge University Press, 1991.

Low, D.A., and J.M. Lonsdale. 'Introduction: Towards the New Order 1945–1963'. In *History of East Africa: Volume 3*, edited by D.A. Low and Alison Smith, pp. 1–63. Oxford: Clarendon Press, 1976.

Lowry, Donal. 'Rhodesia 1890–1980: "The Lost Dominion"'. In *Settlers and Expatriates: Britons over the Seas*, edited by Robert Bickers. Oxford: Oxford University Press, 2010.

Lubkemann, Stephen C. 'Race, Class and Kin in the Negotiation of 'Internal Strangerhood' among Portuguese Retornados, 1975–2000'. In *Europe's Invisible Migrants*, edited by Andrea L. Smith, pp. 75–94. Amsterdam: Amsterdam University Press, 2003.

———. 'Unsettling the Metropole: Race and Settler Reincorporation in Postcolonial Portugal'. In *Settler Colonialism in the Twentieth Century*, edited by Caroline Elkins and Susan Pederson, pp. 257–70. Routledge: New York and London, 2005.

Lynn, Martin. 'Introduction'. In *The British Empire in the 1950s: Retreat or Revival?*, edited by Martin Lynn, pp. 1–15. Basingstoke: Palgrave Macmillan, 2006.

MacDonald, J.F. *The War History of Southern Rhodesia, 1939–45*. Vol. I, Salisbury: Government of Rhodesia, 1947.

———. *The War History of Southern Rhodesia, 1939–45*. Vol. II, Salisbury: Government of Southern Rhodesia, 1950.

MacDonald, Robert H. *The Language of Empire: Myths and Metaphors of Popular Imperialism, 1880–1918*. Manchester: Manchester University Press, 1994.

Mackay, Robert. *Half the Battle: Civilian Morale in Britain during the Second World War*. Manchester: Manchester University Press, 2002.

MacKenzie, John M. *Propaganda and Empire: The Manipulation of British Public Opinion, 1880–1960*. Manchester: Manchester University Press, 1984.

MacKenzie, John M., with Nigel R. Dalziel. *The Scots in South Africa: Ethnicity, Identity, Gender and Race, 1772–1914*. Manchester: Manchester University Press, 2007.

Magee, Gary B., and Andrew S. Thompson. *Empire and Globalisation: Networks of People, Goods and Capital in the British World, c. 1850–1914*. Cambridge: Cambridge University Press, 2010.

Malchow, Howard L. *Population Pressures: Emigration and Government in Late Nineteenth-Century Britain*. Palo Alto: Society for the Promotion of Science and Scholarship, 1979.

Malherbe, E.G. *Never a Dull Moment*. Cape Town: Howard Timmins, 1981.

Mangan, J.A., ed. *The Imperial Curriculum: Racial Images and Education in the British Colonial Experience*. London: Routledge, 1993.

Mann, Jessica. *Out of Harm's Way: The Wartime Evacuation of Children from Britain*. St. Ives: Headline, 2005.

Marks, Shula. 'Natal, the Zulu Royal Family and the Ideology of Segregation'. In *Segregation and Apartheid in Twentieth Century South Africa*, edited by William Beinart and Saul Dubow, pp. 91–117. London: Routledge, 2002.

Martin, H.J, and Neil D. Orpen. *South Africa at War: Military and Industrial Organization and Operations in Connection with the Conduct of the War, 1939–1945*. Cape Town: Purnell, 1979.

Marx, Christoph. *Oxwagon Sentinel: Radical Afrikaner Nationalism and the History of the Ossewabrandwag*, translated by Sheila Gordon-Schröder. Pretoria: University of South Africa Press, 2008.

Mason, Lisa. 'The Development of the Monday Club and its Contribution to the Conservative Party and the Modern British Right, 1961–1990.' PhD dissertation, University of Wolverhampton, 2004.

McCarthy, Angela. *Personal Narratives of Irish and Scottish Migration, 1921–65*. Manchester: Manchester University Press, 2007.

McClintock, Anne. *Imperial Leather: Race, Gender and Sexuality in the Colonial Contest*. New York and London: Routledge, 1995.

Middlemas, Keith. 'Twentieth Century White Society in Mozambique'. *Tarikh* 6:2 (1979, 30–45.

Miescher, Stephan F. *Making Men in Ghana*. Bloomington and Indianapolis: Indiana University Press, 2003.

Mlambo, A.S. *White Immigration into Rhodesia from Occupation to Federation*. Harare: University of Zimbabwe Publications, 2002.

Money, Duncan, and Danelle van Zyl-Hermann. 'Introduction: Rethinking White Societies in Southern Africa, 1930s–1990s'. In *Rethinking White Societies in Southern Africa, 1930s–1990s*, edited by Duncan Money and Danelle van Zyl-Hermann, pp. 1–22. London: Routledge, 2020.

Mongia, Radhika Viyas. 'Race, Nationality, Mobility: A History of the Passport'. In *After the Imperial Turn: Thinking with and through the Nation*, edited by Antoinette Burton, pp. 196–214. Durham: Duke University Press, 2003.

Moodie, T. Dunbar. *The Rise of Afrikanerdom: Power, Apartheid, and the Afrikaner Civil Religion*. Berkeley: University of California Press, 1975.

Morley, Sam. *Back to Durban … 50 years on! The 'Lady in White' Memorial Visit of March '92*. Northaw: Aedificamus Press, 1992.

Munro, Archie. *The Winston Specials: Troopships via the Cape, 1940–3*. Liskeard: Martime Books, 2006.

Murphy, Philip. *The Empire's New Clothes: The Myth of the Commonwealth*. London: Hurst and Company, 2018.

———. '"Government by Blackmail": The Origins of the Central African Federation Reconsidered'. In *The British Empire in the 1950s: Retreat or Revival?*, edited by Martin Lynn, pp. 53–76. Basingstoke: Palgrave Macmillan, 2006.

Nairn, Tom. *The Break-up of Britain: Crisis and Neonationalism*. London: Verso, 1981.

Nasson, Bill. *South Africa at War: 1939–1945*. Auckland Park: Jacana, 2012.

———. *Springboks on the Somme: South Africa in the Great War, 1914–1918*. Johannesburg and New York: Penguin, 2007.

O'Reilly, Karen. *The British on the Costa del Sol: Transnational Identities and Local Communities*. New York: Routledge, 2000.

Ovalle-Bahamón, Ricardo E. 'The Wrinkles of Decolonization and Nationness: White Angolans as Retornados in Portugal'. In *Europe's Invisible Migrants*, edited by Andrea L. Smith, pp. 147–68. Amsterdam: Amsterdam University Press, 2003.

Palfreeman, A.C. *The Administration of the White Australia Policy*. Melbourne: Melbourne University Press, 1967.

Parker, Kenneth. 'Fertile land, romantic spaces, uncivilized peoples: English travel-writing about the Cape of Good Hope, 1800–1850'. In *The Expansion of England: Race, Ethnicity and Cultural History*, edited by Bill Schwartz, pp. 198–231. London: Routledge, 1996.

Paul, Kathleen. *Whitewashing Britain: Race and Citizenship in the Postwar Era*. Ithaca: Cornell University Press, 1997.

Payton, Philip. *The Cornish Overseas: The Epic Story of Cornwall's 'Great Emigration'*. Exeter: University of Exeter Press, 2020.

Peach, Ceri. *West Indian Migration to Britain: A Social Geography*. Oxford: Oxford University Press, 1968.

Peberdy, Sally. *Selecting Immigrants: National Identity and South Africa's Immigration Policies, 1910–2008*. Johannesburg: Wits University Press, 2009.

Perry, Kennetta Hammond. *London is the Place for Me: Black Britons, Citizenship, and the Politics of Race*. Oxford: Oxford University Press, 2015.

Philips, Mike, and Trevor Philips. *Windrush: The Irresistible Rise of Multi-Racial Britain*. London: Harper Collins, 1999.

Phimister, Ian. 'Zimbabwe: The Path of Capitalist Development'. In *History of Central Africa Vol. 2*, edited by David Birmingham and Phyllis Martin, pp. 251–90. London: Longman, 1983.

Pickles, Katie. 'Empire Settlement and Single British Women as New Zealand Domestic Servants during the 1920s'. *New Zealand Journal of History* 35:1 (2001), 22–44.

———. '"A link in the great chain of Empire friendship": The Victoria League in New Zealand'. *Journal of Imperial and Commonwealth History* 33:1 (2005), 29–50.

———. 'Pink Cheeked and Surplus: Single British Women's Inter-war Migration to New Zealand'. In *Shifting Centres: Women and Migration in New Zealand History*, edited by Lyndon Fraser and Katie Pickles, pp. 63–80. Otago: Otago University Press, 2002.

Portelli, A. 'What Makes Oral History Different'. In *The Oral History Reader*, edited by Robert Perks and Alistair Thomson, pp. 32–42. New York: Routledge, 2006.

Pratt, Mary Louise. *Imperial Eyes: Travel Writing and Transculturation*. London: Routledge, 1992.

Price, Richard. 'One Big Thing: Britain, Its Empire and Their Imperial Culture'. *Journal of British Studies* 45 (2006), 602–27.

Richards, Eric. *Britannia's Children: Emigration from England, Scotland, Wales and Ireland since 1600*. London: Hambledon and London, 2004.

Richards, Jeffrey, ed. *Imperialism and Juvenile Literature*. Manchester: Manchester University Press, 1989.

Richmond, Anthony. *Post-War Immigrants in Canada*. Toronto: University of Toronto Press, 1967.

Robson, John M. *Marriage or Celibacy? The Daily Telegraph on a Victorian Dilemma*. Toronto: University of Toronto Press, 1995.
Roe, Michael. *Australia, Britain, and Migration, 1915–1940: A Study of Desperate Hopes*. Cambridge: Cambridge University Press, 2002.
Rose, Sonya. *Which People's War? National Identity and Citizenship in Britain 1939–1945*. Oxford: Oxford University Press, 2003.
Rush, Anne Spry. *Bonds of Empire: West Indians and Britishness from Victoria to Decolonization*. Oxford: Oxford University Press, 2011.
Ryan, Louise, and Wendy Webster. *Gendering Migration: Masculinity, Femininity and Ethnicity in Post-war Britain*. Aldershot: Ashgate, 2008.
Said, Edward. *Culture and Imperialism*. New York: Vintage Books, 1994.
———. *Orientalism*. New York: Vintage Books, 2003.
Samasuwo, Nhamo. 'Food Production and War Supplies: Rhodesia's Beef Industry during the Second World War, 1939–1945'. *Journal of Southern African Studies* 29:2 (2003), 487–502.
Sapire, Hilary. 'African Loyalism and its Discontents: The Royal Tour of South Africa, 1947'. *The Historical Journal* 54:1 (2011), 215–40.
Särlvik, Bo, and Ivor Crewe. *Decade of Dealignment: The Conservative Victory of 1979 and Electoral Trends in the 1970s*. Cambridge: Cambridge University Press, 1983.
Schofield, Camilla. *Enoch Powell and the Making of Postcolonial Britain*. Cambridge: Cambridge University Press, 2013.
Schofield, Camilla, and Ben Jones. '"Whatever Community Is, This Is Not It": Notting Hill and the Reconstruction of "Race" in Britain after 1958'. *The Journal of British Studies* 58:1 (2019), 142–73.
Schwarz, Bill. *West Indian Intellectuals in Britain*. Manchester: Manchester University Press, 2003.
———. *The White Man's World*. Oxford: Oxford University Press, 2011.
Seekings, Jeremy. '"Not a Single White Person Should Be Allowed to Go Under": *Swartgevaar* and the Origins of South Africa's Welfare State, 1924–1929'. *The Journal of African History* 48:3 (2007), 375–94.
Seyd, Patrick. 'Factionalism within the Conservative Party: The Monday Club'. *Government and Opposition* 7:4 (1972), 464–87.
Shakespeare, Geoffrey. *Let Candles be Brought In*. London: MacDonald, 1949.
Sherington, Geoffrey, and Chris Jeffery. *Fairbridge: Empire and Child Migration*. London: Woburn Press, 1998.
Shutt, Alison K. *Manners Make a Nation: Racial Etiquette in Southern Rhodesia: 1910–1963*. Rochester: University of Rochester Press, 2015.
Slater, Roland. 'Die Maatskappy vir Europese Immigrasie: A Study of the Cultural Assimilation and Naturalisation of European Immigrants to South Africa 1949–1994'. Thesis, University of Stellenbosch, 2007.
Smith, Andrea L., ed. *Europe's Invisible Migrants*. Amsterdam: Amsterdam University Press, 2003.
———. 'Introduction'. In *Europe's Invisible Migrants*, edited by Andrea L. Smith, pp. 9–32. Amsterdam: Amsterdam University Press, 2003.
Smith, Evan, and Marinella Marmo. 'Uncovering the 'Virginity Testing' Controversy in the National Archives: The Intersectionality of Discrimination in British Immigration History'. *Gender & History* 23:1 (2011), 147–65.

Smith, Jean P. 'From Promising Settler to Undesirable Immigrant: The Deportation of British-born Migrants from Mental Hospitals in Interwar Australia and South Africa'. *The Journal of Imperial and Commonwealth History* 46:3 (2018), 502–23.

———. 'Persistence and Privilege: Mass Migration from Britain to the Commonwealth, 1945–2000'. In *The Break-up of Greater Britain*, edited by Christian Damm Pederson and Stuart Ward, pp. 252–71. Manchester: Manchester University Press, 2021.

———. 'Race and hospitality: Allied troops of colour on the South African home front during the Second World War'. *War and Society* 39:3 (2020), 155–70.

———. '"The Women's Branch of the Commonwealth Relations Office": The Society for the Overseas Settlement of British Women and the Long Life of Empire Migration'. *Women's History Review* 25:4 (2016), 520–35.

———. '"Young blood" and "the blackout": Love, Sex and Marriage on the South African Home Front'. In *Home Fronts: Britain and the Empire at War, 1939–45*, edited by Mark J. Crowley and Sandra Trudgen Dawson, pp. 93–110. Woodbridge: The Boydell Press, 2017.

South African Bishop's Commission for Justice and Reconciliation. *The Case Against Immigration to South Africa: The Ugly Reality of Apartheid*. Dublin: Dominican Publications, 1983.

Stewart, Andrew. 'The British Government and the South African Neutrality Crisis, 1938–39'. *English Historical Review* 123:503 (2008), 947–72.

Stockwell, Sarah. 'Greater Britain and its Decline: The View from Lambeth'. In *The Break-up of Greater Britain*, edited by Christian Damm Pederson and Stuart Ward, pp. 192–212. Manchester: Manchester University Press, 2021.

Stoler, Ann Laura. *Along the Archival Grain: Epistemic Anxieties and Colonial Common Sense*. Princeton: Princeton University Press, 2009.

———. *Carnal Knowledge and Imperial Power: Race and the Intimate in Colonial Rule*. Berkeley: University of California Press, 2002.

———. 'Tense and Tender Ties: The Politics of Comparison in North American History and (Post) Colonial Studies'. *The Journal of American History* 88:3 (2001), 829–65.

Stone, John. *Colonist or Uitlander: A Study of the British Immigrant in South Africa*. Oxford: Clarendon Press, 1973.

Stultz, Newell M. 'Evolution of the United Nations Anti-Apartheid Regime'. In *Readings in the International Relations of Africa*, edited by Tom Young, pp. 93–103. Bloomington: Indiana University Press, 2016.

Sutcliffe-Braithwaite, Florence. *Class, Politics, and the Decline of Deference in England, 1968–2000*. Oxford: Oxford University Press, 2018.

Swaisland, Cecilie. *Servants and Gentlewomen to the Golden Land: The Emigration of Single Women from Britain to Southern Africa, 1820–1939*. Oxford: Berg, 1993.

Swanson, Maynard W. 'The Sanitation Syndrome: Bubonic Plague and Urban Native Policy in the Cape Colony, 1900–09'. In *Segregation and Apartheid in Twentieth Century South Africa*, edited by William Beinart and Saul Dubow, pp. 25–42. London: Routledge, 2002.

Tavuyanago, Baxter, Tasara Muguti, and James Hlongwana. 'Victims of the Rhodesian Immigration Policy: Polish Refugees from the Second World War'. *Journal of South African Studies* 38:4 (2012), 951–65.

The Christian Institute of South Africa. *White Immigration to South Africa*. Johannesburg: Zenith Printers, 1974.

Thompson, P.S. *Natalians First: Separatism in South Africa, 1909–1961*. Johannesburg: Southern Book Publishers, 1990.

Tinley, J.M. *South African Food and Agriculture in World War II*. Stanford: Stanford University Press, 1954.

Tischler, Julia. *Light and Power for a Multiracial Nation: The Kariba Dam Scheme in the Central African Federation*. Basingstoke: Palgrave Macmillan, 2013.

Tomlinson, Jim. 'Inventing "Decline": The Falling Behind of the British Economy in the Postwar Years'. *Economic History Review* XLIX:4 (1996), 731–57.

———. 'Thrice Denied: "Declinism" as a Recurrent Theme in British History in the Long Twentieth Century'. *Twentieth Century British History* 20:2 (2009), 227–51.

Uusihakala, Katja. 'Rescuing children, reforming the Empire: British child migration to colonial Southern Rhodesia'. *Identities* 22:3 (2015), 273–87.

Van-Helten, Jean Jacques, and Keith Williams. '"The Crying Need of South Africa": The Emigration of Single British Women to the Transvaal, 1901–1910'. *Journal of South African Studies* 10:1 (October 1983), 17–38.

Veracini, Lorenzo. 'Introduction: Settler colonialism as a distinct mode of domination'. In *The Routledge Handbook of the History of Settler Colonialism*, edited by Edward Cavanaugh and Lorenzo Veracini, pp. 1–8. Abingdon: Routledge, 2017.

———. *The Settler Colonial Present*. London: Palgrave Macmillan, 2015.

———. *Settler Colonialism: A Theoretical Overview*. London: Palgrave Macmillan, 2010.

Vickery, Kenneth P. 'The Second World War Revival of Forced Labour in the Rhodesias'. *The International Journal of African Historical Studies* 22:3 (1989), 423–37.

Voeltz, Richard A. 'The British Boy Scout migration plan 1922–1932'. *The Social Science Journal* 40:1 (2003), 143–51.

Wagner, Gillian. *Children of the Empire*. London: Weidenfeld and Nicolson, 1982.

Ward, Stuart. 'Introduction'. In *British Culture and the End of Empire*, edited by Stuart Ward. Manchester: Manchester University Press, 2001.

Waters, Chris. '"Dark Strangers in Our Midst": Discourses of Race and Nation in Britain, 1947–1963'. *Journal of British Studies* 36 (1997), 207–38.

Webster, Wendy. *Englishness and Empire, 1939–1965*. Oxford: Oxford University Press, 2005.

———. 'Home, Colonial and Foreign: Europe, Empire and the History of Migration in 20th-century Britain.' *History Compass* 7 (2009), 1–19.

———. *Imagining Home: Gender, 'Race', and National Identity, 1945–64*. London: UCL Press, 1998.

———. *Mixing It: Diversity in World War Two Britain*. Oxford: Oxford University Press, 2018.

Welshman, John. *Churchill's Children: The Evacuee Experience in Wartime Britain*. Oxford: Oxford University Press, 2010.

Wetton, C.E. *The Promised Land: The Story of the Barr Colonists*. Lloydminster: Lloydminster Times, 1955.

White, Landeg. *Magomero: Portrait of an African Village*. Cambridge: Cambridge University Press, 1987.

White, Luise. '"Normal Political Activities": Rhodesia, The Pearce Commission, and the African National Council'. *Journal of African History* 52 (2011), 321–40.
———. 'The Utopia of Working Phones: Rhodesian Independence and the Place of Race in Decolonization'. In *Utopia/Dystopia: Conditions of Historical Possibility*, edited by Michael D. Gordin, Helen Tilley and Gyan Prakash, pp. 94–116. Princeton: Princeton University Press, 2010.
Williams, Wendy. *Windrush Lesson Learned Review*. London: HMSO, 2020.
Wills, Clair. *Lovers and Strangers: An Immigrant History of Post-War Britain*. London: Allen Lane, 2017.
Wills, Sarah. '"When Good Neighbours Become Good Friends": The Australian Embrace of its Millionth Migrant'. *Australian Historical Studies* 35:124 (2004), 332–54.
Wilson, Francis. 'Southern Africa'. In *The Cambridge History of Africa*, edited by Michael Crowder, pp. 251–330. Cambridge: Cambridge University Press, 1984.
Wintle, Claire. 'Career Development: Domestic Display as Imperial, Anthropological and Social Trophy'. *Victorian Studies* 50:2 (2008), 279–88.
Woollacott, Angela. *To Try Her Fortune in London: Australian Women, Colonialism and Modernity*. Oxford: Oxford University Press, 2001.
Yow, Valerie Raleigh. *Recording Oral History*. Lanham, MD: Altamira Press, 2005.
Zahra, Tara. 'Lost Children: Displacement, Family, and Nation in Postwar Europe'. *The Journal of Modern History* 81:1 (March 2009), 45–86.
———. *The Lost Children: Reconstructing Europe's Families after World War II*. Cambridge: Harvard University Press, 2011.
Zembe, Christopher Roy. 'Migrating with Colonial and Post-Colonial Memories: Dynamics of Racial Interactions within Zimbabwe's Minority Communities in Britain'. *Journal of Migration History* 2 (2016), 32–56.
Zweiniger-Bargielowska, Ina. *Austerity in Britain: Rationing, Controls, and Consumption, 1939–1955*. Oxford: Oxford University Press, 2000.

Index

Note: page numbers in *italic* refer to illustrations.

abolition of slavery 115, 192
accents 9, 172, 175, 177, 178–80, 184–5, 188
African nationalists 108, 110
Afrikaner nationalists
   anti-British sentiment from 51–2
   British migrants and 38, 39, 53, 63–4, 99, 113
   child migration schemes and 62, 82
   neutrality crisis and 27, 29
   public holidays and 116
   rhetoric of 74, 83, 86
   white English speakers and 117
Afrikaners 39, 61–2, 70–1n43, 76, 82, 90, 98n81, 100, 114, 115, 116
Algeria 172, 188
Aliens Act (Southern Rhodesia 1946) 89
Aliens Acts (United Kingdom) 11, 22n44
Aliens Control Act (South Africa 1937) 75, 84
Aliens Control Act (South Africa 1991) 155
Allied troops (Second World War) 36, 39, 43–4n12, 47n68
Almanzora 51, 55, 103
Amery, Leo 106
ANC Youth League 70n39
Angola 127–8, 149–50, 152–3, 156, 159, 172, 188
anti-apartheid movement 16, 126, 149, *150*, 158, 160, 161–2, 163, 192–3

anti-colonial activism 61, 110
anti-colonial forces (Rhodesia) 4, 127, 149, 152, 165–6, 178
anti-racism 7, 186–7, 192
apartheid 93n8, 121n63, 129–30, 144n15, 144–5n18, 187, 192
Arundel Castle 78, 84
asset restriction 5–6, 152, 156–7, 158, 162
assimilation 13, 62, 81, 88, 90–1, 111, 152
atheism 153
Atlee government 103
Australia
   'Bring Out a Briton' scheme 111
   child migration schemes and 56, 68n17
   Dutch immigrants to 80
   migrant recruitment by 13, 106, 124, 132–3
   migration to 3, 28, 92n4, 139
   racial kinship and 164–5
   racial policies of 128
   settler colonialism and 10
   shipping companies and 118n8
   South Africa majority rule and 173
   subsidised migration to 59–60, 77, 101, 107, 142, 150. *see also* 'Ten Pound Pom' scheme

Bailey, E.A.S. 37
Bailkin, Jordanna 29

Ball, G.M. 49n85
Bantustans 6, 121n63
Barclays 161–2
Basner, Hyman 64, 71n58
Battle of Delville Wood 115
BBC 35, 109
Beaverbrook, Lord 106
Bedford, Tommy 190n20
Belgium 16, 61, 80–1, 82, 133
Belich, James 13
birth rates 62, 113
Black African MPs (Rhodesia) 156
Blacking, Alfred 39
Black migrants 51–2, 60
Black servants 130
  see also servants
Black service personnel 15, 51, 53–5, 61, 67
Black South Africans 137, 155, 162
Black workers 99, 110, 149, 162–3
Boer War 115
Bonnynge, Anne 177, 179
Bonnynge, Brien 176–9, 181
Botha, P.W. 155
Botswana 186
Bradlow, Edna 14
'brain drain' 5, 8, 139, 140–1
Brexit 164, 193–4
'Bring Out a Briton' scheme (Australia) 111
British Council of Churches 162
British Empire
  migration policies 11–2, 15, 66–7, 104–5
  Natal and 117, 179, 190n20
  racial ideologies 7, 55, 60, 164
  repatriation and 54, 160, 171–2
  Rhodesia and 156
  Second World War and 27, 42
  South African politics and 113, 116
  Southern Rhodesia and 88, 90
British Leyland 149
British migrants
  Afrikaner nationalists and 53, 99
  Anglo-South African identity 115
  apartheid and 131–2, 144n15, 167n8
  assimilation and 89
  assumptions about 54, 60
  Central African Federation and 100, 108
  decolonisation and 188
  1820 Memorial Settlers' Association 114, 134
  migrants of colour and 106
  'Operation Brickie' and 112
  racial hierarchy and 12
  racial logic and 26–7
  recruitment of 11, 13, 28
  Second World War and 38, 51
  serial migration and 171–6
  social mobility of 52, 124
  Southern Rhodesia and 66
  statistics on 1–2, 3, 74, 101, 102
  subsidies and 19n16, 166
  Unilateral Declaration of Independence and 5, 158
British Nationality Act (1948) 5, 6, 11–2, 52, 103, 193
British Nationality Act (1964) 140
British Nationality Act (1981) 140, 151, 165, 193
British National Party 165
Britishness 56, 66, 118, 171, 176
British South Africa Police 176–7, 178
British Travel Certificate 103–4
Brownell, Fred 9, 14, 83
Brownell, Josiah 14, 156, 160
Burnside, Duncan 62
Butler, Rab 139

Canada
  child migration schemes 56, 57–8, 68n17
  citizenship legislation 12, 103
  demobilised soldiers and 59–60
  Dutch immigrants to 80
  migrant recruitment by 13, 28, 77, 101, 107, 124, 150
  migration to 3
  racial kinship and 164–5

Canada (cont.)
  Second World War 30
  settler colonialism and 10–1
CANZUK 164
Cape Town, South Africa 9, 36, 37, 38, 40, 77, 130, 162
Carnarvon Castle 78, 84
Catholic children 80
Central African Federation
  see Federation of Rhodesia and Nyasaland
chain migration 32, 46–7n50
child migrants 82, 90, 189n10
child migration schemes 13, 52–3, 56–8, 61–3, 70n40, 70–1n43, 80–3, 90–1, 175
Children's Overseas Reception Board (CORB) 56–8, 61–3, 68n17, 69n27
Christian Institute 162–3
Churchill government 100, 104–5
citizenship
  British Nationality Act of 1948 and 103
  British Nationality Act of 1981 and 151, 165
  Dominions 12
  Rhodesian migration statistics and 153
  South African Citizenship Act and 113, 121n62
  South African migration statistics and 77–8, 143–4n6, 154
  Southern Rhodesian migration statistics and 19n15, 127
  white Kenyans and 140
City of Benares 56–7, 61
Clarke, Marieke 9, 186–7
Clarkson, Charles 63–4, 65
class
  child evacuees and 57
  decolonisation and 117
  identities and 8–9
  lifestyle and 130, 150–1
  migration policies and 5, 11, 160
  mobility and 3
  racism and 54
  scholarship on 22–3n52
  in southern Africa 39, 40–1
  in United Kingdom 39
Cold War 67, 105, 106, 166
Colonial Development and Welfare Acts of 1940 and 1945 56
Colonial Development Corporation 56
Coloured people (South Africa) 145n19
Commonwealth
  colonial development in 6
  migrants from 1–2, 5, 99, 100, 170n63
  migration policies 11–2, 125, 151, 193
  migration to 105, 141–2
  Rhodesian migration to 157
  South Africa's exit from 171
  Southern Rhodesia and 88
Commonwealth Immigrants Act (1962) 99, 125, 139
Commonwealth Immigrants Act (1968) 125, 140
Commonwealth Relations Office 106, 120n45, 141
Commonwealth Settlement Act (1957) 106, 142
communism 153
Conservative Party (United Kingdom) 147n69, 151, 165
Constantine, Learie 51
Constantine, Stephen 13
Conway, Daniel 14, 128
Coventry, Edward 40
culture
  Afrikaner nationalists and 63–4, 99
  child migration schemes and 62, 81
  decolonisation and 173, 188
  diaspora and 13
  empire and 42
  institutional racism and 193
  migration policies and 91
  Natal separatists and 117
  networks and 9

Index

Rhodesian settler 176, 178, 186
settler colonies and 93n9
in southern Africa 7–8
of wartime South Africa 37

Dane, Fred 34, 41
Dawson, Mark 38
Day of Reconciliation (South Africa) 122–3n78
Day of the Vow (South Africa) 115, 116, 122–3n78
decolonisation
  assets and 182–3
  identities and 171, 172, 174
  implications of 188
  legacies of empire 148n83
  migration politics 4, 143
  phases of 6
  racism and 16, 125
  settler colonialism and 178
  state anxieties over 8
  United Kingdom and 192
  white migration 5
demobilisation 31, 46n40, 52, 53–4, 55, 58, 59, 65–6, 67n1, 87
demographic governance 4–5, 118
Department of Immigration (South Africa) 133, 154–5, 161
diaspora 13, 15, 172
Dietse Kinderfonds (Teutonic Children's League) 82–3
Dingane (Zulu leader) 115
Dingane's Day (South Africa) 116
dislocation 171, 173, 181, 182, 189n10
domestic servants 36, 40, 135
Dominions
  British Nationality Act (1948) 6
  child migration schemes 56–8, 63
  citizenship legislation 12, 103
  competition for immigrants 64
  demobilised soldiers and 59–60
  evacuation of children to 52–3
  migrants to United Kingdom from 139
  migration to 13, 92n4, 99, 141–2
  racial kinship and 164–5

Donald, Grahame 54
Donges, Eben 83–4
dual nationality 174
Dubow, Saul 78, 88–9
Duncan, Patrick 31
Dunlop 149
Durban, South Africa 26, 30, 33–7, 70n39, 77, 82, 128, 162, 179, 189n9, 190n20
Dutch East India Company 116
Dutch migrants 114, 134

Eccles, A.F. 31
economic development 66, 88, 105–6, 108, 117, 121n63, 162
economics 151
Eden government 100
1820 Memorial Settlers' Association 56, 62, 63, 78, 82, 109, 114, 115–6, 134
Elizabeth II 36
emigration
  anti-apartheid movement and 161
  British interest in 2–3
  from Central African Federation 112
  limits on 79–80, 103
  from Rhodesia 127
  from South Africa 113
  from Southern Rhodesia 88
  from United Kingdom 15–6, 92n3, 126, 140–1
Empire Day 116
empire settlement 105
Empire Settlement Acts 59, 106–7, 142
employment
  Black migrants to United Kingdom and 52
  British migrants and 124, 131
  Central African Federation and 108, 111–2
  child migration schemes and 62
  competition for 53
  discriminatory advertising and 160–1
  Immigration Council and 77–8

employment (*cont.*)
  migrant concerns about 31
  migrants of colour and 103, 104, 139
  pass laws and 70n39
  for postwar British migrants 40
  South African migration policies and 63–4, 75, 80, 83, 84, 132–4, 155
  Southern Rhodesia migration policies and 89
  subsidised migration schemes and 61
  in United Kingdom 59
  white minority rule and 11
eugenics 54, 81
European immigration
  to Rhodesia/Southern Rhodesia 86, 87, 108, 127, 153
  to South Africa 82, 83, 96n57, 113–4, 134
European migrants 11, 78, 85–6, 88, 108, 153, 160
European Union 194
evacuees 29, 57–8, 61, 64, 68n17, 69n27, 70–1n43, 180–1

Fairbridge Memorial College 90–1, 175
Federation of Rhodesia and Nyasaland (1953–1963) 3, 6, 10, 14, 100–1, 102, 107, 108–9, 111–2, 124, 126, 147n78
Fedorowich, Kent 13
First World War 31, 52, 58, 59, 115
Foggit, John 114
Foreign and Commonwealth Office (FCO) 159
foreign investment 167n4
Forrester, Henry 59
Forsyth, Douglas 65
Founder's Day (South Africa) 116
France 2, 80–1, 83, 133
Fuller, Alexandra 179–80

Gardner, Alford 51
gender 130, 135–7, 186–7
George VI 73
German orphans 82–3

Gibson, Perla (Lady in White) 35–6
'Go Home' vans 193
Goldberg, Benjamin 110
Golley, John 37
Great Trek 115
Guest, E. Lucas 87, 88
Gunn, Simon 3

Hammerton, James 13, 128
Hampshire, James 118
Harare, Zimbabwe 37, 112, 156–7, 182–4
Haskell, A.I. 40
Hastings, Carolyn 129–30, 187
Heist, Hetty 40
Henderson, Henry 181
Hobsbawm, Eric 115
Home Office 193
hospitality 26, 30, 35–9, 47n68, 52, 58
housing shortages
  South Africa 113, 136
  Southern Rhodesia 87–8, 89, 111
  United Kingdom 55–6, 60, 92n4, 106, 131, 137
Huggins, Godfrey 98n81
Hughes, David 182
Hughes, Stephen 40–1
Hungary 114
Hunt, David 105
hyper-mobility 3

identities 7, 56, 116, 171, 172, 174, 175, 177–8, 182, 184–5, 188
Immigrant Regulation Amendment Act (Southern Rhodesia 1948) 89
Immigrants' Regulation Act (South Africa 1913) 84
Immigrants Regulation Act (Southern Rhodesia 1948) 89
Immigrants Selection Committee (South Africa) 84–5
Immigration Act (United Kingdom 1971) 140, 151, 163–4
Immigration Council (South Africa) 75, 77–8, 84, 85

Index

immigration officers 104–5
imperialism 12, 16, 56, 59, 66, 192
imperial mindset 176
incentives
  debates over 80
  decolonisation and 6
  demobilised service members and 59, 87
  to leave Rhodesia 159, 160
  limited impact of 10
  migrant motivations and 128
  migration policies 4–5
  in Southern Rhodesia 126–7
  white flight and 3
  white migrants and 132–4, 142, 193
India 104, 139, 172
Indian migrants 108
Indonesia 114
Inter-departmental Advisory Council Concerning Immigration Matters (South Africa) 75, 84
Inter-Departmental Committee on Migration (United Kingdom) 59
Intergovernmental Committee on European Migration (ICEM) 108, 114, 155, 160
international law 158
interwar period 6, 56, 59, 85, 93n8

Jamaica 67n6, 104
Jervois, William 174–6, 181, 183, 189n13
Jewish children 80–1, 82, 83, 95–6n43
Jewish immigration 64
Jewish refugees 69n27
Johannesburg, South Africa 185–6
Jones, Ian 130, 133, 184–6
Jones, Philip 131

Kariba Dam 108, 184
Kenrick, David 14
Kenya 134, 140, 143–4n6, 189n9, 191n43
Kilpatrick, T.S. 37
King, Sam 51

Kock, Wickus de 156, 168n25
Kruger, Paul 116

labour activism 61
labour shortages 53, 100, 103, 105, 141–2
Lady in White (Perla Gibson) 35–6
Lambert, David 171–2
Lambert, John 115
language tests 11
Law, Kate 183
Lawrence, Harry 61–2
Leggate, William 65–6
Leonard, Pauline 14, 128
Lester, Alan 171–2
letters 29–30, 31–2
Lewis, Alun 39
lifestyle
  apartheid and 132
  Central African Federation 111
  migrant motivations and 1, 128, 130, 150–1, 166
  migration policies and 91
  migration propaganda and 2, 134–7
  nostalgia for 183–5, 187, 188
  'poor whites' and 53, 88
  racial hierarchy and 11, 26–7, 110
  Rhodesian white prestige and 112
  Scouting and 65
  Second World War and 15, 28, 29–30, 33, 38, 41
  South African white minority 75
  Southern Rhodesia white minority 86
Lin, Patricia 57, 172
Lindsey, Lydia 104
Livingstone, David 109–10
Lloyd, Bernard 39
loans
  for migrants to Canada 11, 75, 77, 150, 166n2
  for returning South Africans 133
  Samorgan and 114
  for skilled migrants 100, 109, 112
Louw, E.H. 64

222   Index

Maatskappy vir Europese Immigrasie (Organisation for European Immigration) 114, 122n72, 134
Mackie, Moira 38
Macmillan government 139, 141, 147n69
Magee, Gary 13
majority rule 125, 152, 156, 159, 160, 166, 171, 173
Malan, D.F. 74–5, 76, 80, 82, 83–6, 91–2
Malawi 100
  see also Nyasaland
Malherbe, E.G. 31
Malone, W.J. 36, 38, 39
marriage 30, 32, 46nn43–4, 60, 67n2, 179
May, Theresa 193
McCarran-Walter Act (1952) 104
McCarthy, Angela 13
Melvin, K.A.C. 34–5, 38
memoirs 29–30
migrants 9–10, 51, 91, 117–8, 126, 138–9, 140, 141
migration, motivations for 1, 144n12, 172
Migration Council 106, 107
migration policies
  decolonisation and 125
  effects of 91–2
  racial ideology of 4–5, 7, 46n49, 55, 160, 193
  selectivity of 5–6, 11, 61, 64–6, 78–9, 83–5, 99–101, 107–8, 110–3, 151, 153, 156, 194
  South Africa 74–86
  United Kingdom 13, 103–7, 138–42
  see also restriction
migration schemes
  debates over 61, 64, 67, 87
  for demobilised service members 31, 52–3
  employment and 59
  failures of 155
  funding for 106–7

migrant motivations and 13
  participants in 184
  public support for 105
  in receiving countries 28
  subsidised 4, 11, 101, 133, 150, 166
  see also child migration schemes
migration statistics
  for British emigrants 17–8n6, 44nn13–4, 74, 92n3, 102, 127
  collection of 19n15
  decolonisation and 143–4n6, 152
  of Oversea Migration Board 141–2
  Rhodesian 153
  South African 96n57
  Southern Rhodesian 97n61
Miles-Cadman, Cecil 62
Mine Strike (1946) 70n39
minority rule
  decolonisation and 192
  end of 157, 171, 193
  in Federation of Rhodesia and Nyasaland 6
  immigration policies 75
  migration and 66
  Natal separatists and 117
  opposition to 158–63, 166
  pressure to end 125
  racial basis of 4, 5
  resistance to 7
  white migrants and 11, 60–1, 151–2
minority settler colonialism 10–2
missionary societies 162
Mlambo, Alois 14
modernisation 56
modernity 7, 39, 40
Monday Club 125, 141, 143, 147n69, 151, 164
Moodie, T. Dunbar 115
Mozambique 143–4n6, 149–50, 152, 156, 159, 172
multiculturalism 193
Murray, R. Haldane 62–3
Muzorewa, Abel 158–9

Natal, South Africa 116–7, 190n20
National Front 125, 143, 151, 165
National Party (South Africa)
  British concerns about 105
  British migrants and 28, 113
  demobilised soldiers and 63
  Dutch migrants and 80
  migration policies 64, 74–5, 85, 99, 114
  political power of 115
  white English speakers and 117
National Society for the Prevention of Cruelty to Children 62–3
National Union of Students 161, 162
Netherlands 61, 79–80, 114, 126, 160
networks 8, 13, 15–6, 20n27, 30–3, 46n42, 46–7n50, 166
New Zealand
  child migration schemes 56, 68n17
  demobilised soldiers and 59–60
  migrant recruitment by 13, 28, 77, 101, 107, 124, 150
  migrants to United Kingdom from 139
  racial kinship and 164–5
  settler colonialism and 10–1
  South Africa majority rule and 173
Nichole, S.S. 62
Northern Rhodesia 89, 100, 173, 174
  see also Federation of Rhodesia and Nyasaland; Zambia
Norton, P.M. 32
nostalgia 172, 173, 182–7, 188, 191n43
Nottingham riot (1958) 139
Notting Hill riot (1958) 139
Nyasaland 89, 100, 120n45
  see also Federation of Rhodesia and Nyasaland; Malawi

Occupation Day (Rhodesia) 115
Operation Brickie 112
oral history 8–10, 21n33, 129, 172–3, 174
O'Reilly, Karen 128

Ormonde 103
orphans 62, 63, 80–3, 88, 95n32, 95–6n43
Osborne, Cyril 140–1
Ossewabrandwag (Ox-wagon Sentinel) 38, 39
Oversea Migration Board 141–2
Overseas Settlement Board 59, 141

Pakistan 104, 139
pass laws 70n39
patrials 140
Paul, Kathleen 125
Payton, Philip 13
Peberdy, Sally 14, 78, 84
people of colour
  Commonwealth Immigrants Act (1962) 139
  immigration restrictions on 6, 11, 15, 140–1, 151, 163–4. *see also* Black migrants
  migration of 1
  repatriation and 165
  in United Kingdom 124, 128
Perry, Kennetta Hammond 192
pieds noirs 172, 188
Pioneer Day (Rhodesia) 115
political views 188
'poor whites' 53, 61, 64, 80, 88, 110
Portelli, Alessandro 172
Portugal 159
Portuguese migrants 127, 152
Powell, Enoch 125, 139
Pratt, A.E. 33
public holidays 115, 116, 122–3n78
Public Holidays Act (South Africa 1952) 116

Queen's Birthday 116
quota systems 74, 76, 90, 100, 101, 108, 110, 121n61

race 7, 15–6, 60, 129
race patriotism 88–9
Race Relations Act (1968) 164

Race Relations Act (United Kingdom 1968) 160
Race Relations Acts of 1965, 1968 and 1976 (United Kingdom) 7
Race Relations Board (United Kingdom) 161
racial discrimination 107, 155
racial fitness 110
racial hierarchy 5, 10–1, 12, 16, 67, 88, 129
racial ideology 130–1, 143, 153, 160, 164, 194
racial labour hierarchy
　Black workers and 110
　changes in 155
　minority rule and 76, 86
　selective migration policies and 99
　South African 59–60, 113, 130
　white migration and 162–3
racial politics 129, 187
racial privilege 39–42, 76, 86, 129, 132
　see also white privilege
racial solidarity 33, 113, 115, 117
racism
　against Black migrants 52
　Churchill government and 105
　decolonisation and 16
　disagreement with 39
　migration decisions and 128–9
　migration policies and 142–3
　migration schemes and 60
　repatriation and 53–5
　in United Kingdom 192
　during wartime 51
recruitment 11, 15, 99, 107, 124, 126, 132–8, 142, 154–5
Reeves, Ambrose 131
refugees 62, 64, 69n27, 114, 160
Reid, Alfred 180
repatriation
　assistance for 159
　of Black service personnel 53–5
　British right-wing groups and 143, 147n69, 151, 164, 165
　of Commonwealth migrants 5

'hostile environment' policy and 193
from Southern Rhodesia 89
statistics 170n64
Republic Day (South Africa) 116
restriction 11, 12, 22n44, 88, 90, 124, 143
　see also migration policies
retornados 172, 188
Rhodesia
　anti-colonial war 165–6
　decolonisation and 125, 192
　emigration from 149–50, 152, 167n8
　migrant recruitment by 13, 132, 137–8
　migration statistics 127, 153
　migration to 3–4, 4, 130
　minority rule 6–7, 10–2, 126
　Monday Club and 147n69, 164
　sanctions on 158
　settler culture in 176
　United Kingdom connections 151
　white privilege 128
　see also Federation of Rhodesia and Nyasaland; Southern Rhodesia; Unilateral Declaration of Independence (Rhodesia), Zimbabwe
Rhodesia Association of South Africa 190–1n34
Rhodesia House 87, 108–9
Rhodesian Air Force 175
Rhodesian Association of the USA 184
Rhodesian Front 112, 158–9, 168n29
Rhodesian High Commission 111
Rhodesian parliament 156
Rhodesian Pioneer Club 190–1n34
Rhodesian Unilateral Declaration of Independence (UDI) see Unilateral Declaration of Independence
Richards, George 64
right-wing populist movements 165
riots of 1919 53, 68n9
'Rivers of Blood' speech (Enoch Powell 1968) 139
Robson, Harold 32, 182–4

Robson, Thelma 182–4
Ross, A. G. 32–3

Salisbury, Rhodesia *see* Harare, Zimbabwe
Salter, Penny 26, 34
sanctions 149, 152, 158, 167n4
Savoury, Alan 168n29
Schwarz, Bill 7, 29, 187
scientists 141
Second Chimurenga 127
Second World War 14–5, 26–7, 30–3, 51, 56–8, 70n39
segregation 39, 71n58, 93n8, 128–9, 163
self-presentation 173
'Send Them Back' campaign 165
separate development 6
separatism in Natal 116–7
serial migration 157, 171, 173, 180
servants 36, 40–1, 67n6, 135–6, 137, 186–7
  see also Black servants
Settler '74 campaign (Rhodesia) 155
settler colonialism 10, 14, 27, 39, 42, 178, 182, 186–7
settler nationalism 189n15
Settlers' Day (South Africa) 115, 116
Shakespeare, Geoffrey 56, 57–8
Shankanga, Moses 110
Sharpeville massacre 122–3n78, 131
shipping companies 103, 118n8
Simmonds, Eric 58–9
Simon's Town, South Africa 37
Smith, Andrea L. 172
Smith, Andrew 173–4, 181
Smith, Ian 156, 159
Smith, Robert 32
Smuts, Jan
  Dietse Kinderfonds and 82–3
  George VI and 73
  migration policies 28, 64, 74–80, 85–6, 91
  Second World War and 33
  Union-Castle shipping line agreement 84

social engineering 10, 142–3
social mobility
  apartheid and 132
  for Black South Africans 155
  migration decisions and 3, 73, 135–6, 150–1
  racial privilege and 39–41, 52
Society for the Overseas Settlement of British Women (SOSBW) 56, 109, 142
  see also Women's Migration and Overseas Appointments Society
soldier settlement schemes 31
Sons of England 82
South Africa
  anti-apartheid movement 152, 160
  apartheid 7, 129–30
  child evacuees to 70–1n43
  child migration schemes 56, 58, 61–3, 68n17
  citizenship legislation 121n62
  declaration of republic 100–1
  decolonisation and 125, 188, 192
  demobilised soldiers and 59–60
  economy of 167n4
  emigration from 89, 100, 121n61
  identities and 178
  migration policies 5, 6, 13, 76–86, 107, 113–7, 124, 132–7, 145nn35–6, 166
  migration statistics 74, 85, 92n3, 96n57, 102, 127, 143–4n6, 154
  migration to 3–4, 3, 31–3, 44n13, 126, 150–1
  Monday Club and 147n69, 164
  opposition to migration to 149
  Rhodesian migrants to 157, 181
  sanctions on 158
  Second World War 26, 27–8, 33–8
  separation from United Kingdom 73
  serial migration and 175
  shipping companies and 118n8
  United Kingdom connections 151

South Africa (*cont.*)
  white minority rule 29–30
  white privilege 128
South Africa Communist Party 71n58
South Africa House 65
South African Boy Scouts Association 64–5
South African Citizenship Act (1949) 113
South African Immigration Organisation (Samorgan) 114, 134, 155
South Africanism 78, 88–9
South African Senate 63–4
South African War 116
South African Women's Auxiliary Service (SAWAS) 36–7
South Asia 1, 28, 30
Southern Africa League 134
Southern Rhodesia
  child evacuees to 70n40
  demobilised soldiers and 59–60, 61, 97n61
  emigration from 126
  Federation of Rhodesia and Nyasaland 100
  immigration policies 5, 75–6, 86–91
  migration schemes 65–6
  migration statistics 74, 89–90, 92n3, 102, 127
  migration to 3–4, 44n13, 101
  patriotic societies in 177
  post-war era 26
  Second World War 27–8
  selectivity of 107
  serial migration and 173
  South African migration to 121n61
  wartime abundance in 34
  wartime hospitality in 37–8
  wartime travel 30
  white migrants from 167n8
  white minority rule 29–30
  see also Federation of Rhodesia and Nyasaland; Rhodesia; Zimbabwe
Soweto Uprising 122–3n78, 144n7, 149, 163, 167n4

Spain 2
standard of living 40, 132
Statute of Westminster (1931) 10
stereotypes 49n106, 54
Stokes, John 164
Stoler, Ann 8
Stone, John 14, 38, 130–1, 132
Stumbles, Albert 87–8, 112
subjectivity 8, 21, 172–3
subsidies
  Dominions and 150
  ending of 125
  First World War 31
  South Africa 19n16, 101, 114–5, 145n35, 184
  Southern Rhodesia and Rhodesia 86–7, 126, 156
  support for 64
  white migrants and 4, 11, 132–3
Switzerland 160

'Ten Pound Pom' scheme (Australia) 59, 101, 106, 142, 150
Thompson, Andrew 13
Thompson, Edith 62
Thomson, Alistair 128
Tomlinson Commission 113, 121n63
Transa 114, 155

unemployment 59, 104, 128
Unilateral Declaration of Independence (Rhodesia)
  British response to 5
  decolonisation and 16, 176–8
  migration trends and 14
  naming conventions and 18n7
  settler colonialism and 10, 125
  United Kingdom and 29
  UN's failure to recognise 168n34
  white emigration and 112, 171
union activism 161
Union-Castle shipping line 78, 79, 83–4
Union Day (South Africa) 116

United Kingdom
  anti-apartheid movement in 149
  citizenship legislation 121n62
  decolonisation and 188
  economic difficulties 151
  emigration from 1–2, 13, 44n13, 73, 76–7, 92n3, 100–1, 124, 126, 164, 167n8, 171
  lifestyle in 185–6
  migration policies 5, 6, 11–2, 103, 125, 138–42
  migration statistics 102, 127, 154
  racial attitudes 53–5, 128–32, 192, 193–4
  sanctions on Rhodesia 152, 158
  social mobility in 3
  South Africa and 161, 173
  Southern Rhodesia and 86–7
  white Rhodesians and 157, 159–60, 176
United Nations
  on apartheid 160
  on minority rule 125
  pressure on Britain from 6
  Rhodesia and 15, 149, 158, 168n34
United Party (South Africa)
  British migrants and 113
  child migration schemes and 62
  electoral strongholds of 121n62
  minority rule and 75
  post-war immigration under 28, 73–4, 77, 83, 85, 91
  segregationist ideology and 93n8
United States 3, 6, 13, 64, 80, 105, 141, 173
Uys, Stanley 134–5

Van Riebeeck, Jan 116
Van Riebeeck's Day (South Africa) 116
Viljoen Commission 113
violence 1, 6–7, 16, 52, 54, 150
Voortrekkers 115
Vorster, John 149, *150*

Ward, Stuart 12
Webster, Wendy 7, 29, 52
Weddell, T.J. 36
Weighill, John 36
Welensky, Roy 98n81
West Germany 82–3, 114, 133, 134, 160
West Indian migrants 103, 104
West Indian RAF personnel 55
white flight 3, 128
white migrants 10–1, 52, 106, 114, 117, 127–8, 131–2, 142, 155–7, 167n8, 173
white migration 149, 155, 157, 158, 159, 162–3
white nationalism 7, 118, 193
whiteness 7–8, 9, 22n47, 66, 80–1
white privilege 22n47, 128
  see also racial privilege
white racial solidarity 113
white Rhodesians 89, 155, 157, 183, 186, 189n13
white supremacy 85, 143, 156
white women 135–7, *136*, 186–7
white workers 5, 99, 149, 161, 162
Wilkins, Derek 34
Williams, Wendy 193
Winchester Castle 78, 84
Windrush 103, 193
Winston's Specials 30, 37
Witthoft, Jan 33
Wolfe, Patrick 10
Women's Auxiliary Air Force 54
Women's Migration and Overseas Appointments Society 142
  see also Society for the Overseas Settlement of British Women (SOSBW)
Women's National Service League 36–7
Women's Royal Navy Service 181
Woollacott, Angela 181
Wright, Charles 40
Wynn, Laura 181

Zambia 100, 129, 173, 174
  see also Northern Rhodesia
Zimbabwe
  archives of 8, 14, 44n21
  British migrants and 175
  decolonisation and 188
  emigration from 149–50, 152
  independence of 18n7, 155, 171, 178
  migration statistics 143–4n6
  restrictions on journalists in 9
  see also Federation of Rhodesia and Nyasaland; Rhodesia; Southern Rhodesia
Zimbabwe Rhodesia 158
  see also Rhodesia

EU authorised representative for GPSR:
Easy Access System Europe, Mustamäe tee 50,
10621 Tallinn, Estonia
gpsr.requests@easproject.com